C000181994

DAMAGED

IT BEATS
WORKING

Winner of the 1996
Timo Makinen Trophy
presented by The Guild of Motoring Writers
for outstanding motorsport coverage

As part of our ongoing market research, we are always pleased to receive comments about our books, suggestions for new titles, or requests for catalogues. Please write to: The Editorial Director, Patrick Stephens Limited, Sparkford, Nr Yeovil, Somerset BA22 7JJ.

IT BEATS WORKING

MY 35 YEARS INSIDE MOTOR RACING

EOIN YOUNG

Foreword by Jackie Stewart, OBE

Patrick Stephens Limited

To Denny and the Mushroom Cloud Society

First published in August 1996
Reprinted in January 1997

British Library Cataloguing in Publication Data
A catalogue record for this book is
available from the British Library

ISBN 1 85260 460 3

Library of Congress catalog card no. 96 75821

Patrick Stephens Limited is an imprint of Haynes Publishing, Sparkford, Nr Yeovil, Somerset, BA22 7JJ.

Designed & typeset by G&M, Raunds, Northamptonshire.
Printed in Great Britain by Martins the Printers, Berwick on Tweed.

Contents

'If you look as though you're working hard,
you ain't working hard enough.'

Gene Kelly

Foreword
by Jackie Stewart

EOIN YOUNG IS read in almost every corner of the world. The syndicated articles he creates are informative, but much more importantly, amusing and compelling to read.

I met Eoin in 1964 when I had just started to drive for Ken Tyrrell in Formula 3. I had met Bruce McLaren on my very first try-out in a single-seater car at Goodwood, driving a Cooper Formula 3 in March of 1964. Naturally he was one of my heroes, after all he was a Formula One driver; glamorous, and charming with it. One of Bruce McLaren's friends and an integral part of the McLaren operation, was Eoin Young. I went to a party, I think it was after the Guards Trophy at Brands Hatch that same year, in a house where it seemed all of the New Zealand motor racing fraternity lived. Chris Amon was there, Wally Willmott, Denny Hulme, Bruce McLaren and of course Eoin Young.

To me in those days there was no doubt, Eoin Young knew what it was all about! He lived in the fast lane, he knew all the right people, the sort of man that a young, ambitious, up-and-coming racing driver would love to have around, to give him advice, help him with contracts and possible future deals. That story is told in this book by Eoin. I don't know if my version is different, but I believe that we both missed an opportunity of not joining forces at that time, as I am sure each of us would have gained handsomely!

Eoin has seen them come and go; has missed few of the highs that motor racing can provide and has surely suffered the lows that death would bring to so many friends in those days. Eoin has survived all of that. His knowledge of the Sport is perhaps unequalled. He looks at himself and sees himself as other people see him – sometimes with amusement! He lives well, he enjoys good food and good wine, has known the commercial side of the Sport from its early and complicated days to what we know today. He has known the powerbrokers since they were amateur enthusiasts, most of today's drivers since they were in short trousers, and has remained friends with those who have been able to keep the pace and still be around.

The ones who have entered the Sport, whether in journalism, or through being mechanics, engineers, team managers or owners, all enjoy Eoin Young. He has great tales to tell, wonderful reminiscences, and insight, as much into today's players as those of the past.

If you knew Eoin Young as I know him, you would enjoy him just as much as I am sure you are going to enjoy this book.

Jackie Stewart
31 May 1996

Preface

THE HARDEST WORDS to write in this book were the three that made up the title. Darryl Reach at Haynes Publishing was searching for a suitable title and rejecting my feeble ideas as I rejected his. We were asking people we knew to come up with a title, but there simply didn't seem to be one out there. I finally found it in the most unlikely place: a taxi on the way to Adelaide Airport after the Australian Grand Prix.

It was early on the Monday morning after a long night before. The last race in the season was over and I was catching the red-eye out of Adelaide. The taxi driver was from some forgotten Middle European country, but demanding conversation the way they do.

Had I had a good weekend?

'Yes.'

Did I enjoy my stay in Adelaide?

'Yes.'

Had I gone to the Grand Prix?

'Yes.'

Where was I going?

'Home.'

Where was home?

'England.'

Whaddyado?

Since monosyllables seemed unlikely to stem his pressing early-morning need for my personal details, I told him that I travelled a fair amount of the world each year going to glamorous places and writing about racing people and their cars. His mouth dropped open.

'Jeez!' he said, when the power of semi-Australian speech returned. 'Whadda great job . . .'

I confessed that it did have its plus points and added as an afterthought, 'I guess it beats working.'

Somehow it made the whole dawn taxi journey worth the tip. I realised I had found the title to my autobiography and it was more or less downhill from there, a statement that my long-suffering publisher will dispute, saying that it must have been a very gentle slope since it took him all of three years, maybe nearer four, to prise the final words of the manuscript from me so that the book would reach the readers before the end of 1996 . . .

Introduction

THIS BOOK BEGAN at home in East Horsley, Surrey, around 4 am on Sunday 5 October 1992. The telephone rang in the chill pre-dawn darkness and woke me. In my experience early morning telephone calls never bring good news: Denny Hulme had died during a 1,000-kilometre touring car race at Bathurst in Australia a few hours before and the word was spreading to his friends around the world. I took in the details of how 'The Bear' had been racing a BMW in pouring rain and had a heart attack at the wheel. The car had veered to a stop against the guard railing and Denis was dead at the wheel. A racer's way to go. If you had explained it to him he would have agreed that was the way to do it.

I tried to go back to sleep but it was pointless. Heartless almost. There was much too much to think about, too much of Denny to remember. I lay there numbed but wide awake now, on a flick action replay in my mind remembering the way Denny had been involved in my life through the years. He and Bruce McLaren had been, off and on, essential elements in both my life and my career. It was as though I had been able to enjoy my own personal 'Bruce & Denny' show, as their rollicking domination of the Can-Am sports car race series in North America was known in the late 1960s.

I had met Denny almost by accident in the small hours of the morning after a prize-giving function following a 1960 Tasman race near Invercargill in New Zealand. I was drunk, lost, and sitting at the side of the road waiting to be rescued. The first car to stop was a Mini driven by Denny Hulme with five or six of his mates already squeezed in. Whoever I was, I could get in as well if I could.

I first met Bruce McLaren in 1958 as a very junior motor racing journalist covering the New Zealand series, and was inadvertently responsible for introducing him to Patty, the girl from my home town, who later became his wife. Denny had taken me with him for his

1961 season in Formula Junior when I had only just arrived in Britain, escaping from being a bank-teller in New Zealand for the rest of my life.

Bruce hired me as his secretary in 1962 and I worked with him and the fledgling McLaren Racing team through its formative years. When my daughter Selina was born in 1971, Denny and Patty McLaren were godparents; Bruce had been killed in a testing crash at Goodwood the previous summer.

When Bruce died I vowed that I would never get close to another driver or shed tears for any bloke again. We used to talk about it on those endless shuttles back and forth across the Atlantic to Can-Am races, and I'd say to Denny that, even though we were good friends, I wouldn't cry for him. I lied. In fact the only time I had cried since Bruce's death had been one Christmas morning when news came through that Denny's son, Martin, had drowned in a lake accident near his home in New Zealand. Denny and Martin had been at Adelaide for the Grand Prix and I spent some time with the 21-year-old, meeting for the first time in years and the first time as a man. I had been vastly impressed with him, and this made his death so much harder to accept.

It was the same with Denny. Latterly our paths would cross perhaps once a year when he stayed overnight on his way to or from a race in Europe, but we spent a week together sharing a room at Monaco during the 1992 Grand Prix, and it was to that week I looked back as I lay there trying to take on board that Denny had died.

It was a time-warp week, as though we were still knock-about Kiwis 30 years before. Some people are like that, aren't they? You don't see them for years, and yet you slot straight back in as if you'd never been apart, picking up the conversation as though you'd just slipped out of the room for a minute. We talked about old escapades long into each night. He tittered now and then, and eventually fell asleep. In the morning he'd wake up and say 'My *God*, Eoin, it's just like the old days. *Bloody* good, isn't it?' The shame of it was that it wasn't bloody good for long enough.

Denny was pretty much a forgotten hero even at home. A Sportsman's Hall of Fame had been created in New Zealand a few months before and Denny wasn't included, although he had won the World Championship in 1967. There had never been a book on 'The Bear'. He probably would have told any prospective author that there wasn't a book in him, but in fact Alan Henry had meetings with him in our room at Monaco and they were on the point of penning an autobiography. It died with Denny.

Later, when I was in Auckland for Denny's memorial service, several people asked if I was writing a Hulme book and I resolved to explore the idea, but the ashes of enthusiasm were already growing cold in the publishing world. *Autosport* reporter Nigel Roebuck and I discussed the subject at length over several glasses of wine on the flight from Auckland to Adelaide for the Grand Prix in 1992. We decided that if a book devoted to Denny might not be viable, why shouldn't I write a book on racing as I had known it in the 1960s, which would incorporate Denny and Bruce and the whole racing circus as it was then, a very different animal from the professional circus it is today. After discussions with Darryl Reach at Haynes, that book has evolved into my autobiography, a vehicle for writing down all those stories I've been telling across dinner tables for what seems like most of my life.

When I told *Daily Telegraph* journalist Tim Collings over lunch in the paddock at Monza in 1993 that I was writing my autobiography, he almost spilled his wine and spluttered, 'But you haven't *done* anything!' This may be true, Timmy, but I've known a lot of people who have . . .

Michael Caine wrote in his autobiography *What's It All About?* that he wanted to be regretting the things that he had done, not the things that he hadn't. It must be awful to look back over your life and wish you had done so many things differently, or even just to have done so many things. If I had my life to live over, I think I'd do it all the same way. Jackie Stewart jokes now that in 1964 he offered me a job as his manager for 10 per cent of everything he earned, and I turned him down because he was only a Formula 3 driver. I tell him if I'd taken the job we'd have killed each other by now.

Life is what you make of it. Mark Blundell said in a recent interview that he wanted to be around for a good time, not for a long time. There's something in that. This life is not a rehearsal for the next one, it's the real thing and it's on now, live.

Denny's philosophy latterly was that 'you've got to be *happy*', and although his personal philosophy didn't make everybody happy, at least he was happy with his lot. So this book is being written while I still enjoy the life I lead rather than waiting until I become jaded and morose. My friends never imagined I would reach 20, and when I was 30 I imagined the good times would be ending, but at 40 I had started my business in rare motoring books, and at 57 the weekly 'Diary' in *Autocar* that I have been writing since 1967 is still fun to write. I've always maintained that if something is fun to write it's going to be fun to read. That's the way I'll be writing this book.

CHAPTER ONE

Deadlines down under

TO PUT ME in a motor racing perspective, I was born 16 days before Richard Seaman was fatally injured while leading the Belgian Grand Prix at Spa in a factory Mercedes-Benz on 25 June 1939. Being so young I was unaware of this. I was also probably as far from Spa as it was possible to be, in a maternity hospital in the seaside town of Timaru in the South Island of New Zealand.

My colleagues may find this hard to believe, but family history insists that I was so small at birth that I was brought to my mother in a milk jug. I've never liked milk since. Defying my current robust stature, the doctors advised my mother to wait a few days before placing a birth notice in the local paper. They thought I might not make it, and my mother could save the cost of the announcement.

I was eventually named Eoin Spence. Spence was a family name on my father's side; Eoin has defied pronunciation and spelling ever since. Before you ask, my family has always pronounced it as the English 'Ian', and I cautiously tell enquirers that it's an old Gaelic name that could have Scottish origins as well. Paddy Hopkirk is more forthright. He says it's an old Irish name and is pronounced 'Owen'. But it's my name and I'll pronounce it my way.

I was actually named after the son of a family friend, Eoin Little, who was killed in a fighter plane during the Second World War. It is a phonetic puzzle. Those who can't pronounce it, certainly can't spell it either. I can spell it carefully letter by letter and watch it being just as carefully written E-I-O-N because that's the way it *sounds* and that's the way they want to write it.

I suppose because there is this problem with the spelling and pronunciation of my Christian name, I have become in a measure paranoid about giving my name over the phone or, say, to the maître d' in a restaurant. I always spell it out. 'My name is Young. Y-O-U-N-G.' A friend pointed out that I don't have to spell it out in England.

Young is an English word. I'm over-compensating because nobody seems to pick up on the way I say 'Eoin', and to foreign ears my name always comes out as 'YongYong'. Marlboro PR lady Agnes Carlier has always called me that. Jean Sage, team manager for Renault when they ran their own F1 cars, says my name is onomatopoeic with the noise a car makes going past on full song down the Mulsanne Straight at Le Mans: 'Yooooonnnnnnnnnnyoooonnnngggggg . . .'

I suppose I cursed my name through school and for most of my first career in banking, but when I started writing I realised I had a built-in trademark. Everyone remembered my name. They couldn't pronounce it or spell it, but they remembered it, which is half the battle in most forms of endeavour. Being remembered.

I was actually grateful that a family friend had christened me 'Buster' as a toddler, and the name stayed with me until I left New Zealand, by which time I was ready to accept my grown-up real name. The nickname stayed in New Zealand until Rob Walker (R. R. C. Walker, famous as the entrant of Grand Prix cars for Stirling Moss and others, and later gaining fame as a motor racing writer in the American *Road & Track* magazine) visited a Tasman race and we were walking down a street in Christchurch when we bumped into an old school friend.

'Gidday, Buster,' he said. 'Haven't seen you for years!'

Rob had never heard me called that before and he's called me Buster ever since.

My father, Herbert Alexander Young, was a first-generation New Zealander and we lived on a 60-acre farm on the outskirts of Cave, a township of probably 200, 20 miles inland from Timaru on the road to Mount Cook. Now the road is a tourist trail, but when we lived there tourism hadn't been invented. My father earned his living trapping rabbits and selling the skins to tanners and the carcases to butchers. Later the rabbits became so prolific that he laid trails of poisoned carrots and I went with him in the spring cart as a junior spotter of small corpses along the trail. The butchers weren't so keen on the poisoned carcases . . .

The one-eyed cob horse and spring-cart gave way to an Austin A40 pick-up truck, which my father bought new around 1951 and in which he taught himself to drive. He taught me, too, and I was driving on our deserted country roads undetected from the age of 12 or 13. At least I *thought* I was undetected until I went for my licence at the age of 15, terrified at the prospect as one is, only to receive a blistering lecture from the local traffic cop, a doughty old Scot, who told me that he was well aware of my under-age activities and by rights he should be giving me a ticket, not a licence. It did heaps for my morale as I stammered off into the test.

A river ran along one boundary of our farm and the local lads and I swam in it and fished out of it. Salmon swam up beyond Cave to spawn and we would stand in the rapids watching them crashing up past us, battered and on their last gasp but determined to reach their spawning ground. Our fishing wasn't always by the approved method. We didn't understand why grown men would stand in the river for hours fly-fishing when we could hook trout out in minutes with a gaff, or seconds with a sawn-off .22 rifle that everyone told me would split asunder and kill me if fired with the muzzle under water in a trout's ear. But it never did.

I was once taken fly-fishing with my Uncle Charlie, who lived for his fishing. He gave me a rod and flies, some basic instruction, and sent me off to a stretch of river on my own. The trout were not remotely interested in the fly, but when I dug a worm out of the bank it was a different story. I went back with three fish to Uncle's none, and he was vastly impressed at how well I had done with his coaching. When I explained my personal method he was appalled, and refused to take me fishing ever again.

These lateral tactics have worked throughout my life. I once gave my mother an airgun for her birthday, and when she said that she didn't want it, I said I'd have it instead.

My mother Emily was a sweet lady and I always thought I conned her, but looking back from a position of parenthood today, I realise that she must have seen through all my tactics and played along. When I came home in the small hours after a night with the lads visiting various pubs and parties, she would say, 'You haven't been drinking, have you?' And every night I'd swear total abstinence when I must have smelled like the local brewery.

When I had twin carburettors fitted to her Austin A30 I explained that these were to improve the fuel economy and were really nothing to do with the fact that I had joined the local car club and wanted to race it. In an effort to maintain some form of parental control, mother would agree to loan me the A30 on a Saturday night, providing she could note the mileage reading so that she could give me an 'allowance' of miles depending on where I said I was going. I soon found out how to disconnect the speedometer after my 'allowance' had been used up, which meant that we could go to parties much further afield.

It's odd how time distorts perspective. Then I thought the A30 to be the epitome of a compact and speedy small saloon. Now when I see one on the road I can't believe how slow they are. But perspective distorts both ways. I bought an Austin A35 on a whim to remind me of misspent youth and thought daughter Selina would think it was a joke. She loved it and claimed it for her 21st birthday present. I suppose to her it was a vintage car in the same way that I regarded my various 1920s Austin Sevens as vintage in the 1950s.

These days my family firmly believes that my mail might as well be delivered to The Barley Mow, a period pub dating from the 1500s and my regular watering hole in West Horsley, Surrey. Drinking came upon me in an oblique manner, but it stayed. My father was by no means a boozer, but he presumably spent a sporting amount of time in the Cave pub drinking with the locals. My mother was a staunch Presbyterian and instilled into me the evils of drink from my earliest days, to the point where I couldn't even stand the beery smell from an empty bottle in our wash-house. That part stayed with me. I was never going to drink beer.

After my father died, we sold the farm and moved to Timaru where, coincidentally, we bought a house in Kiwi Drive from well-known local racing driver Ernie Sprague, but in the mid-1950s I hadn't discovered racing. As I was a non-drinker with a car – mother's A30 – I was a useful chauffeur for a group of local Catholic lads who were trained from birth to fancy a drop.

In those days in New Zealand there were Catholic kids and Protestant kids and the two usually didn't mix. You went to a High School or a Convent and the only time you met was on the rugby field, and it usually ended in a fight. Being a country lad, sheltered from this mildest of religious gaps, I worked it out that the Catholic lads seemed to have more fun than the guys I knew at Timaru Boys High, so I ferried them to parties. It dawned on me equally quickly that the more they drank the more fun they seemed to have, and while I was enjoying it, I wasn't enjoying it as much as they were.

They drank beer, so I was set against joining them, but I decided that if I drank whisky I could take it like a rather strong cough medicine and toss it back in one gulp; this at age of 17, when the minimum drinking age in New Zealand was 21. The pubs also shut at 6 o'clock every night, resulting in a daily drinking race as soon as the offices emptied at 5. The police seemed to accept after-hours drinking as a fact of life and there was always one pub in every town that was known as a 'safe place' to take a drop after 6. The other accepted lore was that you rang the doorbell three times to gain admittance. The police rang only once. Woe betide the newcomer who inadvertently rang the doorbell once for an after-hours tipple. Thinking it was a police raid, the bar would clear instantly, with erstwhile illicit drinkers clearing back fences, hiding between rows of potatoes or locked in lavatories, leaving an impenetrable haze of cigarette smoke and rows of half-empty glasses with the landlord balefully regarding the sole hotel resident legally allowed to be there.

At 17 I could match my mates drink for drink, my Scotch to their 8-ounce (about half a pint) beer. It's taken years of practice. They could never get me back into that milk jug now . . .

A succession of teachers despaired of ever making me learn. Every morning at 8 o'clock we formed a ragged queue of six or eight to get on a school bus to take us 9 miles to Pleasant Point District High, which took children from all over the local farming area. By that time in the morning I had milked two cows, ridden my bike to the local store and delivered the *Timaru Herald* to the local householders I had coerced into forming a small round. After school I would buy magazines at the local newsagent and deliver those with the papers the following morning, adding a few pence for the service. I wasn't learning at school, but I was taking it on board before and after.

School Certificate was the equivalent then of the English O-Levels. As I recall an average 50 per cent pass was required in four subjects. I topped the class in English, failed miserably in mathematics, history and geography and scraped through with a pass of 51 per cent.

My problem was that I have never been able to learn anything in which I have no interest. In the same way I love buying things, but I hate to be sold something. Mother insisted that I learn the piano when a music teacher appeared at Pleasant Point District High, and I was one of her small group of pupils picked to play at an end-of-year school evening. My heavily practised piece was 'Turkey In The Straw'. I could play it in my sleep – which was perhaps my undoing. When I reached the end, I couldn't for the life of me remember the closing chords and I kept playing the chorus over and over again. I could see the piano teacher in the wings nearing hysteria and making graphic throat-cutting gestures indicating that I should finish now, but with no suggestions how I should achieve a suitable ending if the appropriate chords had been stricken from my mind.

I eventually solved the problem by standing up and walking off the stage to uncertain applause. The piano teacher thought I'd done it on purpose to embarrass her. For the next recital she told me to learn the national anthem so that I could play it at the start of the evening and avoid any chance of creating mayhem during her concert. This time my brain froze at the start instead of the finish – I couldn't remember the opening chords. The audience was standing expectantly while I frantically tried to imagine how the anthem began. I was saved by the headmaster's wife who quavered shakily into 'God Save Our Gracious Queen . . .', and everyone else joined in. So did I. By the time the anthem ended I was in fine form, pounding away and even managing to end when everyone else did, but the piano teacher was still furious with me, thinking I had deliberately sabotaged the start of the concert instead of the end.

The following year I went to Timaru Boys High to study for the University Entrance in my first and last year at this prestigious seat of local learning. There was a procedure whereby if you showed enough promise during the year, you would be accredited – given a pass without having to sit the exam.

I knew two things from early in that year: a) that I would never be able to pass the exam, and b) that I wasn't going on to university anyway. The accrediting was based on results in school exams held a month before the national University Entrance exams, so 6B1 held a sweepstake on who would scrape through. Only one person picked me, and that was myself. In fact, I was so certain that I would fail that I'd taken two bets and left my name off the second one.

For the few weeks between the exams and the accreditation announcement we were exhorted to keep working in case we needed to sit UE. I knew it was over as far as I was concerned, so I sat in the back of the class at every lesson and read a thriller. The day of the accreditation was awaited with bated breath by my more academic friends, who actually enjoyed school and learning, and I think they were as disappointed in the system as I was totally amazed when my name appeared at the bottom of the list of those who had passed. They thought I was going to be a drain on the educational system. I knew I had won the sweepstake and would be launching myself on the world of banking the following year.

Banking and I were not a natural pairing. My mother always erred on the side of conservatism, and she felt that a career in banking would be safe as well as being a good deal more rewarding than whatever I had in mind as an alternative. Which was nothing.

School returned almost immediately when we were told that we could jump a grade in pay as soon as we had achieved a Bachelor of Commerce degree at night school. Propelled by an urge to earn more so easily, I took five subjects in the first year. And passed none. The second year they suggested that three subjects might be a more realistic goal. I passed none. The third year they said, 'Why don't you try Secretarial Practice on its own because it's the easiest subject?' And I flunked that. The fourth year they asked me not to come back because I was a disruptive influence on the newer students.

Banking was boring. When I was doing it, it was what I did as a job, and in those days everyone had to have a proper job and stick to it. Being sacked was like getting divorced – you had to leave the neighbourhood under a cloud. When I later arrived in London I couldn't believe the number of office workers in pubs at lunchtime. If you came back to the Australia & New Zealand Bank in Timaru after lunch with the merest hint of an alcoholic beverage on your breath, you were summoned to the manager's office.

Banking and writing about motor racing came together by a bizarre combination of events. On my way home I cycled up Sefton Street where a young guy of about my own age was sometimes polishing an immaculate BRG XK120 Jaguar drophead. I learned that his name was also Young, so that made the excuse to stop and chat. From that day on everyone assumed we were brothers, and it didn't always seem worth telling girls that my brother didn't own an XK120 at a time in New Zealand when it was like owning a XJ220.

I asked him if he went to motor races and he said no, because he didn't have anyone to go with. I volunteered – as one does, always anxious to be kind to lonely people. We drove to a few races and David got the bug. He entered for a beach race near Christchurch and won by half a mile from the aforementioned Ernie Sprague in his modified Ford Zephyr.

The headline in the *Timaru Herald* the next morning read 'Timaru Man Second In Beach Race'. I was outraged. My mate had won the race going away and he wasn't getting recognition. More to the point, he had been totally ignored. To the extent that a 20-year-old can stomp, I stomped into the editorial office and demanded that the matter be put to rights. They said, in so many words, 'If you're so clever, why don't you write it?'

With a promise that it would appear the next morning I spent what seemed like hours composing the most perfect 200-word race report you have ever read. In fact nobody read *my* words because the sub-editor re-wrote it, but it was a start and, as Denis Jenkinson later pointed out, I've never had a proper job since.

In 1959 my race reports graduated to a weekly column on motoring and racing. I was working at a tiny sub-branch in the north of Timaru, tapping out the column on the bank's typewriter while my elderly colleague snoozed. This was life in the slow lane.

Every weekday morning we would walk the half-mile to the sub-branch with £5,000 in various denominations of notes in a large gladstone bag. In the bag with the money was the biggest revolver I had ever seen, but in hindsight any robber who grabbed the bag also got the gun. Which probably saved a lot of people being hurt, because I had never fired it and I never knew of any member of the staff who had pulled the trigger . . .

Then came the Christmas holidays that led to my being exiled to a branch in Dunedin. I was a teller and on Christmas Eve it was understood that everyone balanced quickly and we all disappeared for seasonal festivities. My cash was £100 over. I couldn't understand the fuss. Everyone had to stay behind and check and double-check and still my cash stayed obstinately too much by £100. They gave up eventually, glowered at me en masse, and left late for Christmas. On New Year's Eve, as fate would have it, I was £100 under in my till. I could more or less understand the reason for the staff unrest this time, and made a barely audible offer to make up the difference, even though it was probably the equivalent of at least £1,000 in today's money. The manager said that wasn't the point. A mistake was a mistake and I'd made two of them. I wondered if one didn't cancel out the other, but this seemed to be another point I'd missed, that one mistake didn't cancel another.

I was banished to Dunedin, the Glasgow of New Zealand, and I hated most of it. Except for a man named Quinn who ran the overseas desk and took me under his wing, pointing out all the ways to stay employed in the bank without actually doing anything much in the way of work. Quinny and I hit it off well, and I kept in touch for several years after I went to England.

I had my 21st birthday party in Dunedin, and I remember a fair amount about it, including going to the movies with two friends and being summarily ejected by the management when we were half-way down the darkened aisle. Apparently the movie had been running for an hour and there was something wrong with the song we were singing lustily.

I think I may have resigned from the bank around this time with a view to sailing to England with David Young and like-minded friends to explore the real world of racing. I asked the *Timaru Herald* for a six months' experience job in editorial, but said I wanted to be a reporter. I was signed on as a second-year reporter, leapfrogging the system, which stipulated making the tea for the first year. The guy who made the tea was not at all happy with me to begin with.

I suffered the disease of all budding journalists. I imagined I could write. Sub-editors were creatures with shells like armadillos, appointed to tell people like me our shortcomings. There are readers now who will leap to their Conway Stewarts and avow that I have not improved with age or experience. I hated the chief sub, Ken Andrews, with a vengeance as he hacked my masterpieces apart night after night, yet years later I went back to see him and thanked him for cutting me down to size. I probably still can't write, but at least I write better than I used to.

To me in those days, the *Timaru Herald* had the power I imagined *The Times* must have if I ever got to London. Indeed, it had an advantage over 'The Thunderer' in that it was the *only* paper in town. Readers either like or loathe journalists. I found that out early on. One angry reader's letter about my weekly motoring column (which was signed 'Dipstick' in the days when personal bylines were simply not allowed, rather in the manner that *Motor Sport* never goes beyond the writer's initials), suggested that any dipstick had to be withdrawn, wiped, then dipped again before being believed.

I now know the pace at which Fleet Street writers work. In Formula 1, anyway. It all happens on deadline. Days of swanning about and enjoying the sponsors' hospitality and suddenly it's all heads-down work. It wasn't quite like that in Timaru, but it probably seemed as though it was. My best scoop came when word came through from Australia that the £12,000 third prize (a fortune then) in the Melbourne Cup Sweepstake had been won by someone living in the Waimate area, 20 miles from Timaru. By sheer chance one of my drinking cronies was a farmer in the area and knew the prize-winner, and I was soon on my way in the company van, armed with a plate camera. I knew all newspaper photographers used plate cameras, but I had never used one. I had maybe 2 minutes' instruction as I was pushed out the door, and by 9.30 that night I had tracked my quarry, a 63-year-old Maori who had been bedridden for 20 years and was looked after by his sister.

He didn't want his photograph taken, while I had been told not to come back without a photo, so there was a localised problem here. I solved it by saying that I didn't want to take his photo anyway, that I didn't know how the camera worked, but if he'd just pose a bit perhaps we could get it all over with, and I could tell the editor that there had been a problem with the camera. The photo was perfect. My first scoop!

My scrapbooks now show numbing headlines that must have seemed like triumphs at the time. 'Owner of Timaru-based Ketch Swept Overboard and Drowned.' 'Timaru Company Seeking Dutch Support for Eels.' 'Bacteriologist Retires After 33 Years' Service.' It could only get better.

Motor racing journalism is an odd line of work where most writers on the specialist papers have had no journalistic training in the strict sense of the word. They started as enthusiasts and became writers as they went along; and the enthusiasm still shows through. The trained journalists on what used to be called the Fleet Street papers can write to time and length, but their work lacks the glow of enthusiasm that shines through a piece by Nigel Roebuck in *Autosport* or Denis Jenkinson at his best in *Motor Sport*.

I have always maintained that you should measure the worth of a piece by seeing if it has a rhythm, if it sounds right, if it flows. Never mind the grammar, how does it read? How does it sound? How does it scan? If it feels good reading it, it's been written well. That's a homespun philosophy but it has served me better over the years than any formal grammar training I never had at High School.

My daughter Selina had always been interested in art, but at 20 she discovered she could write delightful stories for children and began illustrating them. Her problem was that she had never been able to spell. The stories sounded great, but the spelling was atrocious. Her agent told her not to worry – they had editors who knew how to spell. Her gift was the art of story-telling.

Which is really what writing is all about. Story-telling. Spinning a yarn. My weekly columns on racing are all based around what people want to hear in the pub. They've already watched the race on television and read the report in Monday's newspaper by the time I get back to The Barley Mow on Monday evening. They want to know what really happened, the paddock gossip, the Grand Prix scandal, the stuff that never makes the pages of the papers or the magazine reports because there is never enough space or it probably isn't true anyway. That has never put a stopper on a good story. If it's a quiet week you can always run 'I gather there is no truth in the rumour that . . .', and you can follow it a week later with the denials from the people who'd never heard the rumour you'd made up in the first place.

At Pleasant Point we were offered French as one option. French? Was this a joke? Who would ever go to France? We rejected the option and probably took something like science, which was an alternative total mystery to us. Years later I worked for 15 years in motor racing public relations for the French Elf Oil Company and never learned a word of their language.

That is not entirely true. I actually learned a French word on my first day in France with Denny Hulme and his Formula Junior Cooper in 1961, and I've never forgotten it. Denny was of the press-on-and-eat-when-we-get-there school. I insisted that if we were in France we should have a French picnic for lunch at the roadside. He grudgingly stopped in a village and I bought a French loaf, cheese, tomatoes and a bottle of wine. Even more grudgingly he stopped again for me to create this minor feast . . . which was when I discovered that we didn't have a corkscrew or any means of asking for one. We stopped at the next hardware shop and I asked in broadest New Zealand for a corkscrew while all the time miming the extracting of a cork from a bottle.

'Ah, m'sieu – un tire-bouchon!'

Wonderful word. Served me well ever since.

CHAPTER TWO

Early days in Europe

THE GOOD SHIP *Ruahine* took five weeks to reach Southampton. In that time I had one breakfast and lost my virginity for 4 dollars. The two happenings were not related. I had breakfast on the first morning but immediately slipped into shipboard routine that did not include any form of early morning activity. We rose around 11 am, shaped up to a morning pint at the bar to prepare for lunch, which was always a jolly affair in the dining room with a bottle or two of wine, took a siesta in the cabin until 5-ish, then back to the bar to loosen up for dinner, after which there was always a party just starting in the bar and it was the wee small hours of the morning by the time we were trying to find our cabin to sleep away what was left of the night. On balmy evenings we slept on deck.

The cost of my losing my virginity was not engraved on my mind for life – I found that I had noted the cost in my diary of the trip. A dusky young Panamanian girl in the Rock & Roll bar charged 4 dollars to allow me membership of a club to which I assured my friends I had belonged for years. Safe sex as far as I was concerned in New Zealand was making sure her parents didn't know about it. I must have known what to do but I didn't know how, and I wasn't able to ask since it was generally established that I *knew*. I thought sleeping with a girl meant that. I must have made very chaste company, so I apologise retrospectively to any former girlfriend who thought I had amazing self-control. I just didn't know where to start.

Was it Dr Johnson who said, 'Keep a diary, my boy, because one day it will keep you?' Someone like Dr Johnson, anyway. And it's true. The only problem was that I didn't. Not after the diary of my boat trip and my first year in Britain – but then *every* colonial keeps a record for the first year overseas. After that any form of record becomes passé. You are assumed to be an old hand at foreign travel and beyond writing it down. This is why the chapters on 1961 will be more detailed than later years, but also because 1961 was the year when everything was new and novel. You were allowed to be impressed in your first year, but after that you were supposed to belong and to have graduated from being a tourist. Which may account for the fact that, like most of the motor racing circus, I have travelled the world most of my life and seen almost none of it. An airport, a plane, a hire car, a hotel, a race track. Every second weekend is the same during the summer. There isn't the time to *look* at anything.

The *Ruahine* sailed from Wellington on 10 March 1961. We were travelling by boat because the fare of £110 was half the price of flying. We had more time than money. I was sharing a six-berth cabin with David Young, Tony Vial, a schoolteacher and a father with his six-year-old son. I can imagine that the father would not have chosen us as cabin-mates, given the choice, but then we wouldn't have chosen him.

Our first port of call was Tahiti, and our cabin steward was at pains to instruct us on how to behave when we landed. The place to drink was Quinn's Bar, but we were not to start drinking anywhere on the island before 7 pm. According to the steward the local Hinano beer, with an onion base as I recall, was dynamite, and a 7 pm start guaranteed a slightly longer night. A Canadian friend, sharing a cabin with David's mechanic friend Colin Kyle, had either not heard our briefing or chose to ignore it, and by the time we arrived at Quinn's Bar he was already several Hinanos ahead of us, out of his brains in fact, and had a colourful Tahitian damsel on his knee.

'Shake hands wi' m'frens. Shake hands wi' m'frens!' he kept slurring, totally oblivious to the fact that the young lady only had one arm and it was round his neck . . .

The *Ruahine* then stopped at Panama and Curacao, where us young bloods let ourselves off the leash and behaved badly. Then it was back on board and deck quoits, deck golf, deck tennis, swimming, cards, Scrabble, quizzes, movies, dances. And a lot of drinking and sleeping. According to the names in my diary I must have endeavoured to date every female on the ship, but the diary also notes a nil success rate.

There was occasional cabin discord. Diary: 'Eric [the father] woke me at 6 am with his electric razor buzzing in my ear. If he does that again I will tear the fitting off the wall and brain him with it.' Come to think of it, I wouldn't have much cared to share a cabin with us either.

On Monday 10 April the *Ruahine* felt its way through the fog to dock at Southampton and we were decanted into a bus for the trip to London. We were amazed at the way the houses were joined together – there were no terraced houses in my part of New Zealand. The Overseas Visitors Club arranged a bed in a dormitory room in Earls

Court (where else?). There was a South African in the next bed and we had long discussions after lights-out. I suggested that the blacks were not treated very well in South Africa, but he replied in a broad Afrikaans accent, 'Och, man. You Kiwis, you got the right idea. You shoot all your kaffirs when you get there . . .' Which I suppose is one way of interpreting the Maori Wars of the mid-1800s.

Londoners regard the underground railway – the 'tube' – as a way of life, but for us first-day colonials it was an adventure. Unless our fathers had been miners we had never been so far under the ground in our lives, and to hear a train coming was eerily exciting. Being told to change at Piccadilly, we climbed out of one train, walked across the platform and got into the next train that arrived, then wondered why we had come back to the station we had just left. We weren't told that we had to find a train on another line. When I lived on the farm at Cave there was only one train – the 'Fairlie Flyer' – which went down the line in the morning and came back at night. There was only one train and one platform. London was a huge rabbit warren full of trains . . .

Then there were the Rolls-Royces. I remember coming out of the tube at Green Park and standing on the footpath counting the Rolls and Bentleys as they slid along Piccadilly. In Timaru it was a topic of conversation if a Rolls-Royce drove through the town. Nobody we knew actually owned one.

The E-Type Jaguar was announced in 1961 and the first one I actually saw in the metal was parked outside Harrods. I braved the Knightsbridge traffic and ran across the road to gawp at its sleek lines. Bruce McLaren bought one of the first pre-production models and he was in love with it. Or lust perhaps, because it was *such* a horny-looking car. But he must have been in love with it because for all its good looks it had so many faults and was forever going back to the factory to be repaired or rebuilt, but Bruce wouldn't hear a word said against it and it *did* motor so wonderfully fast on the open road. He bought a hard top for it when these became an option, and we sold it to an Australian in this form. A few weeks later we had an aggrieved telephone call from Sydney wanting to know where the hell the convertible top was? We had taken it off and stowed it in Bruce's attic and forgotten all about it when the E-Type was sold.

Our first trip outside London was by underground, overground and double-decker bus to the Cooper Car Company at 243 Ewell Road, Surbiton, Surrey, to check delivery on David's Formula Junior car. I remember the address because my mail was sent there for two years. In 1961 Cooper was the holy of holies in motor racing. Jack Brabham had won the World Championship in 1959 and 1960 and, although the wave had crested and they would never come close to the world title again, Cooper was the place to be when we arrived and John Cooper was an important man to know.

He was, and still is, an enormously entertaining man. Working with Bruce in later years I would often go for an after-dinner stroll with John in whatever city the race happened to be. This stroll always included a bar and a brandy. At Rheims I was having dinner with the Cooper party in the Restaurant de la Paix, and Jack Brabham and his new team were dining on the other side of a partition. John and his father Charles had been extremely put out when Jack had left to form his own team, but John soon regarded it as an inevitable fact of racing life and they were still good friends. A huge salver of French fries arrived at the Cooper table during a prolonged session of banter over the partition. The next minute Cooper had pitched the whole thing over the partition and the result was pandemonium. Betty Brabham was most definitely not amused.

One evening on our after-dinner perambulation John was fuming about one of the women at the table who had insisted on trying to order for everyone in French, which was most definitely not her first – or her best – language.

'French! She can't speak French!' spluttered John. 'The only French she knows she learned off the bathroom taps . . .'

We discovered that David's Formula Junior Cooper would not be ready for a month. When Denny Hulme had asked where his Formula Junior Cooper was in 1960, John Cooper had pointed to the rack of tubes. It hadn't been started yet.

John appeared to have a soft spot for colonials and we seemed to be readily accepted as part of the racing family. Ten days after our first visit we were setting out at 4 am for Liverpool with a new exhaust system for Jack Brabham to fit at Aintree. We bluffed our way into the paddock with no passes, just the exhaust system for the World Champion, which seemed to work better than any tickets. Brabham won the race, but we never saw him take the flag. We were fast asleep in the car, exhausted.

New Zealander Angus Hyslop had come over to race a Lotus 20 in Formula Junior, while Denny Hulme had a new Cooper with a Martin-Ford engine, cheaper than a Cosworth but more troublesome as it turned out. There was a suggestion that I would travel to the FJ races with David and his mechanic Colin Kyle when their car was ready, but nothing was firm, and when Denny Hulme asked if I wanted to go with him, I jumped at the chance. He had raced in the European FJ series in 1960, so I asked him what I would need to take. He said I would need a suit for the prize-givings, so I went out and bought one off the peg for 10 guineas.

We set off on our European trip on 24 May 1961. Thirty years ago most privateers towed their race cars on trailers behind their road cars, and Denny had an 80,000-mile Ford Zodiac that he had bought for £300. For some reason it was fitted with a siren, which came in useful for clearing traffic on occasion, but also nearly set the car ablaze. Smoke poured out from under the bonnet and Denny leapt out, saying that it was the fuses. The 'fuses' turned out to be a drill bit and a screwdriver blade . . .

The back seat of the Ford was stripped out and the space filled with tools, spares and fuel cans. The fuel contract for the racing car stipulated that the supply was to be as much as was required at the track, so we always filled the race car, the tow car, and as many cans as we could carry to get us to the next race.

On the way to Dover, with Denny hurrying to make the ferry, he lost top gear and opted to stop and have the gearbox repaired where the mechanics spoke English. We caught a later ferry and drove all night through Germany to meet the Hyslop equipe at the Grossenbrode ferry for the crossing to Denmark. A few miles from the port there was a loud bang and the car lurched down with a broken main leaf in the rear spring. We crawled to the dock and on to the ferry for the 4-hour crossing; on the other side Denny bound the spring with wire.

The race was at the Roskildering, a short three-quarter-mile track with banked corners in what looked like a large gravel pit. It held sad memories for Denny. He had shared the 1960 New Zealand Driver to Europe award with George Lawton, but George had crashed his Cooper at Roskilde and was killed. The marks were still on the track where his car had skidded for 80 yards, then overturned.

I stayed in my first motel in Denmark. I also slept under my first duvet. (Diary: 'The beds have strange feather sheets.') Angus Hyslop won both heats of the FJ race, while Denny battled with assorted engine problems.

Now we headed south in convoy, bound for Rouen. David Piper was staying at our hotel and he took us round Les Essarts circuit, which was made up of French public roads a short distance from the town. He showed us one bend where he had stopped during a race the year before and Innes Ireland had crashed a few laps later, going right over the top of Piper's car and over the banking, landing high in some trees. There was always some 'old hand' anxious to show a new driver the circuit and point out where others had crashed in the past. The Nurburgring was a particular favourite for that.

Angus was third fastest in practice and Denny sixth. The following day Denny moved up to third behind John Love and Henri Grandsire, with Angus fourth. However, neither featured in the race, both dropping out with engine problems.

During practice Denny introduced me to Denis Jenkinson, the bearded *Motor Sport* writer who had ridden sidecar for Eric Oliver's Norton when they were winning world championships in the late 1940s, and had partnered Stirling Moss when he won the Mille Miglia in a Mercedes 300SLR in 1955. 'Jenks' was God to any aspiring motor racing journalist, and I was vastly impressed to meet him.

A few years before I had met Hans Tanner when he came out to the New Zealand Grand Prix with the Temple Buell Maseratis. Tanner lived in Modena and had the inside line on the Ferrari and Maserati factory news, as well as knowing all the racing drivers who based themselves in Modena to be near the factories. At a time when I was still a bank clerk in Timaru using the bank's typewriter to do my weekly column for the local newspaper, Tanner wrote for a number of magazines, so was already a hero. In 1970, after Bruce McLaren's death, when I had written the book on Bruce and the team, I received a letter from Tanner in California saying that he had enjoyed it. And now I had met Jenks.

I was writing the Rouen race report for *Motoring News*, and as it was a weekly from the same publishing house as *Motor Sport* I asked Jenks if he would take my copy back. I thought no more about it until someone expressed amazement that Jenks had taken it because he had a traditional stand-off with *Motoring News* and would never go out of his way to help. There was also a measure of surprise that he had even *spoken* to me because in those days he was very much a loner and wasn't renowned for encouraging conversation with the lower orders of scribblers. Especially a 21-year-old New Zealander still very much wet behind the ears. My advantage was that I was on first-name terms with the top drivers who had raced on the Tasman series. Later Jenks was to come to several of our lunches at The Barley Mow in West Horsley, having switched from *Motor Sport* to the weekly opposition *Autosport* following internal wrangling. Sadly he suffered a major stroke early in 1996 and is still recovering slowly as I write this.

The next race for Denny and Angus was Le Mans. BP had arranged for them to share a works Abarth, but it was made apparent from the moment the two New Zealanders arrived that it was very much an arrangement that had been wished upon the team by their sponsoring oil company. They were given an 850 cc GT when the effort was behind several 750 cc cars, which had the best chance of wresting the coveted Index of Performance from the French. This was a complicated formula that had been worked out to favour small cars, which were predominantly French, since there were no French cars likely to win overall. The 850 cc car was essentially an orphan.

While the cars were being scrutineered and the drivers were having their medicals, I found the track souvenir shop and bought a silk headscarf depicting all the winning Le Mans cars for 7 francs, and an ashtray for 5 francs. (Diary: 'I thought these were quite cheap.') Understatement. When I started dealing in racing books and memorabilia these original scarves were selling for several hundred pounds! I called at the office of the Automobile Club de l'Ouest where I was given free posters from the previous races. Such items from the late 1950s and early 1960s nowadays sell for well over £1,000 . . .

The Abarth GT had not been fitted with a safety harness, so Denny asked for one to be installed. Angus said that the car had very positive steering like his Formula Junior car and had nearly as much performance, but that it was noisier than the single-seater because they were sitting in a closed sound-shell.

The Friday before Le Mans was my 22nd birthday and I was about to see my first Le Mans race, on the threshold of a new career. As I write this my daughter Selina is 22, has just bought a house in New Zealand and is well established as a writer and illustrator of children's books.

Angus started the race and after 2 hours Denny took over with the car in 35th of a field of 53, and 8th on Index. At midnight the drivers were complaining of a clutch problem. By dawn on Saturday morning the clutch had failed altogether, and starting after a refuelling pit stop was a major problem. Denny had been cautioned after grinding away on the starter, so he and Angus worked out a way of starting the engine, then crashing in a gear to get under way. The final hours were a drone as every driver cruised to guarantee a finish. The Hulme/Hyslop Abarth was classified 15th overall and was the only Abarth to finish, which prompted something of a sea-change in Carlo Abarth's appreciation of his colonial drivers.

Denny's next race was at Caserta near Sorrento. We headed over the Mont Cenis Pass and down to Turin to visit the Abarth factory and collect the Le Mans money, then down through Milan and Florence. Approaching Turin we were wondering how we would find the Abarth factory when a Fiat 600 dived inside, carving Denny up on a roundabout. He was busy delivering robust Hulme-style invective when I realised that the Fiat had an Abarth scorpion badge on its door and that the driver was Abarth himself. We shouted and I banged on the door, and Abarth swung round looking most indignant until he realised that it was his favourite New Zealand racing driver, then he was all smiles as we followed him to the factory.

While the starting money, prize money and expenses were reckoned up we were given a tour of the showroom and presented with sales catalogues for the cars, photographs, lapel badges, key rings and a silk scarf illustrated with winning Abarth cars. All this detail comes from my diary at the time. Everything has doubtless since been lost during various moves or more probably just discarded. My later dealer self recoils at the memory of items that I threw away. I still remember sifting through bags of sales brochures, press releases and photographs gathered during the Turin Motor Show in 1966 and dumping the Ferrari Year Book because it was too big and heavy – and in Italian. At the height of the market it became worth around £600!

While we were struggling to find the Autostrada on the way out of Milan we met up with David Piper. He told us that the Caserta race was the next weekend, with practice starting at 4.30 the following afternoon, not the following weekend as we had been told. So it was another all-night drive with the trailer behind. We left Milan at 12.30, went through Florence at 5.30, Rome at just past midnight and arrived at Caserta at 3.30 am, where we stopped in what we thought was a park. We slept like logs until dawn, then discovered that we had inadvertently parked in the grounds of a former royal palace.

We found that David Young was sharing a huge five-bedded room with John Love and Neil Davis. David had already raced at Teramo in Italy with his new Cooper, but had suffered engine and clutch problems and had then gone off the road. Angus's friend and engineer Bill Hannah had taken the Lotus on a trip through Switzerland and had planned to meet Angus at Caserta, but while Angus may have known that the race was in fact a week earlier than we had thought, there was no way of finding his racing car and mechanic in Switzerland.

By some international family quirk, Denny had an Italian full cousin, Giovanni, who was a lawyer in Sorrento and couldn't speak a word of English; we visited him for lunch on the day before practice. (Diary: 'We had a huge feed of oranges, peaches, apricots and cherries, then he gave me a cup of coffee with Cognac in it. During the night I was very ill.') Surprise, surprise.

There was a delay during scrutineering when the doctors would not clear Denny because his heart was beating too fast. I noted this in my diary and realise now that it was an early indication of a Hulme heart condition; there were suggestions before his death that he had been having heart-related problems. However, he qualified fastest in the heat for pole position in the final, while David, having been quick in practice, tangled with an Italian who spun in front of him on the first lap and he was out for the weekend. In the final Denny bent a gear selector and finished third behind Love and Siffert.

The next race on Denny's schedule was Monza, so he decided to check the engine bearings and change ratios while we were in Sorrento. He told me how to take the gearbox off, showed me which ratios he wanted changed, and let me get on with it. I thought I had done quite well to get it all back together and bolted up, and so did Denny when I told him I was finished. But when I told him that I had a few bits over that he might like to put in his spares kit, I thought our friendship had come to an end. He was *furious*! I couldn't understand. I had done exactly what he had told me and saved him a few parts, and he didn't seem best pleased about it. He called into question my abilities as a mechanic and I pointed out that I had never done any mechanical work in my life. So why had I told him I was a mechanic when he asked me to come on the trip with him? I said I'd done nothing of the sort – if he cared to think back, he had asked me if I wanted to come with him and I'd said yes. No mention of being a mechanic. It then all went quiet for about half an hour as he set about taking the gearbox off again to make good my best efforts . . .

We took time off to visit the nearby ruins of Pompeii, buried in lava when Mount Vesuvius had erupted centuries before. We were badgered by would-be guides, but Denny had been there the year before and said we didn't need a guide. His main interest was to visit the buried brothels and bath houses. Most of the buildings of interest were locked and the guides had the keys, but my 'guide' solved this problem by climbing the walls. The next tourist target we saw was the Colosseum in Rome, but this by sheer chance, passing it when we were lost, trying to find our way out of the city.

At Monza we met up with David and Colin again, parked the Cooper in their paddock garage, and joined them for a drive into Milan to see the sights and have dinner. David was driving, and if he was looking for red lights he missed one at an intersection and tee-boned what must have been the only right-hand-drive Fiat 600 in Milan. Italy, even. Nobody was hurt but we brought that part of Milan to a complete stop as the cars were locked together across the tramlines. Trams were backing up in both directions and so was traffic while we waited for the police to come and sort it out.

We were taken to the local police station and when the Italian desk sergeant gave up trying to cope with taking down the particulars of our New Zealand addresses, I persuaded him to let me use his typewriter. The following day David went to find the British consul while we went to the track, to discover at 3 pm that Denny didn't have an entry – mainly because he hadn't sent it in. He had forgotten that he was entered for the Formula Junior race supporting the French Grand Prix at Rheims, so this meant loading up and setting off on another overnight drive.

By 8 pm we were at 6,500 feet crossing the Simplon Pass. I was driving while Denny slept. I was aware that the road was climbing more steeply and becoming narrower, but I didn't risk waking Denny until the trailer guards were brushing both verges. My problem was to explain that a) we were lost, b) there was no place to turn, and c) I couldn't reverse with the trailer. Denny could, and did – for 2 miles . . .

We crossed into France before dawn in thick fog and running low on fuel; because the banks were closed we only had Italian currency. Denny found a small petrol station that opened early and he scrabbled around in a shoebox of mixed coinage gathered during his two seasons of European travelling, getting together sufficient francs for enough fuel to get us to Rheims by 8.15 am. We managed to get a fifth-floor room at the Hotel Cecyl, paying the equivalent of a fiver for the five-day race weekend. In qualifying Angus towed Denny up to third fastest time behind Trevor Taylor's Lotus and Alan Rees.

After dinner Denny took us to the famous Brigitte's Bar where we found Jack Brabham, Bruce McLaren, Trevor Taylor and John Whitmore, and there was a commotion as John Cooper climbed in through the window. Drivers like Mike Hawthorn and Peter Collins had been noisy patrons of Brigitte's Bar in the past, and if the police didn't arrive in force at some point in the evening it was regarded as a quiet night. Cooper announced to the bar that he was going to paint his cars red. When someone asked why, he said it was because they were the only ones going fast. The Ferraris were totally dominant on the long fast straights.

The following morning we went to the swimming pool to find Stirling Moss, Jack Brabham, Bruce McLaren, Jim Clark, Trevor Taylor, Innes Ireland, Colin Chapman and John Cooper already taking the sun. (Diary: 'Moss was very chatty and telling us a few tales that have never got into print.') Imagine that sort of inter-team socialising today – there is probably a clause in driver contracts of the 1990s specifically precluding it. That afternoon we were in the Cooper pit watching Phil Hill in the Ferrari taking pole, then going out again to provide a tow for fellow Californian Dan Gurney in the F1 Porsche!

On the morning of the race Denny and I were leaving our room when a driver in Dunlop blue overalls came out of the one next door, nodding to us as he locked up. I asked Denny who it was.

'Dunno,' he said. 'Never seen him before.'

That afternoon the driver we didn't know drove his way into the record books when he won his first Grand Prix in a Ferrari. It was Giancarlo Baghetti.

Ten days back in England, then we were on the road again, this time down to Messina in Sicily. Forty hours later we were in Rimini to pause for the night, then on to Pescara where Denny took us for a lap of the 16-mile circuit, a combination of mountain sections and a 6-mile straight along the coast. Denny had won the FJ race there in 1960 after a race-long battle with Colin Davis, son of the famous S. C. H. (Sammy) Davis who won Le Mans for Bentley in 1927 and was later Sports Editor of *Autocar*.

I like the story of the FJ race at Monza that year when Colin Davis was leading Denny in the closing laps and Bill Gavin, the New Zealand journalist who travelled with Denny in 1960 as I did the following summer, held out a pit signal as Davis went by: 'HULME OUT'. Davis eased back and Hulme swept past, thinking Davis had problems, and won comfortably. The story goes that Bill was back at his hotel by the time the race had finished and Davis was rather angry at being outwitted by reading signals other than his own. Gavin refuses to confirm this story but I think it's worth re-telling on the off-chance that Bill is being uncharacteristically bashful.

In those pre-transporter days there were always terrifying tales of the trips, which made towing to the race sound more dangerous than the race itself. On the ferry from Reggio Calabria was an American

named Peterson, who had put his car, trailer and new Cooper-DKW
over a bank when he went to sleep. David Piper's mechanic was
towing his Lotus when the lashing ropes broke; the car slid off the
trailer and the mechanic back-tracked 10 miles to find the Lotus in a
ditch but only slightly damaged. Bob Anderson, the racing motor
cyclist who had switched to four wheels, towed his Lotus on a trailer
behind his van with two camp beds bolted to the floor in the back.
Bill McGowan, racing a Lola for the Fitzwilliam team, travelled in the
AC-Bristol he had raced the previous season. The Fitzwilliam
mechanics carried their cars in a converted bus that had a top speed
of 38 mph, its advantage being that the mechanics not driving could
sunbathe on the roof the way Nevil Shute used to on the tail-fins of
the prototype airships during their long, lazy proving flights.

Colin Davis led away in the De Sanctis, but he was out with a
broken con-rod on the 9th lap leaving Bob Anderson, the British
privateer in his Lotus 20, leading from Hyslop's similar car. But
Anderson's engine blew, letting Angus into the lead with Denny in
second place, and they ran that way to the flag. The Italians weren't
sure what to make of the result – New Zealanders first and second.

Back at the hotel I had a couple of bottles of beer sent up and set
to work on my first race report of New Zealand drivers dominating a
race abroad. There would be more.

During this time I had been sharing a bedsitter in Parsons Green
with Tony Vial, but he had moved off to the Continent for a
prolonged trip and I see from my diary that I went to a party at a flat
in Vereker Road, Barons Court. 'It was a flop as there were about 20
girls and three boys. I stayed until about 3 am chatting to a couple of
Pom girls.' Obviously there were flops and there were flops. I
mention this only because the Vereker Road flat returns with a
vengeance later in the year.

Denny's next Continental race was at Karlskoga in Sweden, with a
race at the Roskildering in Denmark the following weekend.
Motoring News agreed to pay for my air ticket to cover both races, so
for the first time I was a 'professional' journalist with someone else
picking up the tab. It would come back to haunt me 30 years on. We
flew in a Comet and I was peering hopefully at the map in the airline
magazine to find Karlskoga, which I imagined to be on the outskirts
of Stockholm. It was the first time I had been in a serious passenger
jet and I was as intrigued as any first-time flier. The novelty would
soon wear off.

I discovered that in fact Karlskoga was a 3-hour drive from
Stockholm, so I hired a Saab 95 thinking that the paper would be
eager for a test on the new model. It cost £20 for the five-day hire,
and was another new experience because it was a left-hand-drive car
but Sweden still drove on the left-hand side of the road at that time.

There was also a non-championship Formula 1 race in Sweden,

and all the top teams had entered. Peter Arundell had practised his FJ Lotus during the F1 session and was credited with fastest lap, but the organisers changed their minds at the last minute and disallowed his times. Colin Chapman was furious and stood with arms folded in front of the FJ grid until Arundell was put back on the front row. The organisers refused, Chapman backed down, and the race started. But the Arundell saga didn't end there. He tangled with the driver of one of the front-engined, front-wheel-drive Saabs at the end of the pit straight and was punted through the haybales. Love and Maggs finished an easy 1–2 in their Tyrrell Coopers and Denny was fourth.

In the F1 race Jim Clark's Lotus was on pole with Moss on the back of the grid in his UDT-Lotus, having missed practice while winning the TT at Goodwood in a lightweight Ferrari 250GT Berlinetta. Stirling showed the style that made him a legend as he sliced through to fourth on the first lap, second on the following lap, and on lap 3 he was 2 seconds ahead of Jimmy. This was Moss in his heyday, dealing with the opposition the way that Jimmy would handle it after Stirling's Goodwood crash the following Easter. The Lotuses of Clark and Ireland were both out by half distance and former motor cycle ace Geoff Duke rolled his Cooper, having already rolled it during practice! The final order was Moss, Bonnier, Surtees, Salvadori.

I then flew down to Copenhagen and met up with the racing gang again. Some time during an evening with Jack Brabham's mechanic Tim Wall and Stirling's UDT mechanic Tony Robinson, I hatched a plan to go to the F1 races at Modena, Monza and Zeltweg (I spelled it 'Selweg' so I obviously wasn't too sure about it!) by transporter. I phoned this idea through to Stuart Turner, then at *Motoring News* and later to mastermind rallying and competition programmes at BMC, Castrol and Ford. He said he would cable back an answer. I had tried to cash in my air ticket but couldn't, then a cable arrived from *Motoring News* saying that they wanted copy from Modena, but no mention of expenses. I cabled back asking for clarification. That night John Love, Tony Maggs and their Tyrrell mechanic Neil Davis piled into the Maggs Mini and we went into Copenhagen looking for entertainment (Neil is now works manager with Tyrrell and 30 years on I still see him occasionally at The Barley Mow).

My plans seemed to change by the hour. The transporter trip to Modena was off, and I was considering going to Zandvoort for the Dutch GP or the Nurburgring with Andrew Hedges and John Whitmore. French stunt driver Jean Sunny was doing his two-wheel act and a series of spin turns at the track, prompting UDT-Lotus driver Masten Gregory to observe that he could do just as well. 'You do too,' said Tony Robinson, 'but you don't get paid for it!'

Stirling Moss won all three heats of the F1 race in his UDT-Lotus and John Love won the Formula Junior trophy overall. I wrote the *Motoring News* report that night while the others partied and prepared to leave next morning for the 500 km touring car race at the Nurburgring with John Whitmore in his racing Mini. It was to be the most frightening experience of my life to date. And that was just the trip down.

Whitmore, now Sir John, had the first of the fast private racing Minis. We were ready to leave around 7 am and I was less than encouraged to see him buckle into his harness while I didn't have one. He cruised at 85 mph, which included tight corners and blind brows, reaching the ferry port at Gedser at 8.15 am having averaged over 70 mph.

This needs putting into perspective. It was the 1961 equivalent of being invited by Paul Radisich to ride in his racing Mondeo by road to the next race and being driven at racing speed the whole way. I had never been driven so fast for so long. The Danes and the Germans weren't ready to be passed and certainly not by such a tiny car – the Mini was still a relative novelty in Europe. A Mercedes driver on the Autobahn took particular exception at being overtaken and John finally let him by at about 95 mph, then latched on to his bumper, slipstreaming up to 100 mph and looking like a Brockbank cartoon. The Mercedes driver then slowed, but blocked every attempt by the Mini to pass again, so John dived off into a service station, flew straight through an empty lane of pumps and out the other side in front of the German, who was still looking in his mirror to see where we had gone! If this was frightening in daylight, it was just a foretaste of what it was like in darkness. The Valkyries had it easy.

We arrived at Adenau to meet Christabel Carlisle, the incredibly quick lady who raced a Mini and usually beat the men. John and Christabel were to share her car in the race, but as she had never been to the 'Ring before, John planned a comprehensive track training session on the daunting 14.2-mile mountain course.

Looking back, it was the ideal introduction to the 'Ring. We went three-up in Christabel's Mini while John pointed out all the corners. Clip the grass on this apex, take this one late, this one flat, turn into this one before you get to it. There was one important tree to line up with on the horizon as you approached the Karrusel, the steeply banked corner that you actually dropped into if you were going fast. If you kept the tree lined up on your approach you would take the Karrusel right. Get off line and you would be flung out off the banking too soon.

I remember Denny Hulme taking Laurence Edscer and I round the 'Ring in a Sierra Cosworth and explaining the importance of lining up with landmarks. 'The first time I raced there I was told that you lined up one important series of corners with a house . . . and do you know, all the years I raced there, I *never* saw that house!'

It was hard work for Christabel, trying to absorb the complexities of the circuit, then being quizzed by John next time round as to which corners were coming up. Then John put his helmet on and went off for a fast lap, and Christabel and I drove round to see how much we could remember on our own. We found that we knew a lot of the corners, but of course the ones that we had forgotten could have meant we never made it to the next corner. A daunting prospect for the petite young English girl. The following day John and Christabel concentrated on learning in her car, which they would race, and I did a few laps in John's racing Mini.

Porsche was also using the track for testing, and while John and Christabel went off together, Jo Bonnier took me round in his Porsche 1600 road car, pointing out where some of the more spectacular accidents had happened. He told me about coming through one section on his first lap testing with Porsche to find a family having breakfast in the middle of the track!

Andrew Hedges arrived with his racing Sprite trailered behind an Austin A40, and called by our hotel that afternoon. As he was leaving, John filled a wastepaper bucket with water and tipped it over him from our second-floor window. Christabel thought this was a hoot, and the next day, when she spotted Andrew arriving, she filled the narrow-neck water jug in her room, went on to the balcony and flung it over him. Unfortunately she had reckoned without the laws of physics relating to a mass of water in movement, and the jug swung itself upright and emptied straight down – over the landlady who was scrubbing tables below! Christabel did what any red-blooded public schoolgirl would do in the circumstances. She screamed and fled, locking herself in her room.

When official practice started, John got down to 12 min 34.6 sec in Christabel's car, but he had done 12 min 31 sec with me as passenger in his own more highly-tweaked Mini.

As the cars lined up on race morning for the Le Mans-style start, Whitmore found that he was beside Bill McGowan in a works Abarth. It was left-hand drive and they joked about tangling doors, but John said that he planned to wait and fasten his seatbelt so it wasn't going to be a contest. After all the learning and the preparations for the race, poor Christabel never got a drive in her own car as John retired the Mini with gearbox problems during his first stint.

We drove back in convoy with Christabel's Mini presenting the driver with a variety of gears, and John's car loaded with the spares. We missed the ferry at Ostend, so drove to Dunkirk at midnight and got aboard after a terrific argument. I slept in the car and must have been totally exhausted – a truck loaded with speedway bikes a few feet away caught fire and there was pandemonium, but I slept through it all. Christabel's Mini limped as far as London, sometimes in first gear, sometimes in top, and sometimes selecting reverse by itself and jarring to a halt. I rushed by tube to *Motoring News* just as the Editor, Cyril Posthumus, was processing final copy.

As far as I was concerned I thought I had done a good job for the paper. Having agreed to do the races in Sweden and Denmark, I had delivered a Saab touring story and the 500 km Nurburgring report as well as a feature on the hectic Mini trip with Whitmore, but the proprietor, Wesley Tee, somehow decided that I had overcharged on the Swedish hire car and misappropriated the unused portion of the air ticket, and when *Motor Sport* published a feature of mine on driving the 1922 TT Sunbeam in New Zealand in 1993, he issued an edict that I was not to appear again in any of his publications! At least there is nothing wrong with his memory . . .

My diary notes that on Sunday 10 September I went to Madame Tussauds and the Planetarium with someone called Debbie, and when we came back to the flat in Cromwell Road (into which I had moved with Peter Jackson and Richard Melville) we heard on the news that Wolfgang von Trips and 14 spectators had been killed in the Italian GP at Monza.

This flat was really more of a large bedsitter with a high turn-round of visitors, all racing Minis or Sprites, and nobody seemed to have a front door key. Entrance was by climbing over the windowsill from the front doorstep and sliding in the window. Exit was more conventional using the front door.

In mid-September I moved again, into the aforementioned flat in Vereker Road. This flat has to be explained. It was on the second and third floors on a corner block in Barons Court, and when I arrived there were 14 in residence, seven girls and seven boys, all New Zealanders. Oh, and there were *two* bedrooms. If this sounds like a den of iniquity, it wasn't. A Christchurch girl called Adrienne ruled the flat with a rod of iron, and anyone who disputed her authority found themselves with bags packed and on the pavement very quickly. There were *no* in-house romances that I was aware of, except, ironically for Adrienne, who shared the big cupboard under the stairs with Hank, who worked for John Sprinzel on his Austin-Healey Sprites; they eventually married and now live back home in Christchurch. Even I find this hard to believe as I write it now, but it is absolutely true. All-in board was 30 bob a week, and Adrienne kept a duty rota so that the boys took everyone's washing to the launderette on Saturdays (God help anyone else in the area who wanted washing done, because we commandeered most of the machines), then did the food shopping. It was like shopping for an army.

One particular party sticks in my mind. I remember that we borrowed a piano from somewhere, manhandled it up the stairs into the lounge and invited everyone we could think of. There was a bloodcurdling shriek of tyres at about the time the party was due to start and we ran to the balcony to see Paul Hawkins coming off a 360-degree spin through the intersection in his Austin-Healey.

Hawkins was a hewn-from-granite Australian, a determined racer, a good man to have at your side if the company looked like cutting rough, and enormous fun. We realised that we might run out of glasses, so Hawkins grabbed an airline bag and a tea-towel and asked me where the nearest pub was. I took him, and as I was ordering a couple of beers I realised that he had the towel over his arm like a waiter and was systematically clearing the tables of all the empty glasses – into the airline bag. It was Hawkins who, during a police raid on Brigitte's Bar in Rheims, took advantage of the mayhem to undo the nuts on one of the wheels on the Black Maria, with predictable results. Irrepressible. His death in a fiery race crash in a Lola at Oulton Park in the 1969 TT robbed the racing world of one of its great characters.

According to my diary, Christabel and I were going out together at this point: 'Christabel called round in her mother's Mini and she let me drive to Warren's place.' I can't remember who Warren was, and he's probably pleased about that. The entry continues: 'The party there was a shambles with Warren trying to put the stone lions in the street. He wasn't very impressed when we put his Mini on the footpath. When we left he was fighting with a taxi driver. Christabel and I had a long talk and she said she is keen to drive a Sprite so that she can go to Sebring.'

Switching to rear-drive cars turned out to be her undoing. She crashed a Sprite at Silverstone and a race official was killed. I don't think she raced again after that. But she was some racer in a Mini!

Two days later I made a note that I had been to 'Chater & Scott, the motoring booksellers. I spent half the day there and bought £3 worth of books, but I think I will get a few more before I go home.' I'll bet the owner, Frank Stroud, was pleased to see me, spending half a day and three quid. When I started dealing in old motoring books we became close friends in the business.

I was trying to put together a package that would enable me to cover the races in New Zealand and Australia in January and February 1962. Peter Garnier at *Autocar* had offered £75 for the four races in New Zealand, and there was a chance that I could do the Australian races as well.

My next trip was to Paris for the Coupe de Salon at Montlhery with Andrew Hedges, and we met up with Fitzwilliam in his 3.4 Jaguar with Bill McGovern and Sally Weston on board. First call was to L'Action Automobile, the Paris equivalent of The Steering Wheel Club in London. Jabby Crombac was also there, and I noted that I chatted with him about writing for the new magazine he was starting. *Sport Auto* is still going, but Jabby has retired as editor although he still covers all the Grands Prix as the senior scribe on the series.

After dinner and copious amounts of wine (Diary: 'The meal and wine cost a small fortune, still I reckon I'll never see Paris like this again so I might as well make the most of it') we piled into Fitzwilliam's Jaguar and on the Rue St Denis he drove right in behind one of the rear-entry Parisian buses so that none of the passengers could get on or off. At that time of the night after that sort of dinner it seemed hilariously funny – except to the gendarmes, who were watching from the front door of the police station! They came pouring out in force and, to make matters worse, Fitzwilliam reversed into the car behind him. He was dragged from the Jaguar and frog-marched to jail. We made valiant efforts to get him freed, but a gendarme with a gun behind a concrete barricade dissuaded us from further efforts. We took a taxi back to the hotel, and Fitz appeared at breakfast next morning having been lectured on his behaviour and sent home about 1.30 am.

Tony Maggs and John Love dominated the Formula Junior race in the Tyrrell Coopers and McGovern crashed and retired in the second heat with the Fitzwilliam Lola. Actually, the dinners were more exciting than the motor racing. After a hectic meal in Paris on race night we piled into Crombac's Hispano Suiza with some of us on the roof and set off for a trip around the sights, but perhaps Jabby didn't approve of his rooftop passengers because he parked the car round the corner and walked back to the restaurant. McGovern slipped in behind the wheel to drive the Hispano, but was apprehended by the constabulary trying to drive the wrong way up a one-way street. I borrowed 200 francs from Andrew Hedges the following morning and caught an Air France flight back to London with my race report for *Motoring News*.

Motor Racing magazine offered 70 guineas for coverage of the New Zealand races, while *Motoring News* was offering £10 a race, and I had paid a deposit on a passage on the *Bretagne*, which arrived at Sydney on New Year's Day. Perhaps it was the cost of this venture that prompted me to get a job in a company that produced business directories (by lifting entries from other directories as far as I could make out). It was the first job I'd had in six months, and it was crashingly boring. Come to think of it, it was probably the *last* proper job I've had . . .

On 28 October, a day worth remembering, Roger Tregaskis, who had been showing up in my diary for a few weeks as 'Trig', arrived at Vereker Road to announce that he was flying home to Tasmania with Gavin Youl in a single-engined Cessna 180 and there was a seat available. I wasn't sure what a Cessna looked like, but I said I'd go. It would cost £25, and I queried how it could cost this much. Apparently Gavin had worked out that it would take five days, so that was five nights in hotels at a fiver a night. Looking at it like that it sounded reasonable. But of course it didn't work out quite that simple . . .

CHAPTER THREE

Bruce McLaren

BRUCE MCLAREN APPEARED in my life a year before I met him, and dominated it beyond his death ten years later. When I was the motor racing writer in my local paper in New Zealand, I discovered by incredible good fortune that Bruce's sister Pat, then married to John Hunter, lived in Timaru and received regular letters from her brother. Pat would phone when a letter arrived and I would be allowed to digest this straight-from-the-horse's-mouth information. My columns perked up each time Pat had a letter.

Bruce had been picked as the first New Zealand Driver to Europe in 1958 by the International Grand Prix Association in Auckland, the organisation that staged the annual GP on the Ardmore airfield circuit near the city. He was the ideal driver at the ideal time, a trained engineer with a natural talent as a racing driver who could be relied on to bring the car home, and with the talent to win if the opportunity presented itself. Jack Brabham was the first to rate McLaren's ability when he raced in New Zealand, although perhaps it would be fairer to say that Jack recognised Les McLaren, Bruce's dad, as a likely customer for the spare cars the overseas drivers always brought to the colonies to help make ends meet. Which always meant 'make a profit'.

Bruce's first proper racing car was a bob-tailed Cooper 1500 centre-seat sports-racer bought from Brabham and raced with success in local events in 1957. Bruce had kept in touch with Brabham by letter and agreed to buy a 1750 cc ex-works Formula 2 Cooper that Jack was bringing out to New Zealand with his 1960 cc Formula 1 machine in 1958. Armed with this Cooper single-seater, Bruce drove his way into the overseas scholarship, earned a works Formula 2 drive with the Cooper team in Britain and Europe during that 1958 season and joined Brabham in the Cooper Formula 1 team for 1959.

Bruce would win the last race of the 1950s (the US GP at Sebring),

the first race of the 1960s (the Argentine GP), and a car with his name
on the nose would win the last GP of that scintillating decade (Denny
Hulme in Mexico). A year later, on 2 June 1970, Bruce would die at
the wheel of his latest Can-Am sports-racer, the fastest racing car in
the world at that time. The rear body-panel flexed under the pressure
from the new rear wing, the tail billowed open at top speed on the
back straight at Goodwood and the car was flicked into an unused
solid concrete flag marshal's post.

Everyone seems to remember where they were the day John F.
Kennedy was assassinated. I remember 2 June 1970 in the same way.
I had taken the train to Waterloo and walked along Stamford Street to
the offices of *Autocar*. When I went into the office, Martin Lewis said,
'Have you heard the news on the radio? Your mate's been killed at
Goodwood.' That moment became engraved on my mind. Not even
so much the news, but the way I received it – both barrels, short
range. I walked straight back to Waterloo, got on the next train and
rode back to Horsley in tears. The worst day of my life. It was like
losing a brother. I vowed then never again to get close to a racing
driver.

Bruce became the dominant figure in my life and work from the
days when I dogged his sister for news. We met briefly in 1958 at the
Teretonga race near Invercargill, the southernmost circuit in the
world, when I had somewhat diffidently approached him for details
of his entry in our local loose-metal hill-climb the following weekend.
This needs to be put into perspective. I was the lad from the local
paper and he was an international sporting star. Diffidence didn't last
long. He turned out to be one of us, a regular bloke. His ability to put
people at their ease was one of his endearing and enduring features.
I didn't think I needed to bother him with the fact that I was also
entered in the hill-climb – in my mother's Austin A30! I won my class
and Bruce didn't. There was only one other entry in my class and he
didn't turn up, so my gentle ascent of the hill guaranteed me a class
victory. Bruce had filled the Cooper differential with plumber's lead
to lock it, but the transmission failed on the line for his second run
and he couldn't approach the times of local driver Maurice Stanton in
his supercharged air-cooled aero-engined Stanton Special.

Being a local lad and fancying myself as something of a Man About
Town in Timaru with a captive sports personality in tow, I laid it on
thick. I told Bruce that I would take him to the Saturday night dance
at the Bay Hall on Caroline Bay, the beach that made Timaru a
holiday centre in the summer. I probably assured him that the local
girls were breathtakingly beautiful. Well, some of them were. One girl
in particular took Bruce's fancy. Pat Broad had won local beauty
contests and was most certainly the class of the evening. There was a
mutual attraction, but local custom decreed that the first male admirer
to request the last dance of the evening and be accepted was allowed

to escort said lady home. Bruce left his run late and was furious at being turned down.

'She said she's going to a party,' reported the spurned swain. 'Where would it be? Let's go and find it.'

He was driving his father's new 2.4-litre Jaguar, then the equivalent of a Rolls-Royce among unaffordable and unobtainable cars in a country still stricken with import quotas. I thought the idea of the Jaguar might aid his quest. But we never found Pat's party. Then it became a Cinderella quest. He had to find her. If he had had a glass slipper in his hand he couldn't have made it plainer when he came round to our house the next morning.

I thought perhaps a cautionary phone call might be better than appearing on the lady's doorstep first thing on a Sunday. Pat answered the phone. Did she want to see this racing driver again, I asked, with Bruce leaning forward trying to hear the answer. Well, yes, she supposed so. Where had she been last night? Mind your own business. The course of true love never did run smoothly, but this was the start of a romance that was to lead across the world, to marriage and a daughter, Amanda, before that tragic day in 1970.

They say that 'Those who can, do. Those who can't, write about it.' That stands good for me. I was never going to be a racing driver and I was never going to be bank manager, but the gypsy life of motor racing held a definite appeal and I was immensely fortunate in being in the right place at the right time. The circumstances would never be repeated. In the 1950s and 1960s New Zealand enjoyed a unique position in world motor racing when all the top drivers came south to enjoy the off-season in the sun while Britain froze. Through Bruce I met all the Grand Prix drivers who had only been names I had read about. The races were serious affairs, but life away from the tracks was a laid-back series of barbecues and parties, and I got to know all the international celebrities on first-name terms. This paid off when I arrived in Europe in 1961 and could chat comfortably with the likes of Jim Clark and John Surtees.

I worked with Bruce in 1962 and stayed with him until 1966, when I was well established and could start my own company, maintaining my links with him by working with his sponsors. The 1966 season was to see the emergence of the first McLaren Formula 1 car, built for the new formula when the engine size doubled from 1.5 to 3 litres. It's history now that Bruce felt that the aluminium Oldsmobile engine he used in his Can-Am sports cars would not work as the basis for a Grand Prix power unit and embarked on a scheme aimed at luring Ford into Formula 1. Jack Brabham picked up the Oldsmobile and had Repco in Australia convert it into an engine that would win world championships for Jack and Denny Hulme in 1966 and 1967.

Bruce was working closely with Ford on their Le Mans programme (he won the 24-hour race with Chris Amon in 1966), and he wanted to bring Ford behind his Formula 1 programme. No official help was forthcoming, so he decided to make a gesture that would surely bring the blue-oval boys into his corner. He commissioned a project to reduce a 4.2-litre four-cam Indianapolis Ford V8 engine to 3 litres, but it was an expensive disaster. They had been aiming for 330 bhp, but the engine was heavy, unreliable and could only just summon 300 bhp at the peak of a very narrow power band. Everything they didn't need. The car debuted at Monaco where the megaphone exhausts made an incredible noise, but it was a failure. Howden Ganley, the New Zealand mechanic who worked on the build of the car and would later race BRMs in Formula 1, recalled over a Barley Mow lunch in 1996 that the Ford engine, bell-housing and gearbox in that first Formula 1 McLaren weighed more than Jack Brabham's complete car! It must have irritated Bruce beyond measure a few months later when Ford commissioned Keith Duckworth to build a Formula 1 engine that would be used exclusively by Lotus in 1967.

McLaren used various engines to stay in Formula 1, but it was not until they could buy the Ford-Cosworth DFV V8 engine in 1968 that their fortunes would change. Bruce won the 1968 Belgian Grand Prix in his own McLaren car and scored second places in Canada and Mexico. Denny Hulme had joined the team for an all-Kiwi line-up and he won the Italian and Canadian GPs that summer for McLaren. Bruce won the Can-Am championship for the second time in 1969 and he was planning a car for Indianapolis.

The Can-Am series was in some ways a mirror of the Tasman series, where the drivers enjoyed themselves as much off the track as they did on it. Formula 1 in Europe was serious and hard work, but in the late 1960s, when Can-Am success was coloured the orange of the McLarens, and Bruce and Denny were dominant, it was lucrative recreation. I remember the night before the race at the old-fashioned Siebkins Hotel in Elkhart Lake when I was sharing a huge three-bedded room with Bruce and Denny. I had been late in the bar and was creeping in, opening the door ever so carefully so as not to disturb the sleeping drivers. But as I put a foot in the door I heard a 'shhh' from the direction of the big drop-sash window. The two drivers, who I had imagined sleeping dreamlessly in preparation for race day on the morrow, were both at the window with the shade raised an inch, watching the progress of someone on the verandah outside pleasuring his lady . . . So much for pre-race sleep. But that was the way it was. It may even have been that weekend at Elkhart when the two McLarens set times well clear of the field on the first day of qualifying and ignored the second day altogether, the drivers spending the time on a lake water-skiing.

Bruce's goals were becoming more those of an engineer, and he was considering retirement as a driver to concentrate on the potential of his team. A pair of M15 Offenhauser-engined McLarens ran at

Indianapolis in 1970, but they were not on the pace, and on the flight back to London Bruce and designer Gordon Coppuck pondered the special problems of the spookily fast four-cornered oval.

Two days later Bruce was testing Denny's Can-Am McLaren at Goodwood when the fatal crash happened that sunny midsummer day on the Sussex circuit. The following year the McLaren team went back to Indianapolis with a radically new car and immediately re-wrote the record books at the Brickyard. It was a tribute to that amazingly great guy who gave the team his name.

CHAPTER FOUR

Flight
to Tasmania

BACK IN OCTOBER 1961, although I didn't know what a Cessna was, I knew that Gavin Youl was a Tasmanian who had raced the first Brabham Formula Junior. The car was originally called an MRD (for Motor Racing Developments, Jack Brabham's company), but it was Jabby Crombac who pointed out that the pronunciation in French came perilously close to *merde* ('shit')! Jack was one of the first racing drivers to fly, and he had sold his Cessna 180 to a farmer in Tasmania, part of the deal being that Gavin would deliver it at the end of the 1961 season.

I knew nothing about aeroplanes, and when Gavin drove me up to McAlpine's hangar at Luton Airport I was blithely strolling round looking at some of the impressive twin-engined executive aircraft.

'It's over here,' said Gavin from a far corner of the hangar where the smaller planes were parked.

It was *tiny*. He unlocked the door and I looked inside. The cabin seemed smaller than the inside of the Ford Zephyr in which we'd driven down from London. (Diary: 'We took a new wireless set with us and Gavin showed me the plane. Fairly small, but it looks as though we should have a lot of fun in it. He is getting a long-range tank flown from America for it.')

It soon became apparent that flying to Tasmania would be the easy bit. First came the paperwork. Sheaves of forms for visas for India, Indonesia, Lebanon, Thailand – you name it, we needed paperwork in triplicate for it. The route through the East called for more fuel capacity than the Cessna had as standard, and Gavin cabled Warren Olsen in California to arrange for a long-range tank to be flown out from the Cessna factory. Warren had managed Lance Reventlow's Scarab F1 operation. (Diary: 'The extra tank fits in the luggage compartment.') More later.

We paid a visit to the Royal Aero Club for route instructions, much as one would check with the Royal Automobile Club before setting out on a trip to Cornwall. Only further. At the Aero Club we met a Mr Black, a big chap with an aviator's handlebar moustache and a nagging concern for our safety. He was worried about Albania. 'Don't cross the Albanian border or you'll be shot down or forced down.' I wasn't sure where Albania was, but now didn't seem to be the time to ask. Gavin mentioned that we would have to fly along the border of Saudi Arabia and Iraq as flight over both countries was forbidden. Mr Black pointed out that on some maps the border petered out with a cryptic note that the boundary was not clearly defined.

Our basic route was down through France, across to Corsica, Rome, Athens, Rhodes, Cyprus, Beirut, Kuwait, Sharjah, Karachi, Calcutta, Rangoon, Singapore, Jakarta, Darwin, Adelaide and home to Launceston. If you said it quickly it didn't sound far or long, but if you thought about it at all you probably wouldn't have gone. Not 30 years ago. Not with a pilot who didn't have a night-flying rating. Back then I thought if you could fly, you could fly. Like riding a bike or driving a car. I didn't know that there were degrees of flying capability and that one didn't set off to the other side of the world in just about the smallest passenger plane on the market without knowing a good deal about it. Basically, Gavin could fly; his mate Roger Tregaskis and I couldn't. This was putting your head in the lion's mouth big-time, but in my case ignorance was bliss.

We needed inoculations against smallpox, cholera and yellow fever. Shell arranged to make fuel available at all our many stops for a total of £200. Today that is less than my monthly petrol account with Bell & Colvill in West Horsley!

We visited a ship's stores in Royal Mint Street to stock up with emergency rations, but looking at the shopping list now it's hard to imagine what sort of emergency Gavin was anticipating. We bought tinned butter and chocolate. The guy behind the counter didn't sound very enthusiastic about the ship's biscuits, so we halved our order for them. Then we needed a life-raft – presumably so we could eat the iron rations in some sort of comfort. Rafts for four were not available, but they could offer one for 10. Gavin said that was rather too big for the three of us. We could have three singles, but they were £50 each. Another problem to solve. Gavin eventually found a four-man raft through a girlfriend's father who was something high up in the RAF. The arrangement would be that Roger would sit in the co-pilot's seat and I would sit in the back with the life-raft stowed person-size beside me.

It wasn't until we had completed the trip that someone pointed out the absurdity of the life-raft. The Cessna was a high-wing plane and the packed raft was too large to fit through the window if the plane was floating in the sea, so it would have meant opening the door and sinking the plane to get the life-raft out. If it had been inflated in the cabin it would have crushed us against the sides. On balance it was better to discover these things *after* the flight.

We were due to depart early on the morning of Sunday 19 November, later than Gavin had originally planned because of the delays in getting the life-raft; it would now place us at risk in the monsoon season, which was just starting in the area of Indonesia.

On the Friday we met Jack Brabham at Luton and had our photographs taken with him for the *Sunday Pictorial*, the *Daily Express* and papers in Tasmania. Our current girlfriends arrived and we staged a tearful farewell scene on the tarmac, knowing full well that there were better personal farewells to come before the actual take-off two days later. In the event of a suitably large mishap I was to file copy to the *Daily Express*. It was left to me to judge the enormity of the mishap.

An ITN television news crew filmed our preparations for take-off, but we managed to avoid letting them know that while we were stowing our luggage in the hold above the long-range tank, I noticed a small sticker that hadn't been on the door before. It related to luggage stowage with the extra tank fitted. If the tank was empty the luggage hold could be filled. If the tank was full, which it would be on every take-off, *no* luggage could be carried at all in the compartment. We took a joint decision that it was too late to find signs like that, and the luggage was crammed in.

Brabham's instructions to Gavin for the benefit of the TV cameraman was to take off and turn left for Australia. He couldn't have known how close we came to taking his instructions literally. We took off at 10.30 am and recognised Jack's voice from the control tower giving directions. Gavin waggled the wings as we flew over the hangars and congratulated ourselves that so far we had been more successful than a luckless chap who set off in a Tiger Moth after an elaborate public send-off but flipped at the end of the runway on take-off.

Our egg-on-face turn was to come soon. At 2.30 pm somewhere near Paris our new radio and the radio compass went on the blink. The compass needle was lazily circling the dial. Gavin asked if we would prefer to land in France and have the radio fixed or return to Luton. We voted 3–0 to return to Luton. I was nominally the navigator since I was sitting nearest the maps in the back, so Gavin turned round and said, 'OK, where's Luton?'

'Back there,' I said confidently, flicking my thumb over my shoulder in the direction from which I assumed we had come.

But it wasn't going to be that easy. Gavin pointed out that we may have been flying in circles after the radio systems had gone AWOL and England could be in just about any direction.

We studied the ground for assistance and realised that we were flying over a large navigable river flowing down to a city that I recognised as Rouen, where I had been with Denny racing earlier in the year. I could see Les Essarts circuit on the edge of town. England, I announced, was to the right and across the Channel.

This was broadly accurate, but when we crossed the coast we were over a large town and we couldn't decide which one it was. Not much credence was given to my assertion that it was Brighton, because Brighton was the only South Coast town I had been to. We tried flying low enough to read the names of railway stations, but that didn't help, so we decided to fly up England until we found the M1 motorway. Luton, we knew, would then be to the right. This ploy worked until Gavin said over his shoulder, 'If this is the M1, what's that big road over to the right?' We had been flying up the A5, so we had to do some cross-country work before we found Luton.

Gavin hoped to be in the air again before dark, but there was a lot of head-shaking among the radio people at McAlpines so we resigned ourselves to going home to the prospect of seeing ourselves leave on the television news. We arrived at the flat where our girlfriends were staying and let ourselves in just as the news was showing us leaving. The looks on their faces were worth the trip back!

On Monday afternoon we had a call from Luton to say that the problem had been traced to a wire that had not been properly soldered. It made contact on the ground, but the vibration of the engine made it drop away from the connection and lose contact. The *Daily Express* and *Daily Mail* carried short paragraphs to say that we had taken off on our flight to Tasmania. Only the *Daily Telegraph* noted that our trans-world flight had lasted just 5 hours.

It was noon on Tuesday 21 November when we finally took off with all our scheduled stops now awry. We landed at Lyon at 5.20 pm local time and stayed overnight, refuelling in the morning when we were told that we would have to land at Nice to get permission to fly over the sea to Corsica because we had no emergency radio for the life-raft. It was a short flip down to Nice but a long wait while Gavin got the necessary documents. The wind was strong at ground level and the sky looked forbidding. We were in the plane and ready for take-off when word came that we weren't allowed to take off because of worsening weather conditions across our flight-path to Corsica. There was no option but to park the plane, chain it to concrete blocks and leave it. We found a hotel at half summer season rates and I had a room with bath for £2.

We woke the next morning to a howling gale and pouring rain, but we went to the airport on the off-chance. Take-off was out of the question, then we couldn't find our hotel again so we chose another that was even cheaper at 30 bob a night with bath. Gavin sent a cable to Jordan advising of our delayed progress.

We had a 6 am start the next morning, and Gavin announced that we were off – bags packed and bills paid, we were on our way again.

The weather still looked forbidding, but with a slightly favourable forecast at 10 am we were hurrying to prepare the plane for take-off. At 10.40 we headed for a small hole in the clouds that immediately closed behind us and we were on our way to Corsica.

We were trying to fly below the cloud at 1,000 feet when, just before noon, we sighted the island. More accurately, we almost flew into the side of it when it loomed out of the cloud. We had been trying unsuccessfully to raise Calvi on the radio, so climbed to 6,000 feet, but still no response. It was 12.15 by the time we made contact with the tower and spotted the narrow stretch of air-strip carved out of the rough scrub. The airport staff of one handled our landing and paperwork and arranged a taxi to a local hotel.

We were airborne at 9.45 the next morning, passing over Elba at 10.20. We skirted a rainstorm on the way to the Italian coast and made a refuelling stop at Rome. While Gavin was arranging the fuel, two ladies from Reuters arrived in a Healey Sprite to interview us. Through a quirk of language difficulties, we ended up with eight huge steak sandwiches for in-flight lunch as we took off at 1.35 heading for Brindisi on the south-east coast near the spur on the boot of Italy. Our target was Athens that night, but we decided to settle for Brindisi, flying from Rome down to Naples by 1.30 and landing at Brindisi at 3 pm, where the man from Reuters helped with translations while we tied the plane down; he then took us in his Skoda to the Jolly Hotel.

We had hoped for a pre-dawn start, but there was so much official argument as to whether this was permissible that it was daylight as we taxied out on to the runway. We crossed the Straits of Otranto and sighted the coast of Greece at 7.35, dropping in over the hills of Athens at 9.15.

This may all sound fairly casual, but it has to be remembered that small-plane flights to Australia were still relatively novel – novel enough for Reuters to be following our progress anyway – and we were three babes in the air when it came to flying experience, three colonial lads without a vague idea of what lay before us. It became an adventure only afterwards when we realised what we had done. At the time it seemed like a cheap way of getting home, considering that the fifth night had been spent in Nice waiting for the weather to lift.

Take-off was delayed until 11.45 am, and taxying to the end of the runway we saw the burned-out remains of Ron Flockhart's Mustang, which had caught fire after overheating when he was held too long for take-off during his attempt on a record flight. We received clearance to fly over Cyprus and by 6 pm we were on short finals for Beirut, where we stayed overnight. The Beirut taxis were probably the most dangerous part of our trip. They were huge American Fords or Chevrolets and we wondered which side of the road we were supposed to be on. Everyone seemed to drive in the middle with priority to the driver who hooted loudest, longest – and first.

Next day we were refuelled and aboard as Gavin did his final check walk around the plane. He looked into the cabin to ask if we had heard gunfire the day before, because he thought we might have been hit – a wing trim tab had been badly gashed and twisted. It turned out that a Pan Am forklift had swiped our wing while unloading a freighter 20 yards away during the night. Pan Am agreed to fix the damage, paid us $10 each to cover personal costs and picked up the tab for our hotel.

We had planned only to refuel in Beirut because Lebanese visas were almost impossible to arrange in London in the time available, but as we were stuck for a second night we did need visas – these were issued instantly on the spot for 1s 3d each! During our documentation we met up with Bob Banzhaf, an American flying a Cessna out of Damascus, and that night he and his wife took us to an Arab-style restaurant called the Chickenhouse, which was appropriate as it had wire netting for windows, feathers on the floor and only chicken on the menu. The place looked awful but the chicken was wonderful. We had a whole bird each and ate with our fingers. Bob told us that he flew for a Turkish company servicing pipeline installations on the border, and he had been through three local wars in five years. He told us that the Cessna was the ideal plane for pipeline work because he could be up and down again before the jet fighters could be scrambled from either warring side. He also told us that if a fighter approached us and waggled its wings, it didn't mean follow him, it meant land right there or we would be shot out of the sky!

We sampled the local bazaar and returned to the Mayflower Hotel, where there was a message to say that we should be ready for a 3 pm take-off. While Gavin filed a flight plan I collected the hotel bill from Pan Am, which included our bar charges so it didn't look like such a bad accident after all. Much better than being shot. Bob and his wife were also ready for take-off to Damascus, and we were going to fly over the mountains with them, but as we were taxying away Gavin realised that the right hand disc brake wasn't working. The Pan Am mechanic who had repaired the flap damage worked quickly to fit a new washer, filled the reservoir and told us to take off as quickly as possible. It was 4.45 pm and we had only reached 2,500 feet when the tower called to advise that we had to switch from VFR to IFR and fly by the Dacway marker (which we couldn't find on the map because it was still being built!). Gavin misheard the controller and thought he was asking him to fly by the 'back way', and as he didn't fancy creeping under the cloud and over the mountains looking for the servant's entrance to Damascus, we returned to Beirut for another night at the Mayflower.

We were airborne again by 6 am and landed at Damascus 40 minutes later after crossing mountains and barren hills. Everyone was very amiable at the tower, but as we refuelled we found that our requested telegram for permission to overfly Jordan had not arrived, and the authorities were unable to give us official clearance to fly the border to Kuwait because Iran and Iraq were technically at war. We had come too far to go back, and they weren't actually stopping us from flying. It was just that if we were never seen again, it wouldn't be their fault. They hadn't given us permission to fly. And another thing, they said – private flights were not allowed to land in Kuwait, so we would be arrested when we landed. Damned if we did, damned if we didn't.

Just after 9 am we were in the air and heading for Kuwait, uneasily aware that we could see ten MiG jet fighters and camouflaged anti-aircraft guns at the end of the runway. These people were ready to play hardball and aerial tourists could become easy target practice.

We flew over desert stretching as far as we could see with occasional small lakes and groups of tents, people and animals. Nearly six hours later we touched down at Kuwait having seen nothing of anyone's air force but wondering what our reception would be like on the ground. As we had been warned, there was a police car chasing us before the plane had rolled to a stop, and the biggest uniformed policeman I had ever seen wrenched open the door. We were about to offer our wrists for handcuffs when his face broke into a big grin and he said, 'Gidday, you guys. Sorry I can't offer you a cold beer. The place is dry, but welcome to Kuwait!'

He was an Australian and they had been waiting for us to arrive for several days. This official welcome would happen several times on the trip – Gavin's father was well up in Australian politics and the word had gone out that we were making what was turning out to be a leisurely trip across the world.

Next day we had an alarm call at 4.15 am and took off at 6.30. Four hours later we were landing at Sharjah, having followed the coast most of the way. There was a warning of jet fighters in the area but we saw none. After refuelling men and machine, we were in the air again by noon and Gavin decided to aim for Jiwani, which showed on the map as a tiny fishing village on the coast of Pakistan, rather than try to make Karachi in cloud and after dark. After leaving Sharjah we flew over drifting red sand, then over high rocky mountains with updraughts throwing the plane around.

We reached Jiwani at 2.40 pm and were amazed at the size of the airport for such a tiny village. There were buildings sprawling everywhere, explained when we learned that it had been established as an RAF transit base during the war and was now virtually unused, with only about four planes a month stopping to refuel. The Burmah Shell representative invited us to stay at his home and we bounced along a rough track in the airport jeep to the fishing village. We passed camels and veiled women filling pitchers at wells like a page from a bible story. At the entrance to the town a colourful wedding procession – bride and groom were both 12-year-olds – came to a halt to look at the strangers in the yellow jeep without hood or windscreen; the jeep was one of only a handful of motor vehicles in the area. We were taken to the Customs Office, a mud hut where we drank tea and ate biscuits while Gavin filled in the forms by the light of a kerosene lamp.

When we came out the jeep was surrounded by native children, eager to see the foreigners. After a searingly hot Indian meal we were taken for a walk along the beach by the Shell man with a couple of boys carrying lanterns. It was pitch dark but there was a warm wind coming off the desert. We came to a native fishing village with the huts made of palm leaves, and were shown how the fish was salted in a pit then dried on racks. We also saw the long sleek fishing boats that carry a huge amount of sail on bamboo masts. At one point several villagers approached thinking we were planning to steal their fish. They needn't have bothered . . . the smell was appalling!

It was 8 am on 1 December when we left, carrying mail for the outside world (one letter was addressed to 'Mr Ron Coleman, Queensland, Australia.' Wonder if he got it . . .). Two and a half hours later we were sliding into a surprisingly deserted Karachi international airport. We taxied up in front of the main terminal and our reception was fairly offhand. An Indian wandered over, opened the door, emptied a fumigating spray into the cockpit, slammed the door and stepped back, looking very pleased with himself, happy that he was helping to make sure we would be bringing no noxious insects into India.

We took on 54 gallons of fuel, bought some sandwiches for lunch and came out to find that the tail-wheel tyre was punctured. Changing a wheel on an aeroplane is not the work of a moment, so Burmah Shell loaned us a mechanic from a Government crop-spraying company who took the wheel off and discovered that the tyre and the tube were ruined. Then I became aware that planes don't carry spare wheels, and we had ourselves a problem. We took a taxi to the Karachi Aero Club and – I kid you not – they decided that the tyre size might be the same as a First World War Sopwith Camel fighter, and they had new unused spares in the loft. We climbed a ladder and from an old trunk stencilled 'SOPWITH' they produced cartons of tubes, but they turned to dust as we picked them out of their wrappings, 40 years past their use-by date. According to my diary notes I was more bothered about getting ripped off by the taxi driver who had charged us 20 rupees for the trip in his aged Austin A40 instead of the proper fare of 7 rupees. We gave him 10 and a shouting match ensued. Who says foreign travel isn't fun?

We eventually tracked down an American who owned a Cessna the same as ours and he had a spare tyre and tube that he agreed to sell us. The mechanic finished fitting the tyre in the dark while the airport officials were in a panic because all their international traffic was soon due.

We were in the air before 7 am the next morning and headed across India. In terms of our epic voyage, India was easily the most eminently forgettable part. It went on forever. We arrived at Ahmedabad at 10 am and were surprised at the going-over we received by the Customs men, considering that we had only flown 3 hours from Karachi. They checked all the currency we had and stripped our bags from the plane.

By noon we were airborne again. The engine coughed and spluttered when flying through 5,000 feet, giving us a few anxious moments in the cabin until Gavin diagnosed carburettor icing and sorted it out. Nagpur was the next stop at 2.50 pm, where the Shell people had to mix 70 and 100 octane petrol to get the 80 octane we needed. Gavin found that the tail-wheel tyre was punctured *again*, but fortunately a spare was available from the local aero club without having to rummage through cases of Sopwith spares again.

Our bedroom at the hotel had a four-poster bed and two couches, but the four-poster was functional, not mock-Tudor – the posts were to support a mosquito net. It wasn't looking good for Roger Tregaskis and me on the couches with a blanket each. The planes from international flights thundering in and out through the night were more of an irritation than the mosquitoes, and the awful meal we had the night before was to provide an on-going problem. We flew out at 7 am and landed at Calcutta's Dumdum airport at 11.30.

I was ill from food-poisoning the whole morning and the only thing worse than throwing up in such a confined space is to be sitting with someone in such a confined space who is throwing up. My second requirement on landing was an emergency supply of sick bags from the BOAC desk. I had a tomato juice while the others had breakfast. A Reuters reporter met us and said he had been waiting for us since our original scheduled arrival on 23 November – it was now Sunday 3 December. Time flies when you're having fun. Right now I wanted to die. Gavin and Roger would have been happy if I had. At least it would have meant an end to that barfing noise from the back seat.

We left India behind us at 1.30 pm, heading out across the ocean for Rangoon, where we arrived as darkness fell at 6.40. We had to park a long way from the terminal building and could find no chocks, but there was a small army guarding Princess Alexandra's plane beside us so we supposed they would look after ours too, both being British and all that.

The Cessna call-sign is engraved on my mind: Gulf-Alpha-Papa-

Yankee-Juliet. Gavin had to announce it with every radio communication and there were hundreds. Most of the time he had the headphones on and kept all the muffled take-off and landing radio jargon to himself, but on the long stretches he left the radio open through the speakers.

We left Rangoon at 8 am with a scheduled refuelling stop at Phuket Island. My geography could only vaguely grasp some of the places we had been through, but now I was totally lost. None of us had heard of Phuket Island. We didn't even know how to pronounce it, as became clear when Gavin tried to call up the tower.

'Pooket Island, Pooket Island. Come in Pooket.'

Only static. No reply. Perhaps he had it wrong. He tried again.

'Pucket Island. Pucket Island. Come in Pucket.'

More static. And again.

'Fooket Island. Fooket Island . . .'

At which moment a broad Aussie voice burst through the speaker into the cabin from what we discovered was the Australian Air Force base at Butterworth further down the coast. 'Whaddya wanna do with it, mate? Pook it, fook it or fuck it?'

Phuket Island is now a thriving international tourist resort and I'm sure the 747 pilots don't have to swoop over a dirt strip to scare off the cattle the way we did before we could land. There was an eerie silence. No people. Only the cattle we had scared off the strip glaring balefully from the bush. Suddenly we were surrounded by half-naked children, then about 30 monks in saffron robes appeared out of the jungle regarding us and the plane almost ethereally, in a UFO sort of way, as though we might be real and then again we might not. They kept prodding the plane and muttering to themselves. They didn't prod us.

Then a native appeared with a 44-gallon drum on the back of a jeep and the fuel was pumped by a tiny motor that kept expiring in the heat. Roger and I found a village close by the strip and in the local drugstore – thatched roof, open sides, earth floor, chickens scratching, dogs fighting – we bought six bottles of Coca Cola. A badge of civilisation in the jungle. It was like finding Dr Livingstone. The cattle were returning to the strip as we took off and we just managed to clear them. The perils of international aviation.

We headed south for Singapore, but again we were behind schedule and it would have meant arriving there after dark when the airport was closed to light aircraft, so Gavin decided we would head for Kuala Lumpur instead.

'Where is it on the map?' he asked over his shoulder.

I shuffled through all the maps we had and I said it wasn't. 'K-L' (instantly falling into the colonial vernacular) wasn't on any of the maps we had because we had selected strip maps of our route rather as you would ask the AA or the RAC for strip maps of a trip to

Minehead, and you didn't plan on side trips. No K-L. We were flying down the coast with mountainous jungle to our left and sea to our right.

Gavin looked at his watch, worked out how long we had been flying since Phuket and said, 'Well, I reckon if we fly down the coast for another half hour then turn left we should find it.'

Looking back on it, the most amazing thing is that Roger and I accepted this without question. Not that we had much option, I suppose. When I tell experienced pilots that story today, their eyes go wide with disbelief. Disbelief that we found K-L. Disbelief that I'm here telling the tale.

In fact, I soon became aware that there weren't too many flat spaces in those mountains if Gavin's calculations were out by much, but at 5.15 there was K-L suddenly spread out 1,000 feet below us. Gavin landed with the confidence of a man who never doubted he would find the needle in the haystack, and we were greeted by the chaps from the local aero club who appeared to be expecting us and knew our names. How come, I asked, if K-L wasn't even on our route?

'Oh, everybody cocks it up and ends up in K-L, old boy. Don't worry about it. Have another beer.'

We were treated royally and shown to splendid rooms in the Federal Hotel with excellent room service. This was more like it. India seemed a very long way away.

At a leisurely hour the next morning the phone rang. The local newspaper wanted to send a reporter, the Cessna agents offered to have the plane checked, and the flying club chaps were offering to take us sight-seeing. We went to rubber plantations where they were tapping the trees for the white latex that looked like chewing gum, and we saw tin-mining with a giant excavator so far down a huge hole of its own making that it looked like a Tonka toy with tiny people beside it. The ore-bearing rubble was brought up by a conveyor belt that also served as an escalator for the native workers.

'They're not supposed to do that,' said our aero club guide. 'But the boss is always looking the other way at knock-off time so if one of the silly buggers falls off and breaks his neck it isn't the boss's fault.' Quite.

We stayed two days and left refreshed at 10 on the Wednesday morning, arriving 2½ hours later at Singapore. This was when things started to come unravelled again. Laying about in K-L had been the calm before the cock-up. It seemed that the cable Gavin had sent from Rangoon requesting clearance to fly over Indonesia had been scrambled so that Singapore had received a request for us to land and Indonesia had been sent an advisory note to say we were coming. The Civil Aviation authorities got on the job, but it was two days before they received a reply, and then it was to say that application had to be made through the Australian embassy. The British embassy took the matter up and by Saturday afternoon they had clearance for us to fly, but by then our bill at the Strand Hotel was more than we could afford to pay and we had to wait until Monday for Gavin to arrange a bank transfer.

Because we had no money at all, the hotel arranged a tab for us at the Chinese restaurant across the road, assuring the proprietor that we would pay as soon as the bank transfer arrived. Gavin's original optimistic five nights at a fiver a night had long since ceased to be a joke, but fortunately Gavin was bankrolling the flight.

Of course we knew all about Chinese food. We ate it two or three nights a week in London because it was all we could afford. Our first meal in Singapore was a wonderful comedy of errors. We looked down the menu: pork, chicken, fish, duck, chop suey, chow mein. We would order one of each as we did in London and share it around. Thinking back, the waiter's eyebrows did rise a notch with each item ordered, and there was a row of heads around the kitchen door and much Chinese hilarity when the order was delivered, but we thought little of it. Meanwhile, the restaurant owner taught us how to use chopsticks by showing us how to hold them, then set us to practise picking up salted peanuts. This is the ultimate test of chopstickery. If you can pick up a peanut you can pick up *anything*.

It took some time for the food to arrive, but when it came we were stunned and the staff were crying with laughter. A whole duck, a whole chicken, a whole fish, a suckling pig . . . there was enough food to feed an army, and it lasted us for lunches and dinners for the rest of our stay!

We left Singapore at 6.45 am in a rainstorm heading for Jakarta and skimming 200 feet above the sea to keep below the cloud. Indonesia is a banana-shaped island petering out into a chain of small islands hanging alongside the Singapore peninsula and below Borneo. It rained most of the 5-hour flight and we landed in Jakarta as a bomber was taking off. Dozens more were parked along the runway. There were soldiers and officials everywhere, but nobody seemed to know the procedure to deal with us despite all the red tape necessary to get permission to fly there in the first place. There was no passport check, no documentation requirement and we were refuelled and away again at 12.45 into the teeth of another storm. We were cursing the life-raft. If we hadn't been delayed waiting for it, we would have been ahead of the monsoon season. Now we were uncomfortably in it.

It was so bad that Gavin tried to climb above it, but he eventually gave up and spiralled down to creep along above the jungle at 200 feet. This took us a fair way off our course and well off the air corridor, but we managed to get to Surabaya where we touched down having given up trying to make Denpasar. Now we had more problems and we had to contact the British consul before we could leave. He was a pleasant young Chinese called Frank Ong who cleared us through Immigration and Customs and took us into the town in the embassy car to find a hotel. An armed guard was posted outside our door and we were sent a cold dinner that only Gavin could face. That night we all fed the mosquitoes.

The consular car arrived at 5.30 am, and we were in the air at 6. Half an hour later we were in Denpasar. Only the right tank needed topping up and we were away at 7. Five hours later we were in Kupang and anxious to put Indonesia behind us. The landing strip was rough and there were no other aircraft in sight. The refuelling was chaotic. The petrol was run 30 yards from the tank in a hose, which meant that when the native nozzleman at the plane's tank signalled 'stop', there was still a hose-full of petrol coming through. There was as much fuel on the ground as there was in the plane, and they were enjoying this hugely.

The prospect of the sharks in the Timor Sea between Kupang and Darwin seemed a worthwhile risk rather than spending another night in any part of Indonesia. There was a 3½-hour flight over sea ahead of us and thunderstorms were predicted. About an hour from Darwin it started to get dark and we could see the thunderstorms ahead. Lightning was forking all around us, sending the instruments haywire, and as the plane was being thrown around in the storms Gavin was worried that we might miss the signals from lighthouses on the Australian coast and that the compass needle was following the lightning flashes. It meant there was a chance that we could fly parallel to the coast, miss Darwin and get the chance to use our raft . . .

We picked up the 9-second signal at Charles Point, then Gavin sighted the lights of Darwin up ahead, which made Roger and me feel better, but Gavin was now worried that he was landing after dark and he didn't have a night-rating on his licence. He needn't have worried. When we touched down authority arrived in the form of a uniformed official who opened the door, said 'Well, you're bloody game, I'll say that for you,' sprayed the interior of the plane and shut the door again, as they had done in Karachi. The difference was that now we felt we were home, as opposed to half-way there.

It never really occurred to me that we had done something considered unusual in the 'real world' until the fumigation man had made his remark and a small boy at the airport, watching us unloading our bags, asked where we'd come from. We told him we'd flown in from England and he looked incredulous.

'What? In *that*?'

I suppose it did look a bit titchy for such a trip.

I was surprised at how small Darwin was. I had been expecting a city, but it was more a coastal village with houses on stilts to cope with the heat. We stayed at a fair dinkum Aussie pub with the stale smell of beer from the bar and at last a real breakfast of sausages and eggs to put memories of India and Indonesia behind us.

We may have thought we were home but the local pilots made us aware that the most dangerous bit was yet to come. The sharks in the Timor would be as nothing if we had to put down for any reason in the desert between Darwin and Alice Springs. Life expectancy would be measured in hours if we left the plane in the baking heat.

We took off at 10.30 am and an hour later we were passing over Catherine, originally a sheep station of 80,000 square *miles*! We were flying at 10,000 feet over the desert and even up there it was 60 degrees. The heat was making for a bumpy ride with the Cessna tumbling hundreds of feet in some of the gusts.

Nearly 7 hours after take-off we sighted Alice Springs behind a range of hills looking eerie in the heat haze. It was like stepping out into an oven. Ground temperature was 99 degrees in the shade, if you could find any. We stayed overnight in an impressive air-conditioned hotel in the middle of nowhere – 'The Alice' had a population of only 1,500 in 1961 – and on Friday 15 December, what should have been the last day of our epic adventure, we were up at 5.30 am and waiting in the baking heat to leave at 7.30.

These Australian legs were the longest of the trip and the flight down to Adelaide took 6½ hours. We passed over the southern tip of Lake Eyre at 10.25. Gavin was poised for a quick turn-round at Adelaide and a direct flight plan across Bass Straight to Launceston, but we couldn't get a meteorological clearance to fly because there was cloud forecast from 2,000 to 4,000 feet, which we regarded by now as kid's stuff after all the water we had crossed in far worse weather on the way here. The Met people were not impressed and we had to stay overnight. So near and yet so far. We were disappointed.

We were up at dawn the next morning but were still refused permission to fly Bass Straight because of the weather. We could fly across to Melbourne, however, and 2½ hours later we were on the ground refuelling and being interviewed by the *Herald*. By now I was getting used to being interviewed instead of doing the interviewing. Heady stuff. We found that several Cessnas were being cleared for the crossing to Tasmania, so after lunch we set off on the final 2½-hour leg of a trip that had taken nearly a month instead of five days.

About 80 miles out we picked up Launceston tower talking to other light planes and realised that they were coming out to meet us. After weeks of being the only plane in the sky there seemed to be planes everywhere, and as Gavin was asking permission to land he was amazed to hear all the other aircraft getting permission to land beside us. We let down safely for the last time and Gavin taxied to our final stop in front of a sizeable crowd of well-wishers, reporters and TV crews. We discovered that we had been in the Tasmanian newspapers ever since our first efforts to leave Luton, and were fêted as local heroes for a few days.

At the time the trip was a cheap way for me to get home for Christmas, because I flew on to New Zealand, but looking back with hindsight it was a pretty impressive achievement for Gavin, flying round – or more correctly, down – the world in a single-engined plane. It probably wasn't entirely our fault that we survived to tell the tale, but I wonder how many people have made the trip with one engine since the record-makers in the 1920s?

As a postscript, the Cessna was refused a Certificate of Airworthiness when an inspection revealed so much corrosion that the wings were in danger of falling off, a sobering thought considering the buffeting we had endured over the Indonesian Sea and the desert between Darwin and Alice Springs. A few months after the plane was cleared to fly the farmer who had bought it hit a horse while landing in a field. The farmer was unhurt, but the horse had to be put down and the Cessna was beyond repair. Cancer claimed Gavin some years later. Roger Tregaskis is selling real estate in Queensland. I'm writing this book.

CHAPTER FIVE

Surrey in the 'Sixties

I HAD CONTRACTED to cover the 1962 Tasman Series for various magazines and for the *Daily Telegraph*. (Years later a Spanish journalist gave me an umbrella that his wife had bought in a Barcelona department store. The pattern was newspaper cuttings from various countries, and the English cutting was one of my Tasman race reports!) Bruce McLaren was racing a Cooper owned by the English private entrant C. T. 'Tommy' Atkins, and Wally Willmott, a friend from Timaru, was helping to prepare the car with Atkins's mechanic, Harry Pearce. Willmott proved to have such a natural aptitude that Bruce arranged a job for him with Atkins, and he planned to talk to me about working for him when the Series ended at Sandown Park, on the outskirts of Melbourne.

I wasn't aware of this, and while we were in Tasmania for the penultimate race – Willmott and I were sharing an attic room in Austin Miller's Monaco Hotel in Launceston – I was discussing employment as motoring editor with the *Mercury* in Hobart and the *Examiner* in Launceston. (Diary: 'However, the annoying thing is that I still want to go back to England.') Our local publican out there raced an early leaf-spring Cooper fitted with a large American V8 engine, and he worked on it in the barn behind the pub. On the *first floor* of the barn. He winched the car up to the first floor using an outside grain hoist, a highly dangerous operation that was always worth watching.

Bruce and I had two long discussions during practice at Sandown Park the following weekend. The job he had arranged for Willmott was really aimed at grooming him for future work in the team that Bruce was planning for himself. Willmott (he was always Willmott, seldom Wally) had prepared and raced his own Cooper 500 in New Zealand, so he had a good understanding of what was involved.

The upshot of our conversation was that the idea of spending the rest of my life in Tasmania was cancelled and I would go back to England to work as Bruce's secretary. (Diary: 'He says he's not sure what a secretary does, but the other drivers have one, so I can be his.') He told me that he wouldn't have enough work for a full week, so he suggested a 20-hour week for that first year and he would pay me £600. This would allow time for freelance writing and I would also be ghost-writing his columns, which at that time ran in several New Zealand newspapers and later in *Autosport*, for which he would pay me 25 per cent of the column fee on top of my salary. With Bruce's name on the columns they fetched a minimum of £20, a great rate for the time. This also meant that I would go to most of the races with Bruce, and he agreed to pay 75 per cent of my hotel and travel costs. But he wasn't going totally overboard with the largesse. I was in Australia and the job was in England. Bruce advanced me a cheque for £300 for an air ticket, which would come out of my salary, so I was embarking on the best job in the world for probably the smallest salary – £6 a week plus percentages!

The air ticket was for a seat in a slightly larger plane than the Cessna I had flown out in the previous November. I was flying via the USA to take in the 12-hour race at Sebring where Bruce was racing. My main memory of that first visit to a race in the States was walking a mile from the hotel to the centre of Sebring and being asked for identification that I didn't have when I went into a bar for a drink. Faced with a walk back to the hotel for my passport, I went to a milkbar instead. The other Sebring memory was watching mesmerised as Indianapolis driver Lloyd Ruby mixed a bottle of Schlitz beer with tomato juice for his breakfast each morning.

Back in England I found a flat in Claremont Road, Kingston-upon-Thames. In estate-agent-speak now it would probably be a penthouse. In 1962 it was a third-floor walk-up under the roof. There was a bedroom with twin beds, a lounge, kitchen and bathroom. We found a pub called The Gloucester Arms in a side street back from the river near the centre of Kingston. It was walking distance from our flat on a fine night or a short drive in those pre-breathalyser days. Peter Garner ran the pub with his wife Doreen and it became the unofficial headquarters of all the motor racing people in the area in much the same way that The Barley Mow has gained a reputation with the racing fraternity around Horsley.

There was also a fish restaurant called The Contented Plaice with a cockney pianist who played all the old songs, and late in the evening he always had a raucous chorus of racing people helping him out.

When Chris Amon came over a year later to race a Formula 1 Lola for Reg Parnell, he became a regular, and I always used to say that if Chris wasn't singing 'Danny Boy' by 8 o'clock it was going to be a quiet night. Given the chance to refute these aspersions on his character, Richard Becht wrote in his 1993 book *Champions of Speed*:

'Amon's version of events is a little milder on his own antics, a bit richer on Young's performance. "The Gloucester Arms was a great watering hole," he says. "We had a lot of fun in there, perhaps too much. Being only 20, I was pretty much swept along with anything, albeit some of Eoin's stories are exaggerated in that he sometimes thinks everybody else was doing the drinking and he wasn't."'

Neither Willmott nor I were cooks, so we perfected a colonial bachelor concoction that began with lashings of mashed potato in a large saucepan into which went chopped-up fried sausages, peas, a can of soup, steak and kidney pies and pretty much anything else within reach. We always said it tasted amazingly good, but at that time of the evening I suppose it would, the taste buds having by then been successfully blurred.

Jack Brabham had left the Cooper team to build and race his own car, and Bruce was now partnered by South African Tony Maggs, who had graduated from the Tyrrell Formula Junior team. Denny Hulme wasn't as fortunate and he had to slog in the background. Phil Kerr, Brabham's manager, was also a New Zealander, and realised the problems that Denny was having, so arranged for him to work as a mechanic in Brabham's garage. Denny's talent would eventually make him World Champion, but it would take time.

We went down to Goodwood for the Formula 1 races on Easter Monday 1962. Bruce was second to Hill's BRM in the Glover Trophy and won the Lavant Cup for four-cylinder cars, but Stirling Moss's crash at St Mary's in the Glover Trophy cast a shadow over the weekend and the celebrations were muted.

Years later photographer Michael Cooper told me an extraordinary story about the Moss crash. He said that he dreamed the night before the race that Stirling had been killed in a crash. He knew Stirling to speak to but not well enough to tell him something like that on race morning. He showed me the strips of his negatives from that race day. He had concentrated on Stirling. Putting on his gloves, his helmet, checking his goggles, slipping into the cockpit of his Lotus. The next negatives are out at St Mary's, a corner he had never been to before because it was a fast open bend and not favoured by photographers. He caught Stirling's Lotus from the moment it left the track until it hit the bank, and he was first to the wreck, but he was panicked by the sight of Moss's obvious injuries and ran away, coming back when marshals and doctors had reached the scene.

I went to Monaco for the first time that year, staying at the Hotel d'Europe just below the Mirabeau Hairpin. Monaco was everything I had read about. The glamour and the excitement, a street race like no other, a total anachronism still tolerated by the modern drivers only because, well, because it was Monaco. This applied even at the height of Jackie Stewart's safety crusading, when Monaco should have been shut down without question if his requirements for other circuits had been rigidly applied in the principality. The circuit survived because, well, because it was Monaco.

If anyone asked then which was my favourite Grand Prix, I automatically said Monaco because it *was* a special event. Much more than just a motor race. It was a weekend 'happening' with a race thrown in for good measure. Back in the early 1960s everyone dined at Cesar's Restaurant at the top of the town or, further out and more expensively when someone else was paying, at The Pirate. Aptly named, we felt. And afterwards everyone gravitated to the Tip Top Bar on the swoop down from the Casino Square to the Mirabeau Hairpin, actually on the circuit.

But that was then. Now Monaco is a town taken hostage by the race. Too many people chasing too few restaurants, chasing the long-gone chance of seeing the Grand Prix drivers stopping off for a drink at the Tip Top. Now the police are more frequent visitors to the Tip Top than the Grand Prix drivers as bottles and glasses are broken in the street and fights are started. Getting older? Generation gap? Certainly.

In 1962 Monaco was still Monaco. Bruce qualified the Cooper on the outside of the front row beside Jim Clark and Graham Hill, the top title contenders. In those days grid times were in tenths of a second rather than today's thousandths. There were five different makes of car in the first five places: Lotus, BRM, Cooper, Porsche and Ferrari.

The start was then on a stretch of road that is used as the pit lane now, with the field launched straight into a hairpin right, which was difficult enough without the kind of major problem that happened in 1962. Willy Mairesse, the short-fused Belgian who had been brought in as a fourth Ferrari driver, had qualified two rows ahead of team-mates Phil Hill and Lorenzo Bandini. Mairesse had never been so close to a Grand Prix starter's flag, and when it dropped he was storming between Clark and Hill, splitting them, putting them off line, and letting McLaren capitalise on the confusion. Behind them even more confusion reigned. The throttle of Richie Ginther's BRM stuck open, and from the fifth row he triggered a chain shunt into that first corner that took a wheel off his car, wrecked Maurice Trintignant's Walker Lotus and damaged Dan Gurney's Porsche and the Lotuses of Trevor Taylor and Innes Ireland.

Bruce led the opening laps and I was thinking maybe I had backed a winner here – my man was out in front of the Monaco Grand Prix! But Hill's BRM was leading after seven laps, and 20 laps later Clark's Lotus had also passed Bruce's Cooper. Clark was out with clutch failure at half distance and Hill's engine failed seven laps before the finish. Although Graham would win the Monaco Grand Prix a total of six times (1963/64/65/67/68 and 69), Bruce took the prestigious chequer in 1962 with Phil Hill's Ferrari gobbling into his lead to finish just 1.3 seconds behind.

In those days Phil was a driven man, a prisoner of his own reputation with a world championship he perhaps felt belonged to his team-mate Wolfgang (Taffy) von Trips, who had been leading the championship when he was killed in a tangle with Clark's Lotus at Monza the year before in 1961. Phil won that race for Ferrari and won the championship by just a point from von Trips. Ferrari withdrew for the rest of the season. Phil had been racing on his nerves for most of his career with Ferrari. Nerves and motor racing are odd but natural bedfellows if you think about it. Jim Clark used to bite his fingernails to the quick; James Hunt regularly threw up before the start. Phil quit Ferrari at the end of 1962 and in 1965 he would be Bruce's team-mate during McLaren's last season with Cooper. The season was a disaster, but Bruce and Phil had formed a friendship, bonded in gloom perhaps, and shared long-distance drives with Ford, while Phil drove a second McLaren Cooper on the 1965 Tasman Series.

When the chequered flag drops at the end of a Grand Prix today, the next race is for the drivers to complete post-race formalities and press conferences and board their private jets to wherever home is. The day after Monaco in 1962 Bruce and Patty (who had married in Christchurch late in 1961) were water-skiing off the beach at Cap Ferrat and I was typing my reports in the beach bar. Life was probably better somewhere else, but as the waiter brought another glass of wine I couldn't think where . . .

I went to the Belgian Grand Prix with Maggs in his Mini Cooper and we stayed at the Hotel Val d'Ambleve with the Cooper, Lotus and Lola teams. Mairesse was making his presence felt on home ground at Spa when he and Trevor Taylor in the second Lotus traded the lead in the opening laps until Jim Clark came through and drove away into the distance, winning comfortably. The Taylor/Mairesse battled ended in a frightening pall of smoke. The pair had tangled and the Ferrari had somersaulted, catching fire. Both drivers escaped relatively unharmed. Trevor's only injury being a grazed wrist where he caught his watchstrap getting out of the Lotus.

In 1994 singer-songwriter Chris Rea used a photograph of Mairesse's inverted Ferrari at Spa to show how basically simple the 'spaceframe' chassis was. He had a replica of the 'sharknose' Ferrari built to use in a film about the life of his racing hero, Wolfgang von Trips.

Bruce retired at Spa with engine failure, but his next win was just round the corner when he took the laurels at the Rheims Grand Prix, unfortunately not a round of the championship that year. So far in the 1962 season Bruce had started from the front row four times in five races, winning twice.

A dinner meeting with John Blunsden, editor of *Motor Racing* magazine, ended with me taking over Bruce's autobiography, which John had been ghosting. He had run out of time and in the next two months I had to write 70,000 words! I inherited stacks of notes and letters, and *From the Cockpit* started to take shape. It took rather longer to complete than the two months I had promised (rather like this book!) and final notes were included after the Tasman Series early in 1964.

Jim Clark won the 1962 British Grand Prix at Aintree and the celebrations went on all night. At one stage we were on a sizeable ship on the Mersey and Innes Ireland was down below, trying to start the engines! Jim, Trevor Taylor and I had breakfast the next morning sitting at the end of Bruce and Patty's bed in the Adelphi Hotel in Liverpool!

Bruce's 'From the Cockpit' column appeared for the first time in *Autosport* the week after the German Grand Prix, where he had finished fifth in a rain-soaked race behind the battling quartet of Hill, Surtees, Gurney and Clark. Bruce's helmet-bag had been stolen before the race and he had to race in borrowed kit. We had been doing columns for newspapers in New Zealand and they became fun to write when Bruce realised that the readers wanted to know what life was like on the inside of Formula 1 rather than a dissertation on the nuts and bolts of the cars and the races. There were occasions when he would run out of time or (rarely) enthusiasm, and would say, 'You were there, you finish it.' There were the light-hearted columns when he came back from an easy win in a Can-Am race, but there were also the sad times when he worked and thought hard to write exactly how he felt in the circumstances.

The 1964 world title went to John Surtees in the Ferrari, making him the first man to win world championships on two wheels and four. He had won the German Grand Prix on the Nurburgring and the Italian Grand Prix on Ferrari home turf at Monza, taken seconds at Zandvoort and Watkins Glen and a third in the British GP at Brands Hatch. Three British drivers – Hill, Clark or Surtees – could have won the title as they went to Mexico for the final round, but Hill's BRM was shunted at the hairpin by Bandini in the second Ferrari and he lost his championship chance, as son Damon would do 30 years later when he collided with Michael Schumacher in the final Grand Prix of the 1994 season in Adelaide. Clark's Lotus broke down within sight of the flag and Bandini obeyed team orders to let Surtees through to second place behind Dan Gurney's Brabham, earning John enough points to take the title. Bruce hardly featured with the Cooper. He was second in the Belgian GP at Spa, otherwise it was a summer to forget. He had formed his own team now and took two Coopers to New Zealand with Phil Hill as his team-mate.

I flew to Nassau for the Speed Week on the way to New Zealand at the end of that 1964 season. The series was started by Captain 'Red'

Crise with the backing of the Bahamas Department of Tourism, and because he could post serious starting and prize money the entry was strong. Roger Penske won the two major races – one in a lightweight Stingray Corvette, the other in a Chaparral – then announced his retirement as a driver. Penske still makes more money from his motor racing career than anyone else – including Bernie Ecclestone – and he hasn't driven a racing car in anger since the day I watched him win on the bumpy airfield circuit. The reputation he built on the track made him the most powerful figure in the US motor industry; he builds his own Penske Indycars in England, runs his own Indycar team in a hands-on capacity in the pits, owns race tracks, and promotes races. As well as owning giant distributorships for several different makes of car.

In Nassau there were cocktail parties at a different hotel every evening. Bruce taught Phil Hill to single ski and Mike Hailwood, Peter Revson and Chris Amon turned up as spectators. Amon was on his way home and hosted a hectic cricket match on the lawn of his parents' beach house after the Levin race, which Clark had won in the Lotus. Jim won again at Wigram, Teretonga Park, the southernmost circuit in the world near Invercargill, and Lakeside at Brisbane in Australia. While the cars and crews were crossing the Tasman Sea, Jim went ahead to start flying lessons in Sydney. Sadly Lex Davison was killed in practice for the Sandown Park race at Melbourne, and the sport lost a gentleman racer, a wealthy amateur who was one of Australia's top drivers.

In the final race of the series early in 1965 at Longford in Tasmania, Bruce set pole position in the Cooper and won 100 bottles of champagne as well as winning the race the next day, while Phil Hill and Jack Brabham battled to the flag, Hill losing out by a tenth of a second but setting a new lap record on the Rheims-style track with its long, long straights on country roads. This was pre-Armco – the track was lined with barbed-wire farm fences!

The McLaren team felt they had earned a victory party and decided to open a few of their bottles of champagne over dinner. But they hadn't reckoned with the hotel manager, who demanded that if champagne was to be quaffed it would come from the hotel cellars – or not at all. Australian racing driver Bob Jane, now a highly successful businessman Penske-style, argued the case with the manager on McLaren's behalf. I'll never forget his parting shot. The manager had taken exception to Bob's attitude and said, 'Young man, I'm old enough to be your father . . .'

Jane looked up and said, 'You're not *smart* enough to be my father!'

Bruce was eager to extend his business interests beyond the cockpit and asked if I would fly to Japan on the way back to England to see if I could secure the Honda distributorship for McLaren in New

Zealand. Today, with Japanese car-makers like Honda and Toyota enjoying such a dominant position in world markets, it is hard to believe that they were only beginning when I visited early in 1965.

I rode out to the Honda factory in a chauffeur-driven Nissan Cedric – because Honda hadn't made a big saloon yet! The Honda manufacturing plant at Siama outside Toyko had an illuminated sign at the gate: 'HONDA MOTOR WELCOMES EOIN YOUNG'. I saw the first models of the new S600 GT coming off the assembly line and tried one on the test track. It was a bigger 1000 cc version of this engine that Brabham would use in his Formula 2 Brabham-Hondas.

The Honda people were very polite but said that they could not help Mr McLaren (difficult for them to pronounce) because they planned to distribute cars through their existing motorcycle outlets in each country.

Toyota was the next stop. They were the largest manufacturer of cars and trucks in the Japanese domestic market and their sales staff booked me on the new 120 mph Bullet Train to Nagoya, 250 miles north of Tokyo. What I didn't know was that the driver of the Bullet Train effectively had no forward vision in the cab, the Japanese reasoning being that because it took a mile and a half to stop from top cruising speed and he could only see a mile up the line, there wasn't much point in giving him a forward view! I heard a similar theory from Mickey Thompson when I went to Bonneville Salt Flats to watch him run his four-wheel-drive twin-engined record car. It had *no* suspension because the hot-rodder reasoned that at the speeds he wanted to try and achieve, the car would be a mile down the salt before the suspension had reacted to a bump. Better to have none, he reckoned.

I would be met by a Toyota representative on the platform, they said. There seemed to be thousands of Japanese flooding off the train and I couldn't imagine how I would find the Toyota person. Eventually there were only two people left on the platform – me and a Japanese rather dolefully holding a small flag with a badge on it that I didn't recognise because I had never seen it before. I asked if, perhaps, he was from Toyota. He nodded eagerly and pointed at the flag, presumably wondering why this ignorant Westerner hadn't recognised the corporate badge.

I was shown through the factory at Toyota City and told that I was the first British motoring journalist to have been accorded the privilege. I wasn't sure whether that was true or not. At that time the 2-litre Crown and the 1500 cc Corona were being built for Canadian, Australian, Danish and Dutch markets as well as the home market. After pre-dinner drinks, one of the Toyota marketing directors asked how Toyota was regarded in Britain. I was embarrassed to tell them that the British public knew *nothing* about Toyota.

Honda had built their own RA272 Grand Prix car and in 1965

Richie Ginther would win the Grand Prix in Mexico at the end of the year – the first and only GP win for Ginther, the first GP win for Honda, the first GP win for Goodyear tyres and the last race of the 1.5-litre formula.

Ginther had started in the California sports car racing scene with Phil Hill, and both found themselves with Ferrari works Grand Prix and sports car drives. Richie retired from Formula 1 in 1967 and more or less dropped out, living a nomad motorhome life in California. He died in 1989, a forgotten man in Formula 1. He had apparently kept some of his trophies for sentimental reasons, and while I was at the Palm Springs classic races in November 1995 I heard of a very special Japanese trophy from Honda carrying an engraved silver plaque for Richie Ginther celebrating his first Grand Prix win for them. The man offering the trophy for sale for a substantial sum always phoned from a different number, and when these were checked they were public callboxes. 'It sounds as though the guy lives in a motorhome and doesn't have a fixed address,' said my informant. One could only presume that before Richie died he had given the trophy to one of his itinerant friends . . . or it had been stolen after his death.

Jim Clark dominated the 1965 racing season for Lotus. As well as the Indianapolis 500 he won six GPs (five of them – Belgian, French, British, Dutch and German – in succession) with such polished ease in the Lotus that we were told he had made the same set of Dunlop tyres last for three races!

Bruce McLaren Motor Racing Ltd had originally been established in the motor racing equivalent of a biblical stable beside a road grader in a dusty high-roofed building in New Malden, Surrey, near the Kingston bypass, where the Oldsmobile V8 was installed in the ex-Penske Cooper-based Zerex Special, before moving to a 10,000 sq ft factory in what seemed by comparison to be a luxurious modern trading estate at Feltham. It wasn't, but it was sufficiently cheap that we could just about afford it.

Members of our little team had been living in shared flats all round the area and one evening, probably at The Gloucester Arms, it was decided that I would find a flat that we could all share – Tyler Alexander, Teddy Mayer, Willmott and me. Estate agents that I approached were not remotely interested in letting an apartment to four young men who might or might not be the paragons of virtue I portrayed us to be. So I changed tack with the next agent. Did they have a house so big that nobody wanted to rent it? An agent had always come with me to such properties as I had been allowed to view. This time I was tossed a key and told to go and view this house in Corkoran Road, Surbiton. A mite startled, I asked for the number.

'The house doesn't have a number, sir. It has a name . . .'

It was *huge* with a sweeping horseshoe drive so that you could barely see the house from the road. It was also divided so that we were actually renting what amounted to half of this stately home. There were four enormous bedrooms with reception rooms on a grand scale. We called it The Castle and it was £20 a week. I said we'd take it. A fiver each didn't sound bad. I wonder what the neighbours thought.

One memorable party at The Castle was after the Guards Trophy sports car race at Brands Hatch in 1964, and all the Americans came along – A. J. Foyt, Roger Penske, Walt Hansgen and John Mecom – as well as the top 'home' drivers. To give an authentic period atmosphere to the party we produced invitations in Olde Worlde English and bought dummy fibreglass suits of armour as decoration to go with the old swords we had picked up cheaply in antique shops. There was a stately sweeping staircase from the hallway to the first floor landing, and as the party reached its cruising altitude Jimmy Clark donned one of the fibreglass armour breastplates and a plastic helmet, grabbed a (real) sword and challenged Graham Hill to a duel. The pair of them lunged and parried and Graham leapt to the stairs, all Errol Flynn with his dashing moustache, and leaned over the bannister to deliver a mighty thwack across Jimmy's helmet. The clash of real broadsword against the thin plastic helmet had a dramatic effect and Jimmy slumped to the floor, concussed!

Bruce and Patty McLaren lived half a mile away and soon another section of the Grand Prix world appeared, attracted by our communal way of living expensively at an economy rent. The Ditton Road Fliers had arrived: Chris Amon, Peter Revson, Mike Hailwood and Tony Maggs. And any other passing racer who needed a bed. They also rented half a house, but whereas we had the side half of our house, they had the top half. They knew what their downstairs neighbours thought about it because they kept telling them – and the police. Most weekends those who weren't away racing were home having a party, and most Saturday nights around midnight, when the downstairs chap had reached the end of his tether, he would phone the police. They would come up the stairs with a measured constabulary tread, thump on the door, deliver an admonition long enough and loud enough to be heard downstairs, then go in, take their helmets off, have a beer and catch up with the latest racing gossip.

Imagine four Formula 1 drivers sharing today. Amon had various managers who took varying amounts of his income and suggested various schemes for 'investing' the rest. At one stage he was dealing in Mk 2 3.8 Jaguars, buying them cheap in poor shape, having a mechanic 'restore' them at the kerbside, then shipping them to Australia where a ready market waited. One of the advantages of this get-rich-reasonably-quickly (and economically) scheme was that Chris always had the most recently restored Jaguar as his personal transport.

One night he took his ladyfriend of the moment up to London for an evening at the Adlib Club, then *the* place to be seen. You had a fair chance of seeing the odd Beatle or Rolling Stone. That sort of place. For reasons never since entirely clear, Chris took Revson and me with him and his lady, but when our behaviour and the lateness of the hour reached a point where Christopher was starting to lose his sense of humour, he suggested that Revson and I should leave. He may have put it more strongly than that. I pointed out that we couldn't because we were with him. He said to take the car. It was easy to find because he had parked it on the footpath right outside the door of the club. At this point I remembered that the restoration was complete but for a new battery. The bouncers on the door push-started us into the night.

All was well for the first part of the journey, and Revson settled into the sleep of the not entirely sober. I was following the bonnet mascot home when I arrived at the forest of traffic lights at Shepherds Bush. The lights were red and I stopped. Revson stirred and asked why we had stopped. I pointed to the red light.

'But you should have stopped back there – you're across the intersection.'

I explained patiently that he was American and didn't understand. He said that it didn't bother him that much, but perhaps I should explain my theory to the two policemen walking towards us waving their torches.

Is this your car, sir?

'No.'

Who is the registered owner?

'Chris Amon, the racing driver.'

Does he know you've got it?

'He should do, he gave me the keys.'

Would you mind if we looked in the boot, sir?

'Why certainly, officer.'

Now you have to remember one thing about a Mark 2 Jaguar – the ignition and boot keys were *tiny*, and for some reason Amon had about 20 keys (perhaps for his entire Jaguar stock) on the ring. The keys were small, the keyhole was small, it was pitch dark, I was amply refreshed, and the policeman held his torch while I endeavoured to find a key that fitted. Eventually one did. The boot opened and inside was the paraphernalia usually associated with racing drivers of the period. The inside of the lid was adorned with used Fablon racing numbers, peeled off after a race for possible future use. This seemed to confirm my story about the racing driver owner.

By now I thought that there could be a ghost of a chance that we were in the clear, this being aeons before breathalysers. Then a squad car pulled up on the other side of the road and the sergeant called out to ask if everything was OK.

'No problem, sir. Just a couple of drunks on their way home.'

They bade me goodnight (Revson had gone to sleep again), I climbed behind the wheel as they resumed their patrol – then I remembered the flat battery. I called them back and asked if they would oblige with a push as my passenger seemed to be temporarily out of the game, and the strong arms of the law soon had the Jaguar on song and on its way back to Surbiton. There have been occasions recently when I have told this story and the audience flatly refuses to believe it. Different days.

Peter Revson came to spell trouble for me. I was having breakfast with him at Howard Johnson's at Indianapolis early in May 1971 when a huge man I realised was the motel manager thrust himself between us, his face inches from mine. I just knew that, for reasons I would probably soon discover, I was about to have my lights punched out.

'Mr Young?' growled the man who appeared to plan my facial remodelling.

I agreed I was indeed me.

'You wrote the report on the "500" for *Road & Track* last year?'

Guilty as charged.

Then he broke into a big smile. 'Just checking,' he said. 'I wanna shake your hand. I'd been trying to get rid of that asshole of a barman for months. I mailed a copy of your report to Howard Johnson Jr and he had the guy transferred three states away.'

Revvy was curious to know what I had written. So was I. I checked the piece, then remembered writing that 'the nightlife swings at the Holiday Inn Northwest and doesn't at Howard Johnson's across the freeway. HoJo's room service didn't even extend to a pot of coffee. And their barman figured he was doing you a favour just standing there. In Indiana they don't encourage moving drinkers. Signs caution you to drink sitting down. Don't move your drink to another table, buddy, the barkeep will handle that tricky operation.'

What did that have to do with a report on the most important American motor race in the most important American motoring magazine? Local colour. They had asked me for a diary-type report on everything that happened from the moment the plane touched down until it left again after the race weekend.

The Surbiton Castle had large reception rooms and we decided that the owner might like a full-size snooker table instead of his antique dining table, which we would fold against the wall. I had negotiated what I thought was an excellent deal with the landlord of The Rising Sun pub in Surbiton whereby we would buy his snooker table, all cues, rests, sets of pool, snooker and billiard balls, scorers and the period full-size lights, for £10. Dividing this four ways made it quite a reasonable investment, we thought.

I phoned the publican and said we had decided we would take it and asked when he could deliver it. *Deliver* it? Why, yes. He said did we realise that it would cost £1,500 to dismantle the slate bed, load and transport it, then re-install it at our house? Ummm, well, no, we hadn't thought of that and perhaps in the circs we wouldn't be going ahead with the deal . . .

BP were interested in making a film of what their sponsored drivers did between the French and British GPs, and as Amon's 21st birthday fell in this period, I suggested that they might like to film the party at The Contented Plaice restaurant – providing they picked up the tab. Absolutely no problem, they said. With a sponsor for the party, Chris invited most of the people in Formula 1. We warmed up in The Gloucester Arms, then moved across to the restaurant, which we had booked in its entirety.

This was pre-video, so any formal film-making like this was a fair-sized undertaking. The main production problem was that the crew had joined in the party spirit to the point that no usable footage was shot during the entire evening. BP were very good about it. They paid the bill for the dinner party, then paid for a second party with most of the original cast to get *some* suitable film in the can. The BP film eventually came out under the title 'The Time Between'.

Mike Hailwood was something of an individualist. When he moved into Ditton Road he decided to paint his room – each wall a different garish colour. At this stage he was still racing motor cycles as well as driving for the Parnell motor racing team with Amon and Revson. Mike paid to drive the cars, but was well paid to race his motorbikes and he always negotiated handsome cash deals because, in an absurd role-reversal, he was top of the bill at bike meetings but a grid-filler in Formula 1. It made life easier that Mike didn't care. He raced bikes all over Europe and kept wads of banknotes in all known currencies stuffed in a pair of cowboy boots under his bed. His reasoning was that no thief would bother to steal his *boots*.

One weekend he asked Amon and me if we would like to watch him win 1,000 guineas. We said yes, but where? He had entered for the major national 'Thousand Guineas' motorcycle race at Mallory Park. I had a new Austin Healey 3000 from the press fleet on road test and it was something of a brute when fully extended. I suggested that Chris may prefer to drive. At any speed nearing its maximum it was using most of the three lanes of the M1 so I was happy at my choice of chauffeur. Mike, as promised, won the race and the money and embarked on a party to celebrate. We were invited but I wanted to get my Healey home. Chris reluctantly agreed to come with me. Roger Bailey, one of Ken Tyrrell's mechanics, had offered Chris a lift back to Surbiton after the party. His driver went under a lorry on the M1 and Roger was badly injured. Years later Roger would be Chris's mechanic at Ferrari in Formula 1 and on the Tasman Series, and he now runs racing series in North America.

Hailwood was a man's man. The fans, who could only marvel at him from the other side of his leathers or Nomex, knew that they had a real hero. He was liquid genius on two wheels, so smooth he made his wins look effortless, but the rent-a-racer cars he drove in Formula 1 effectively masked his talent. He had reached the point in motor cycle racing where there was nothing left to win and it was only news when he lost. It wasn't a climate for a man like Mike to enjoy, so he opted for the gamble. Men like Nuvolari and Rosemeyer had done it. Geoff Duke had failed. John Surtees had succeeded. Agostini and Cecotto had struggled. It wasn't a logical progression.

Even Mike's fiercest fans would confess that he never really made it in cars, and certainly never enjoyed the total command of this environment that he had on bikes. There were times when he was good, better than those about him, and he won the Formula 2 Championship for John Surtees in 1972. He also drove for Surtees in Formula 1, but John and Mike never really 'clicked' on personality or performance. Perhaps it was wrong for either of them to have expected it. They were poles apart. Mike was essentially a social person with his sport as an extension of his personality; John was sternly serious where Mike was always ready for a laugh. John regarded Mike's 'sport' as a business and was sometimes unable to cope with Mike's cavalier attitude, much as he may have tried.

Mike never bothered to capitalise on his talent and at one stage I offered to negotiate some business contracts for him so that he could make his reputation earn for him. I still have a copy of the contract he signed for his Ecurie Sportive in 1965 giving me a percentage of fees earned from promotional endorsements. The figures don't stack very high in today's terms, but we were both pleased when Mike signed a contract to name a pair of motorcycle boots for a fee of £200, and sixpence a pair royalties on sales. Maybe Mike was right and deals like that weren't worth his while chasing.

He won the George Medal for bravery after rescuing Clay Regazzoni from his blazing BRM in the South African Grand Prix at Kyalami in 1973. He was almost embarrassed at the acclaim, saying that anyone else would have done the same thing. Courage was simply a necessary part of his make-up, and he wasn't aware that not everyone had the same measure . . . He had been awarded the MBE for his achievements in motor cycle racing and he told his puzzled Italian mechanics at MV-Agusta that the initials stood for Motor Bike Engineer.

When Mike left Ditton Road he bought two apartments in a tower block in Heston within easy earshot of the traffic roar from the M4 motorway. He lived on the second floor and he rented the apartment on the ninth floor to Willmott and me, as it was within easy commuting distance of the McLaren factory now re-located in a 20,000 sq ft building in Colnbrook beneath the Heathrow flight-path.

Several nights a week there would be a phone call to advise of another party down below. Some nights he would sit there quietly playing his clarinet, accompanying a Chris Barber record on the hi-fi.

The nearest pub was The Master Robert on the A4 Bath Road, which was also a motel and restaurant, and this we frequented since none of us were cooks. Jimmy Lloyd, the owner, was also a dedicated motor racing enthusiast, and as a result he decorated his largest bar with motor racing memorabilia, bits of bodywork, helmets, trophies and signed photographs that would be worth a fortune today. When the bar was remodelled some years later I checked with the brewery and found that all the memorabilia had been scrapped. All the driver's signatures on the ceiling had been painted over.

In the late 1970s, when Mike made his Isle of Man comeback, I flew across to Douglas on a Manx Airlines flight. I was in a window seat and in the opposite window seat was a sun-bronzed chap with silver curly hair who seemed vaguely familiar. As we were standing to reach down luggage from the racks he said that he was sure he recognised me from somewhere. It was world champion motorcycle racer Jim Redman, up from South Africa to see his old mate racing around The Island again. When he found out that it was my first visit to the Isle of Man he took me for a lap of the mountain course in a borrowed car. Denny Hulme was over as well, and Mike drove us all on laps of the circuit.

The sporting world mourned a true hero when Mike was killed in a needless road accident in 1981. His Rover skidded underneath a lorry that turned without signalling, and Mike died with his daughter Michelle.

McLaren Racing was stretched in the payroll area in 1966 and I offered to leave and continue working with the team through the sponsors. I was writing features, columns and race reports for a new weekly paper, *Auto News*, and the money was good. I had recently married Sandra and had moved to East Horsley. We were honeymooning in Nassau, doubling with coverage of the Speed Week, when a telegram arrived at the hotel. I assumed that it would be updated advice on deadlines. It wasn't. It read: 'COLUMN AND RACE COVERAGE NOT REQUIRED STOP 'AUTO NEWS' CLOSED DOWN THIS WEEK STOP REGARDS STOP'. The main thing that was stopping was my income, and we arrived home from honeymoon with me unemployed. The publishing company had decided that it could no longer sustain the paper; it was a case of last in, first out, and *Auto News* was dumped.

The *Autocar* opportunity appeared in the nick of time and a month later I was signed to write a weekly column on Formula 1. It started on 5 January 1967, and included my account of track laps with a 250F Maserati GP car: 'By an injudicious prod on the central accelerator pedal in a rather low gear (I think it was first!) while feeling my way down the straight on the first lap, I managed to invoke tail-slide in a straight line. Being wholly unaccustomed to such violent displays of out-of-control horsepower while proceeding backwards off the road, I stabbed at the brake (which of course was the central accelerator) and simply aided my hurricane progress into the undergrowth. Fortunately we all managed to regain the track unharmed save for a few trailing lupins from the sand dunes that surround Teretonga, and drove gingerly back to the pits to explain the sudden disappearance of the car and the minor sandstorm!'

I am still writing my 'Diary' page for *Autocar*, the longest-running column of its type in the world of motor racing.

CHAPTER SIX

Cars

I HAVE FOUND that there are always two blissful days in the ownership of any car – the day you buy it and the day you sell it. It has been the same with every car I have owned. Total infatuation on the first day, and sheer delight to be rid of it on the day it is sold.

The first car I bought was soon after we moved to racing driver Ernie Sprague's former house in Kiwi Drive, Timaru, in the mid-'50s. We wondered what the boarded-over hole was for in the floor of the double garage. Anyone with the vaguest interest in motoring would have paid more for the house to get a double garage with an inspection pit. Mother and I just wondered what it was for. Rather like Rob Walker at Las Vegas for the first Grand Prix there. He was fascinated that there were mirrors on the ceiling of his bedroom. 'You know, Buster,' Rob explained in his languid way. 'These Americans must be very lazy. I suppose they shave in bed . . .'

The son of our next-door neighbour, Roddie Mackenzie, must have lusted after our garage. He had fitted a GMC truck engine in place of the blown-up engine in his father's sleek little 1930s SS1, the predecessor of the Jaguar. This would be regarded as automotive sacrilege now, but 30-odd years ago it was a simple expedient that kept the car on the road and probably improved performance.

My knowledge of cars was nil, but Roddie was a latent hot-rodder and read all the American magazines. What I really needed, Roddie said, was a Model A Ford roadster into which we could drop a Mercury V8. I looked at all the pictures in his hot-rod magazines and it certainly seemed to be the way to go. Roddie was a mechanic and he had intimated that 'we' would do the work, so I assumed that all I had to do was buy the hardware and he would supply the expertise. This was not an entirely accurate assumption.

Roddie subsequently announced that he had found a Model A roadster in a local car yard for £45. As I recall, it was sort of Granny

Smith apple green. The car dealer offered rudimentary assistance in how to drive the thing, and I set off along Otipua Road, which passed for the top of Timaru's ring road. Current Austins were motoring state of the art as far as I was concerned then, and I was fascinated by the hand throttle lever on the central horn boss matching the spark control lever. This was before cruise control, but it seemed to offer the same assistance, which was fine on straight stretches of Otipua Road and as I turned into Kiwi Drive. The catch was on the tight turn into our drive, and with light throttle locked on as I turned in, the Model A just sledged ahead and took out the gatepost.

My mother probably hadn't been informed about the addition to our motorhouse, so this noisy arrival required something in the way of family diplomacy to explain to her that this, one had to face it, rather decrepid motor car could be transformed into a sporting machine of enormous potential. I could see that she didn't believe it, and by now I was beginning to wonder about it myself. Roddie remained the constant. He was sure the project was going to be a success.

What he wasn't so sure of was the level of professional expertise he was going to provide for the project. It seemed that I had imagined he would be in the pit with his toolbox performing all the mechanical wizardry he had told me about during long winter evenings, but in fact his assistance now seemed to be confined to technical advice sketched on the back of a window envelope.

The first envelope sketch showed how to renew the kingpins which were, according to Roddie, 'shot', and this sort of mundane mechanicking would be necessary before we could drop in the high-powered Mercury V8 in place of Henry Ford's workmanlike four-cylinder. This may have been the first time I had ever had a spanner in my hand with the serious intention of attaching it to anything. It was certainly the first time I had been underneath a motor car in an inspection pit.

The Model A had the grime of ages caked thick on its undersides. I chiselled my way in to where the kingpins seemed to be and began undoing nuts as indicated on my envelope sketch. There are obviously different ways of doing this, and perhaps Roddie had not taken into account that this was my first mechanical adventure. It occurred to me as I was undoing the last nut that a tension seemed to be building up throughout the front end of the car, but I was not prepared for the explosion that happened when the force of the pent-up spring sheared the last few threads from under my spanner, and the car seemed to lurch to its knees over the pit, covering me in 30 years of indescribable grime and falling car parts.

That, basically, was the beginning and end of my career as a mechanic. I explained to Roddie that his envelope instructions hadn't mentioned the chance of death by misadventure beneath this latest

hot-rod that 'we' were building, and I'd had enough of it. I wound
Number 8 fencing wire round the sundered front end of the Model A
and the local wrecker came and took it away.

This should have been warning enough that aged Fords and I
ought not to mix, but a few years ago at Sotheby's auction at
Brooklands there was an immaculate 1928 roadster, a twin of my first
car. It must be some sort of motoring menopause suffered by men of
a certain age, but I had to own it, especially when I discovered that
the rebuild had been a labour of love in Zimbabwe as well as being a
means of exporting funds from the beleaguered country. The owner
was hovering around his car and explained that he had found a
'trucked' rolling chassis that he had restored, then searched for an
authentic body, which he discovered on a neighbouring farm. How
much had he paid for the body? A bottle of brandy. Sound
commercial terms still surviving in the former colonies.

I think I paid £7,500 at the sale, and daughter Selina was
delighted. She was coming up 17 then, and had plans to use it for
her driving test. This was before we tried to drive it home.
Brooklands is only about 10 miles from East Horsley and we
motored over in our Range Rover to collect the new addition. This
was fortunate because the battery on the Model A had been flattened
in its numerous prods into life for prospective customers before the
sale. It tow-started, however, and we set off. I was quite simply
incapable of remembering what the owner had said about the spark
and mixture controls (my 'cruise control' of earlier days!) and we
lurched down Brooklands Road in a series of explosions as the old
engine tried to cope with the confused messages I was sending to it.
And then we ran out of petrol.

The whole thing was a nightmare and even Selina was beginning
to wish she hadn't been so enthusiastic about driving it. If her father
couldn't cope, what chance did she have as a total novice? It was all
too awful. I couldn't believe I had bought a car that I simply couldn't
drive. That night I was still wrestling with the problem when I
remembered that my Uncle Charlie (he who had taken me on my one
and only fly fishing expedition) had driven a Model A truck for most
of his life, and if he could drive it, I certainly could.

The next morning I approached the Model A in a sterner frame of
mind. It would *not* beat me. I came to terms with the spark and
mixture and reached a point where the Model and I were beginning
to be friends. It was then that I realised it wasn't going to work. Forty
miles an hour was an adventure in low speed instability.

I put it back in the garage and phoned my car dealer guru, Mike
Hallowes, who had lunched with me before the auction and
expressed an interest in the Model A. Would he like to sell it for me?
Certainly, how much did I want? I wanted £10,000 in my hand, which
he achieved with alacrity, so I imagine he sold it for 11-ish and it

turned up in a London dealer's ad for £14,000, so it was a tale that ended happily.

I subscribe to the theory of old cars and I enjoy the company of people who own and drive them, but I don't think I'm cut out to be an owner. Rather like motor cycles. I owned a 197 cc James as a lad in Timaru and a 350 cc 3T Triumph Twin over consecutive Christmas holidays. There was some sort of loophole in the licensing regulations whereby you could apply for a motor cycle licence and ride the machine for six weeks before you had to apply for your licence proper, at which point you had to fit L-plates, stay under 40 mph, and not carry a pillion passenger. But for the first six weeks you could pass yourself off as a licence-holder if you dared. I dared two Christmases in a row when the holidays were six weeks, and I sold the motor cycles immediately thereafter.

The James, I remember, had a habit of flinging off its spark lead at speed, and as it had only one cylinder and one spark plug, the performance then dropped off rather dramatically. It was also an instantaneous cure for the malaise of forced drinking in the infamous '6 o'clock swill' before the early closing time in New Zealand; once the plug lead bounced off and I leaned down to put it back on again, thereby getting the full electrical charge up my arm! The Triumph was an elegant machine but it also suffered an electrical problem, this time in the magneto, and there were times when it soldiered on one cylinder and glorious times when it chimed on two. Twenty years later in England, much to the unease of my ladies at home, I had a resurgence of two-wheeled enthusiasm and bought one of those elegant little 400/4 Hondas. My problem then was that when I was driving a car somewhere in the sunshine, I wished I was on the motor cycle – and yet most of the time when I was on the motor cycle, I was really wanting to be in the car with all its comforts and cons. Ex-competition biker Denis Jenkinson naturally approved of my interest in motor cycles. Then my interest waned and the Honda went. A few months later I was in Jenks's company when someone asked why I had sold the 400/4. Jenks said, 'It rained . . .' He was probably right.

I was very much an Austin man in New Zealand, a situation probably fostered by the A40 pick-up in which I learned to drive, then mother's A30. During my enforced bank exile in Dunedin I bought an immaculate 1927 Austin Light Twelve tourer for £40 from an old chap who had given up motoring after years of driving in retirement to his fishing rivers during the summer and pulling it apart to fettle it during the winter. The battery wasn't up to much but Dunedin is built on hills, so roll-starts were not a problem.

The old Austin covered several Dunedin–Timaru return trips, whining through the intermediate gears, then lolloping along in near silence once the hefty gated lever was slotted into top. The clutch

eventually froze across the traffic light intersection in Timaru one
New Year's Eve and brought the town to a standstill while I
telephoned David Young to come and do a clutchless start out of the
chaos I had caused. The 12/4 was traded for an Austin A35, which I
imagined to be a sports car compared with the smaller-engined A30,
and it wasn't until some years later that I saw the car parked at the
kerb on a visit home, and realised that it must have been a rebuilt
wreck when I bought it. The scuttle was cream and the rest of the car
was baby blue.

I also owned a variety of Austin Seven specials, the finest being the
car I bought from Wally Willmott in 1960, the year before I went to
England. It was a car of immense character if somewhat strange
appearance, being, if you can encompass this, a high-chassis version
of a low-chassis Ulster competition model Austin Seven. It had a
rakish two-seater body sitting on the high un-modified suspension,
and had a hood that worked surprisingly well. Austin Sevens seldom
had good brakes and the trick with this car was to throw it sideways
in moments of crisis. This always scrubbed off the necessary speed,
looked incredible, terrified the passenger, and yet the car *never*
turned over.

It was only when we were sharing a flat in England in 1962 that
Willmott confessed to being appalled that I had decided to buy his
little Austin Special, because he had had months of problems with
stripped keys in the rear axle and, in desperation to sell it, he had
welded the keys solid when they were designed to be floating. I
never knew about the problem, never knew what an axle key was
anyway, and never had any trouble with the car for as long as I
owned it.

There was also an interesting extra fitment consisting of a wood-
cased Model T trembler coil mounted in the passenger compartment
and linked to a button on the dashboard and a spark plug in the
muffler that ran along the passenger's side. The idea was to back off
the throttle for a few seconds to let the exhaust gases build up, then
press the button. The resulting explosion was wondrous.

When I arrived in England in 1961 vintage cars were absurdly
cheap compared to prices in New Zealand. I checked out a 1929 low-
chassis 2-litre Lagonda tourer offered for sale by a dealer not far from
the Cooper Car Company premises in Surbiton. It was £275 and
looked like a smaller version of a vintage Bentley. I was entranced
but explained to the dealer my total lack of mechanical aptitude.
Could he guarantee that the car was in perfect condition? He couldn't.
Second gear was a bit dickey, he said, so I regretfully made my
excuses and left. I was recounting the experience to Denis Jenkinson
over lunch one day. He laughed. 'You couldn't buy a Lagonda second
gear for £275 today . . !'

I soon worked out that writing the weekly column for the *Timaru*

Herald gave me the chance to mention people, and most people *love* to be mentioned in columns, so I pressed my advantage and asked to borrow cars to write about them. Thus I achieved my first indicated 100 mph driving a Triumph TR2 on the long straight roads between Timaru and Ashburton, and also learned some of the basic laws of physics applying to cars travelling fast downhill on a gravel road when I nearly put the same TR2 over the bank in a visit to Clellands Hill where I had campaigned the A30. Nearly 40 years later my daughter saw her own first indicated 100 mph at the wheel of our ex-Witte TR2, a car that I had first seen competing at the just-mentioned Clellands Hill. It had been totally rebuilt and drove like new. Its number plate was TRTWO. The 1928 Stutz Blackhawk I had at the same time had the number STUTZ8. In New Zealand you could choose your own number plate providing it had not already been issued.

Which reminds me of driving my Porsche 911T-Lux away from the opening of Tom Wheatcroft's museum at Donington. I stopped for petrol and a Brooklands type pulled up behind me shouting, 'I say, old boy, do you realise you've got Nuvolari's pit signal?' I wondered whether he was crazy or I was, then I realised that he was pointing at the Porsche number plate, NUV 6L, which in a racing context would have meant NUVOLARI 6 LAPS . . .

I think the Stutz may have been the only car I have ever owned that I was honestly sorry to see sold. It had started life as one of a small run of short-chassis Stutzes (perhaps only 30 were built) intended to have a six-cylinder engine but actually completed with a 5.3-litre overhead camshaft straight-eight and right-hand drive and shipped to Britain to be fitted with a lightweight Weyman body. It eventually found its way to New Zealand and came on the market in a sorry state without a body. Allan Bramwell rescued it and had Auto Restorations in Christchurch fit an open tourer body on the lines of the Stutz cars that ran at Le Mans in 1929. Murray Jones, a brilliant local engineer, designed and fitted a supercharger, the worm-drive Stutz differential was replaced by one from a Ford V8 truck, and the original gearbox was replaced by a modern Jaguar XJ6 four-speed unit with overdrive. I wrote a description of the car for the Stutz club magazine in the US and thought other owners might be appalled at the perceived butchery and modification of a rare Stutz, but the only letters were from owners wanting to know how to fit a Ford truck diff in place of the original fragile worm-drive unit!

It was superbly non-original and it drove like a dream, easily able to outpace the likes of 4.5-litre Bentleys. Tragically, Murray Jones was killed in the car on one of its first test runs when a learner driver made a U-turn in front of him. The Stutz hit a kerb, collapsing a wheel, and the car overturned.

I had lived with a racing Delahaye for a couple of years in England, the actual Type 135S that had held the lap record on the Ards TT course in Northern Ireland. In fact, it was the Ards link that landed me tenancy of the car. Maurice Hamilton's father had been one of the moving forces behind the staging of an event on the old circuit to commemorate the Golden Jubilee of the TT races. The race seemed as though it would have all the right ingredients and I wondered whether I could find a suitable car to enter. Only days later I was boarding a plane for a Grand Prix and Rob Walker was ahead of me in the queue.

'Buster, I wonder if you would do me an enormous favour? I've been asked to send my Delahaye over to the Ards Jubilee but I can't take it myself. Would you take it for me?'

Would I! It looked every inch the vintage racer it was with flowing guards and an open two-seater cockpit. The 3.5-litre straight-six gave it effortless power to cope with modern traffic, and the electro-magnetic Cotal gearbox was simplicity to use once you became used to the fact that the 'gear lever' was actually a little toggle switch on the dashboard. I drove the car up to Liverpool and across on the ferry to Belfast in company with Denis Jenkinson in a borrowed Le Mans Lagonda. It seemed to be raining most of that weekend, but the demonstration laps were a wonderful way of revisiting racing history.

Rob didn't seem very anxious to have the car back, and we agreed that I would keep it and maintain it, and use it in suitable events. It is now on display at the Haynes Motor Museum at Sparkford in Somerset.

At one point I owned a Kougar, a Jaguar-engined two-seater capturing the 1950s spirit of a Silverstone Healey or an Allard. In fact the project had started out as a copy of a Le Mans Replica Frazer-Nash using a Triumph Dolomite engine, but official complaints were raised and the car was scaled up into a larger replica of nothing in particular and using a Jaguar engine. It was a spirited performer, but I was never entirely happy with the look of it. It was reasonably shapely from side and rear views, but from the front it was awkward. Then came the day when someone asked me where the spare wheel was fitted and I realised it didn't have one! From then on I was paranoid about getting a puncture and I sold it soon afterwards . . .

I bought the Kougar from Stephen Langton, later to lose his life in a crash at Brands Hatch, and when we had agreed the deal he took me on a tour of his garages. In one was a distinctive little 1950s sports car, which he said was a Connaught and it happened to be the same price as I had just paid for the Kougar. I asked if I could 'own it' overnight, and he agreed. I did hurried research on the car and found that it was one of the original Connaught works racing cars, so telephoned Peter Briggs who snapped it up for his museum near

Perth in Western Australia. Peter bought several racing cars from me including not one but *two* H16 BRMs, those incredibly over-designed and over-engined under-performers that had been built for the 1966 switch to 3 litres in Formula 1.

The first H16 I bought was in a museum in Hanover owned by Bugatti-collector Uwe Hucke, whom we had met at his home near Monaco. Uwe said that the BRM didn't really fit in with his theme of cars, so we struck a deal and I arranged for Dave Wilkie, then running the Elf hospitality motorhome at the GPs, to hire a trailer, collect the BRM in Hanover and bring it to Hockenheim on the way home. It gave me the unique opportunity to be a journalist with my own Grand Prix car in a Grand Prix paddock! The complicated 16-cylinder BRM engine had been swapped for a 5.7-litre Boss Mustang V8, which I pulled out and sold while I cast around for an H16 engine. In the end Briggs bought the chassis – and he never did get an engine for it! Honour was partially satisfied when I managed to buy a BRM H16 that had been built as a non-running show car, and Briggs bought that too, so he now has an 'H16-and-a-half'.

It was over dinner at Bandol in the south of France during a test weekend at the Paul Ricard circuit when Ken Tyrrell was asked by Harry Calton from Ford what he planned to do with one of the March 701 Formula 1 cars he had run for Jackie Stewart and François Cevert in 1970 while his own Tyrrell cars were being built in secret. Ford had gone half-shares in the March cars and the remaining 701 was gathering dust in Tyrrell's shed. Ken was waiting for Ford to make a decision to sell, and Ford was waiting for the word from Ken. I asked the price because it would make an interesting column piece, but when I heard the figure I decided to buy the car myself!

Back in Surrey, I clambered into Tyrrell's shed with a torch and found that the chassis number was '701/2' – the actual car that Jackie Stewart had driven to win the 1970 Spanish Grand Prix at Jarama. Stewart hated those Marches, but the fact remained that this was the only 701 that had ever won a Grand Prix. Allan McCall fitted it with a fibreglass dummy Cosworth V8 and that car also eventually found its way into Briggs's museum.

On the way home from a Grand Prix in Adelaide, while visiting the America's Cup races, I called at the museum, at York, a few miles from Perth, at Briggs's invitation and was puzzling over one of the cars on display. It was a big yellow single-seater and not the handsomest of racing cars.

'What do you mean, "What's that?",' said Briggs. 'You sold it to me!'

It was another of the cars that I had 'owned overnight', but in fact I had never actually seen this one in the flesh, as it were. At a Long Beach Grand Prix I was chatting with a book customer and he showed me a photograph of this yellow racing car and asked if I recognised it or the driver. I peered more closely and realised that the driver was Jim Clark, so it had to be the American-built Indianapolis Vollstedt that he had driven at Riverside on the only occasion that he had raced a car other than a Lotus later in his career. I phoned Briggs from Long Beach and he agreed to buy the car that neither of us had seen, simply on the fact that it had been raced by Jim Clark. And here it was in Western Australia and I was making its acquaintance for the first time!

It may have been that same race weekend at Long Beach when an American collector telephoned to ask if I would like to come and see the McLaren Can-Am cars that he had in his collection. I told him that looking at other people's racing cars was not really my bag, even if they *were* McLarens. He said he would come and collect me, so, having run out of excuses, I agreed. As well as a late-model Can-Am McLaren, he had a 1966 Chevy-engined M6B, which he had made road-legal.

I knew what was coming next. He asked me if I would like to go for a ride in it. Imagine driving on the freeway at 55 mph in a full race Can-Am sports-racing car with the hubnuts of trucks spinning at head-height and the car itself effectively invisible to the drivers of these huge semi-trailers. It was a terrifying experience, but the owner was loving it. After about 10 miles I was delighted to realise that he was aiming for the slip-road, and we would be heading back home. Under the freeway he stopped, leaned across to me and shouted over the roar of the engine, 'Mr Young, you must know more about these cars than anyone else I know, so it would be a pleasure if you would drive my car!'

I probably knew *less* about a Can-Am McLaren than anyone else he knew, I had never driven one in my life and here I was struggling into the driver's seat to cope with the big heavy-shifting Hewland gearbox, to say nothing of the rush-hour freeway traffic . . .

A similar thing happened at Monaco when I was pitchforked into a driving situation that I hadn't requested. Murray Smith was racing Uwe Hucke's four-wheel-drive Bugatti in the historic race preceding the Grand Prix, and it was having a broken differential mended in Hucke's garage high above the town. I had ridden with Smith on the vintage Monte Carlo Rally in his 1928 4.5-litre Bentley, and he had left the car in Hucke's care in Monaco. Now he was picking me up in Casino Square on the 'free Friday' for the drive up to Hucke's garage to check progress on the Bugatti.

As fate would have it, the Bugatti was ready to be driven down to the paddock and Smith announced that I could follow him in the Bentley, a car I had never driven before. He gave me brief instructions and disappeared. I was pondering my possible fate in the Monegasque traffic when the garage door opened and a lanky French youth asked if he could hitch a ride down to the old-car paddock. I said I would rather he didn't and explained that it was my first experience with a car that was supposedly difficult to drive. He climbed in anyway.

I said to him, 'Your father reckoned these cars were the fastest lorries in Europe, didn't he?'

Michele Bugatti laughed and said that his father, Ettore, had meant it as a joke. I was having my first drive in a Bentley in Monaco with Bugatti's son beside me . . .

CHAPTER SEVEN

The people you meet

I ALWAYS THINK the worst speeches are made by people who write their notes painstakingly, then recite them. The best speeches are made from 'trigger notes', words or names that spark a seemingly off-the-cuff anecdote relative to the occasion. If I sit down to write a feature on, say, a racing driver, I will spend time researching through books and files, but if someone mentions a driver or a race or an incident over dinner this often sparks recollection of a long-forgotten tale. This chapter about drivers is therefore very much a collection of after-dinner stories about drivers I have known.

'Stirling has never forgiven you, you know,' said Rob Walker when we were sitting over lunch in a Melbourne hotel during a weekend of old-car racing at Sandown Park. Stirling Moss was at a table nearby. Mildly flabbergasted, I asked Rob what I had done that wasn't being forgiven.

'Oh, I don't know. Something you wrote on the Tasman Series . . .'

But that was 20 years before! Fortified by another glass of Australian red I decided to have it out with Stirling and clear the air. It isn't good when you suddenly discover that your hero is harbouring a dislike. Stirling had always been perfectly affable when we met, but there was obviously something lurking beneath the surface. I went over to his table and asked what the problem was. He said it was something I'd written, but I think it was so long ago that he had forgotten exactly what it was. I suggested that it was time we buried the irritation and got on with the rest of our lives. Mercifully he agreed.

Look at Moss these days and remember him when he was Hill and Schumacher rolled into one, the consummate professional racing driver unfortunately a generation too early to earn his rightful dues. But it's all relative. Before his Goodwood crash in 1962 Stirling's income from racing was what the other drivers only dreamed about.

He would race anything, anytime, anywhere, and be better than anyone else. When he lapped the field and won the 1962 New Zealand Grand Prix in a torrential downpour on the flooded Ardmore airfield circuit, the Saturday evening sports paper headlined him 'BOSS MOSS'. That was Stirling in his heyday.

His crash at Goodwood on Easter Monday, 1962, has never been explained to anyone's satisfaction, least of all Stirling's. The world waited for days for him to come out of his coma. It must be nigh on impossible for the modern generation to appreciate what Moss meant to motor racing then. He was always front page Fleet Street story material when the sport itself had difficulty getting on to the sports pages. I suppose you would have to say that he was a latter-day Nigel Mansell – but with style. He won't thank me for the comparison. Not long ago he was in the foyer of the British Racing Drivers Club at Silverstone and a father was groping to explain to his small son who Stirling was. 'He's . . . He's a famous racing driver . . . He's like . . . like . . . like Nigel Mansell!' I repeated the story to Stirling. He was incensed.

Karl Wendlinger survived a long period in a coma after his crash at Monaco in 1994, but never regained his form. Stirling knows how he felt. 'I think the biggest mistake I made was testing too soon after I left hospital. I went out in a Lotus Monte Carlo sports car at Goodwood and the times that I did were competitive, but I found that my concentration hadn't returned and it didn't really return for two or three years.'

He thinks that if he had been allowed to wait three years rather than being pressured for a yes/no decision by the press, the result might have been different.

'I found out afterwards that the *Daily Express* had a photographer based down there, and if he saw me go out he was to take pictures. There was more pressure than people realise. It wasn't that I didn't want to make a comeback, because I'd returned to racing after worse accidents really . . . I felt that I had to make a definite decision, and that decision was "No", based on the fact that my concentration wasn't good enough. My speed was OK but I could see that I was dangerous. I would go into a corner and think "Christ, I should be braking by now!", and I was scratching around because I had enough ability to do that but I wasn't smooth. I thought then, "I can't do this . . . I'm going to hurt myself . . ." So I announced my retirement. It was a mistake.'

I was interviewing Stirling on his 50th birthday in 1979 when he had been getting offers of touring car and historic drives. He had claimed his insurance pay-out after his Goodwood crash. Was this pay-back a barrier to a comeback?

'It wasn't really. I could have gone back into competitive racing in the state that I left it – in other words as a potential winner – I couldn't have cared less about the insurance. I mean we're talking about £9,000, so it's peanuts. Now it's nothing. In those days it was worth £60,000–£70,000 at today's [1979] values. If I had gone back into Formula 1 with a chance of the success that I had when I left it, I could have written off the £9,000 in a season or two without trouble.'

How the money has changed in 15 years! If Stirling was talking about it today he would be talking about a *day* or two.

Mike Hailwood rather upset the belief that former glories couldn't be recalled when he climbed back on a racing motor cycle and started winning TTs again on the Isle of Man. It proved the theory, if proof were needed, that naturally talented sportsmen never really lose that essential flair. Could Stirling have waited ten years as Hailwood did and made a comeback?

'I think I had the rhythm and the skill to do it, but whether I would have had the adaptability to come back to a totally different type of car, I don't know. Once you go from the car as I knew it with its narrow tyres, to the very wide tyres, you have a totally different character to deal with. I believe it could be re-learned, but whether it would have been feasible for me with the pressures one would have had as a past winner to go in and get enough experience to be able to establish myself in the right way . . . that would have probably made it not viable.'

Mike Hailwood had been in a similar situation to Stirling after a heavy accident in a McLaren at the German GP on the Nurburgring in 1974, which left him with a severely damaged right heel and ankle. In the autumn of 1975 he told me that he wouldn't race again. It had started off as a chat and then an interview, and I became aware that he was working up to saying to himself as much as to me that he wouldn't drive a racing car again.

'I don't think I *can't* race again – I'm sure I *could* race again, but the urge isn't upon me any more . . . When I go to races now I don't get the urge to race again . . . not at all. It's all over. The fire has gone out.'

Five years later the fire was re-lit when he made a sensational return to the Isle of Man and started winning again. He had to re-learn the modern machines, especially the improvement in braking performance. Mike asked Mick Grant to lead him round for a couple of laps. Grant was flabbergasted at the request. He said it was like God asking you to explain a couple of chapters from the Bible. While Mike was running these first comeback races on the Isle of Man the Formula 1 circus was qualifying for the Grand Prix at Jarama, and all the way down the pit lane everyone was asking for news of Mike at the TT. They were much more interested in that than what was happening at their own race in Spain.

John Surtees was a man who made mountains for himself to climb. Very much a Mansell of an earlier generation, if we still need modern comparisons. Hugely skilled but a man who was worried if he had nothing to worry about. He wasn't good with people. He was great at what he did on two wheels and four, and had the trophies to prove it, but he wasn't a great communicator and he tended to brood about people who handled the public better than he did. John believed that his performances should speak for themselves. A measure of his ability is the way he could blend with the bike and simply overwhelm TT races and GPs to win world championships with the effortless, fluid style that Mike Hailwood would later enjoy. The difference between Surtees and Hailwood was that John would step straight off the motor cycle into a car and transfer the same speed and dedication, the same natural skill. Surtees won seven world championships on two wheels and the car world championship for Ferrari in 1964.

John and Mike were chalk and cheese. John was all about dedication. Mike was all about enjoying life, and as far as he was concerned motor cycles or racing cars were part of that life. For a time Mike drove for the Surtees team in an unlikely liaison. On the first day of practice for the 1972 South African Grand Prix, Hailwood was on pole position. Everyone was amazed, Mike among them. He had been staying with Paddy Driver who had a farmhouse near the track.

'Don't tell John for God's sake,' said Mike, 'but I didn't get to bed until 4 o'clock this morning.'

John was obsessed with playing a straight bat, if you'll pardon the mixed sporting metaphor. He was obsessed with playing the game the way he wrote the rules. That wasn't always the way other people saw the game.

By mid-1966 the Ferrari honeymoon was over. The Italian team traditionally suffered success swings that continue to this day. Years in an also-ran wilderness, then a summer of success that wins a world championship and the team is carried away on a tide of euphoria to the point where they seem unable to remember what they had done to make themselves winners. Surtees was the toast of Italy in 1964 when he won the world championship for Ferrari, having brought laurels to MV-Agusta a few year earlier. He was a household name.

I didn't appreciate quite how much the Italians revered their sporting heroes until I went down to Maranello with John in the summer of 1966. He had phoned me at the McLaren factory where I was still on the staff as Bruce's secretary. Could I get a couple of days off to go with him on a secret trip to Italy? Why? It was secret. That was OK with me. I quite liked being privy to a Surtees secret, but I didn't imagine that Bruce would see it in quite the same way. I said that I would have to explain it to Bruce. We were going to Ferrari. More than that he could not or would not say. That gave me a lever for Bruce. I was quite intrigued with the idea of a secret trip to Ferrari in company with their number one driver.

John was paranoid about the trip. He had crossed swords for the last time with the Ferrari team manager at Le Mans during the 24-hour race and decided he had had enough. The Ferrari team managers were notorious for being hired not on their ability to handle team arrangements but for keeping Enzo informed on what was happening. Since the death of his son Dino, Enzo had never been to a Grand Prix, and he relied on reports from his appointee at the track. His man on the scene was more interested in the tenure of his job, which was considered high profile, and it was thought that he tended to tell the Old Man what he would want to hear. If the cars were off the pace it was automatically down to the drivers. As team manager in motor racing's equivalent to a touring opera troupe, he had the power to favour one performer over another.

This had happened once too often at Le Mans and now John was reporting to Enzo formally to offer his resignation. It was something that *nobody* did. It was an honour to be invited to drive for Ferrari. It was something of an honour in those days to be allowed to *buy* a Ferrari road car. Team drivers traditionally only retired on death. John didn't want to wait that long.

We were therefore going to Maranello to confirm the news to the Old Man. John was convinced that he could be arrested at Milan immigration. I carried his briefcase through the official checks. No problem. We stopped at a restaurant on the Autostrada for morning coffee and the Surtees aura was suddenly extremely apparent. As we stood in the doorway waiting to be shown to a table, I was aware of the customers nudging and nodding in John's direction. In a strange wave of public acknowledgement they stood as one and applauded their champion. Make a comparison by imagining Damon Hill stopping at a motorway restaurant on the M1 and having all the diners on their feet clapping. A few coming diffidently to his table asking for an autograph, perhaps. The direct comparison would have been with his father Graham. The motorway restaurant would have buzzed when Graham came in because he was a 'personality' as well as a racing driver and a world champion. Damon might have been BBC 'Sports Personality of the Year' but that doesn't really make him a celebrity. In the public perception being a 'personality' takes a hands-on approach, and modern motor racing doesn't allow the time or space to make yourself a 'personality'. Famous yes, a 'personality' not necessarily.

But I digress. I was painting in the background to our Ferrari trip in 1966 in a way that it could be appreciated in '90s motor sport terms.

We arrived at Maranello and John was ushered in to his audience with Enzo. Franco Gozzi, for years Enzo's confidant and destro-hand man, took me on a tour of the factory while Ferrari and Surtees argued their points. When John came out he was smiling, which was a definite signal that he had won on points. Enzo would never have admitted that his team manager could have been feeding him biased information, but he accepted the truth of the situation from John and accepted his resignation. And probably continued to receive an edited version of what was actually happening from his man in the pit lane for years afterwards.

The reason for my trip to Maranello with John was to phone all the Fleet Street journalists with the news and Surtees quotes, so that the headlines in the London newspapers the next morning would read 'SURTEES LEAVES FERRARI'. Not 'Ferrari Sacks Surtees'.

Jim Clark was the son of a Scottish farmer, and I don't think he ever entirely escaped his role. He may have been one of the most naturally talented and successful racing drivers we have seen, but he always gave the impression that when he had reached a time when he wanted to retire from the world of Formula 1, he would go back to the family farm near Duns in Berwickshire.

Jimmy took over the Moss mantle after Stirling's crash in 1962. Evolved into it, more accurately, from a pace point of view, rather than any effort to better Stirling's earnings. Winning was what fuelled Jim's ambitions. The money came later and probably only as a means of keeping score. In those days, if you could make money as well as being provided with a competitive racing car, you were quids in. These days you have to be millions in before signing on the dotted line. Jimmy was Colin Chapman's ideal disciple. A driver with limitless natural ability but without naked ambition. The antithesis of a Senna.

Chris Amon arrived in Formula 1 in 1963 when Jimmy and the Lotus were the combination to beat. They were similar in that they were both farmers' sons, and the New Zealand back country was a mirror image of the region around Duns in Scotland. I rode with Jim in a Ford Zodiac with Richard Attwood and Frank Gardner on a trip that took us across country to the Hermitage tourist resort at Mount Cook, then down the West Coast to the Teretonga track near Invercargill. I couldn't believe how well Jimmy coped with tar-seal and loose metal roads that he had never seen before – that was until I visited Scotland for the first time, ironically for his funeral.

Jim stopped for petrol at a remote service station and Attwood spotted a large Dunlop poster of the Scotsman in the window. He whispered to the pump attendant that the driver of our car was in fact the same Jim Clark as shown on the poster. He wouldn't believe it! Refused to believe it. Thought Attwood was winding him up.

'Jimmy was the only guy I ever got alongside and felt I could *never* beat,' Amon recalls. 'He always seemed to have so much left within himself. I really felt I could foot it with anyone else on my day, but I never felt that Jimmy had to try that hard. I can only compare him with people in our own era, so I couldn't say whether he was better than Fangio or Prost because I never raced against them. Even on a good day, given equal equipment, I never felt I could compete with Jimmy.

'As a person? I always connect Jimmy with Bruce [McLaren]. I hardly ever heard either of them say a bad word about anybody. You could try and provoke Bruce into saying something bad about someone, but he wouldn't. Jimmy was exactly the same. I think the only guy he ever criticised was himself. When he was out in New Zealand he would relax his guard and enjoy himself. He didn't have the pressures that he had wherever else he went. I probably got to know him better during the Tasman Series, when he came to our beach house and joined in the cricket matches on the lawn, than I ever did over a season in Europe. He certainly did things down here that he didn't do anywhere else!

'I think everyone who races has a feeling of immortality. If you didn't, you wouldn't do it. Jimmy's death was the most profound thing that happened to me in my racing career. I felt that if it could happen to him, what chance did the rest of us have? It got to an awful lot of people. People who had no interest in racing. That was the uniqueness of the guy. He was someone very special.'

Jimmy's fatal crash in a Formula 2 race at Hockenheim tainted the track in many people's eyes for ever, even when it gained Grand Prix status. Perhaps *especially* when it gained Grand Prix status. The awfulness of it is that by rights Jimmy should have been racing the new Ford F3L at Brands Hatch that Sunday. Jimmy was living out his time as a UK 'tax exile' in Paris, and Alan Mann (whose team built the F3L GT prototype using the Ford-Cosworth DFV V8) had flown over to check his availability. He could do one of the two days of practice but not both, and he could do the race. Mann was delighted because Graham Hill, Jimmy's partner at Team Lotus, had also agreed.

Colin Chapman had never been keen on Mann's close relationship with Ford, feeling that all Ford effort and finance should be channelled into Lotus, and when Mann thanked him for making his drivers available, Chapman quickly re-arranged their schedule so that they couldn't do the Brands Hatch race. The F3L was eventually raced by Bruce McLaren and Mike Spence, and they led the race until they had a slow driver change and a rubber doughnut in the transmission let go soon after Spence had taken over.

I was walking down the path towards the paddock with Spence soon after, and I remarked that he seemed unusually upset at dropping out of the race. He said, 'Haven't you heard the news? Jimmy's been killed at Hockenheim . . .'

Mike was signed to drive the STP Lotus turbine car at Indianapolis, and having set the second fastest lap ever around the 2.5-mile oval (169.555 mph), he lost control and hit the wall. The front wheel came

THE PEOPLE YOU MEET

back into the cockpit and Mike died of his injuries. It was a month to the day after Jimmy's death.

We were to have flown up to Scotland for Jimmy's funeral with Chris Amon in his Twin Commanche, but he was committed to a Matra test session, so he arranged for a commercial 747 pilot to fly the plane instead. Bill Bryce, my wife Sandra and I were passengers. Bryce was a pilot so – fortunately – he sat in the front seat and helped read maps. We found the airfield eventually, a broad concrete crucifix that we were approaching from the long end. We could see people and cars waiting at the cross-piece. We were still bouncing as we passed the cross-piece going into the short end of the 'cross'. Our Jumbo pilot had misjudged his put-down, being unused to a small aircraft, and we were now without enough runway to take off – or to stop! Bryce jumped on the brakes on his side to help the pilot and the plane slewed to a stop with its nose actually *over* the barbed wire fence at the end of the runway. A tyre was blown and the landing gear bent.

The pilot was hugely embarrassed and we were hugely angry and relieved in equal measure. The pilot said he'd do his best to have the plane airworthy for our return flight in the afternoon. We said something about no thanks. If we ever get in a small plane again it'll be too soon. We made reservations on a proper airline for the return to London after the funeral. I remember thinking how many things were coming at once when I walked into Edinburgh airport and saw the newspaper billboards headlining 'NEW ZEALAND FERRY DISASTER'. The inter-island ferry *Wahine* had foundered and rolled over within sight of land on the approach to Wellington harbour and 51 people were drowned.

The connections continue. When a journalist who survived wrote a book on the ferry disaster interviewing other survivors and presenting their different personal recollections as separate chapters, I was so impressed that when I came to write *Bruce McLaren, The Man and his Racing Team* after Bruce was killed in 1970 I used the same idea. I let the members of the team recount their memories of Bruce and what life with his team was like from a personal viewpoint.

One of the best interviews I ever wrote was with Brian Redman, and it was perhaps the better for happening spontaneously. It began with dinner in a small restaurant near the Nurburgring where Brian was to drive a McLaren Can-Am car for John Lewis. There had been a mix-up with hotel bookings and I had a room but Brian didn't. I imagined that this wouldn't be a problem, what with Herr Redman being a former Porsche works driver and the hotel being so near the 'Ring. It made no difference. Full meant full. But they could arrange a very nice zimmer for him in a house nearby.

'Times have changed, haven't they, Brian?' I said, making a joke in appalling taste. 'If you were driving for Wyer's team now I would have been giving you my room and staying down the road in the private house. But you aren't and I'm not.'

We had dinner together that night without a notebook or tape-recorder in sight or even in mind, because I had no thoughts of Brian being feature material. It was a dinner that should have been framed. He was so articulate, put so much feeling into his reminiscences. I was so spellbound by the stories he told about his career that I concentrated as hard as I could on remembering what he said, and when I got back to my room, I wrote for an hour trying to re-capture it and the way he had said it.

Talk about a man who had come back from the brink several times! He talked of his first drive at the Nurburgring (14.2 miles, 176 corners) with Peter Sutcliffe and his GT40.

'I had never been round there before and he took me round the circuit. When we got back to the paddock he said, "Two things you've got to remember about this circuit, Brian. The first is that it's *my* car. The second is – remember those bushes blowing about in the breeze at the edge of the track? They've all got 100-foot trunks beneath them!"'

In 1968 Redman was in line for a Ferrari Formula 2 drive. He tested and was offered a race at the Nurburgring south circuit.

'Ten minutes before the end of practice I stopped and told team manager Forghieri I couldn't go any faster. "Go out and try harder, Brian," he said. "You're only in tenth place." So I went out again and tried *very* hard, went a tenth faster – and then found out I'd been fourth fastest all the time.'

In the race Brian was in the lead group battling for position when he was hit in the eye by a stone.

'I felt this tremendous blow in my left eye and I braked, tore off my goggles, and pretty much came to a halt feeling my eye because I was sure I must have knocked it out, the blow had been that hard. I could still see, but it was painful and I drove slowly round to the pits. Forghieri looked at my eye, said it would be OK and asked where my spare goggles were. I didn't have any, so he threw me a pair of Ickx's. They were dark green, which was great in the sun but not so good in the shady sections under the trees where I was pretty much driving blind. I drove like a madman to catch up, set a new lap record and finished fourth. When I got back to the hotel I was absolutely drained, physically and mentally.

'At dinner that night Forghieri said he had been on the phone to Ferrari and they were offering me a Formula 2 drive with the chance of a Formula 1 drive at the end of the season. I said, "No, thank you. If I continue to drive like this I'll be dead by the end of the season."'

As a poignant postscript, when he signed to drive the 312 PB endurance sports cars in 1972, Forghieri told Brian that he was the only driver Ferrari had ever asked twice . . .

A racing album

ABOVE *Myself, aged 2½, with my first racing car, pedal-powered, outside grandmother's house in Pleasant Point, South Canterbury, New Zealand.*

BELOW LEFT *Aged 3, with my father Alex Young.*

BELOW RIGHT *Junior Bradman at the crease in the garden on our farm at Cave.*

ABOVE *My father's Austin A40 pick-up truck. First car!*

BELOW *Bruce McLaren with his first Cooper single-seater at Ardmore in 1958.* (Barry McKay)

ABOVE *Stirling Moss (right) with the laurels after winning the 1959 New Zealand Grand Prix at Ardmore, with second-man Jack Brabham (centre) and Bruce McLaren, third (left).* (Barry McKay)

BELOW *David Young's C-Type passing George Lawton haybaling his Cooper in the 1959 Waimate 50 street race.*

ABOVE *David's 1960 equipe in New Zealand – Mk 1 Zodiac convertible and C-Type Jaguar.*

BELOW *Chris Amon in shirt-sleeves racing his 250F Maserati in the Renwick road race, New Zealand, in 1961.* (Euan Sarginson)

ABOVE *Embarking for England in 1961 – the good ship* Ruahine.

BELOW LEFT *Denny Hulme (left) checking the suspension on David Young's Cooper Formula Junior at Brands Hatch in 1961.*

BELOW RIGHT *Jack Brabham's Cessna in which we flew from Luton to Tasmania in 1961 – an en route refuelling stop.*

BELOW *Congratulating Bruce after
his win at Teretonga Park in 1963.*
(Euan Sarginson)

RIGHT *With South African Cooper racer Tony Maggs during the 1963 Tasman Series.*

BELOW *Chris Amon in the Parnell team Formula 1 Lola in 1963.*

Above *With Jack Brabham at Silverstone, 1963.*
Below *With Engineer Bertocchi at the Maserati factory in the early '60s.*

ABOVE *S.C.H. (Sammy) Davis explaining the famous Le Mans Bentley crash at White House in 1927, with his oil painting of the night scene.*

BELOW *Mike Hailwood clowning on a vintage Brough Superior.*

ABOVE *Eoin Young gives thumbs-up to McLaren Tasman Cooper after first tests at Goodwood in 1964.* (Nigel Snowdon)

BELOW *Jim Clark (centre) with Bill Bryce (left) and myself during the 1965 Tasman Series.*

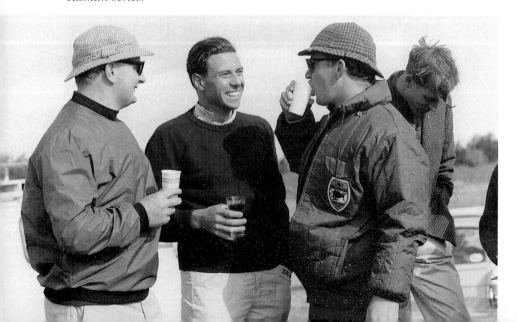

ABOVE *The McLaren Tasman Series team photo at Pukekohe with the first Mini-Cooper Bruce raced. Left to right: myself, Colin Beanland (Bruce's mechanic in 1958), unidentified, Wally Willmott, Harry Pearce, Patty McLaren and Bruce.*

BELOW *Testing a Formula 3 Lotus at Silverstone.* (Geoffrey Goddard)

Above left *John Cooper (left) and myself in the Cooper pit lap-scoring during the Dutch Grand Prix at Zandvoort.*

Above *Jim Clark clowning with my hat at Teretonga in 1965 . . .*

Left *. . . and shampooing in Lake Taupo before a barbecue during the Tasman Series.*

Above right *Team-talk around the wind tunnel model of the first McLaren Can-Am car at Colnbrook. Left to right: Bruce McLaren, Wally Willmott, Bruce Harre, Howden Ganley and myself.*

Right *Bruce McLaren, Teddy Mayer and myself with the Tasman Cooper in the Feltham workshop.* (George Wilkes)

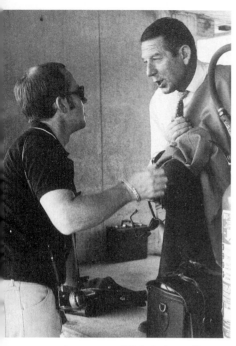

ABOVE LEFT *With Rob Walker, Stirling Moss's entrant, in the pits at Zandvoort.* (Jutta Fausel)

ABOVE RIGHT *In a 1936 V16 Auto Union GP car, talking to the car's engineer, Eberan von Eberhorst.*

BELOW *Bruce McLaren checking his odds before the Monaco Grand Prix.* (Michael Cooper)

ABOVE *Trying Jackie Stewart's Formula 1 Matra-Ford for size at the Tyrrell workshops in 1969.*

BELOW *Bruce McLaren showing the light weight of the F1 car's aluminium tub.*

ABOVE *Ready for a lap of Goodwood with Bruce McLaren in the M6B CanAm car.*

BELOW *With Patty McLaren after the publication of* Bruce McLaren, The Man and his Racing Team *in 1971.*

ABOVE *Chats with Gulf Oil Executive Vice-President Grady Davis . . .* (Michael Marchant)

BELOW *. . . and General Motors head of styling Bill Mitchell, at a Can-Am race in the USA.*

ABOVE *The Adlard's Capri 3-litre I shared with Jody Scheckter in the 1974 Tour of Britain.*

BELOW *Myself and Sandra in Tahitian garb at an Elf Grand Prix party in the South of France in 1975.* (Phipps Photographic)

ABOVE *With Denny Hulme (right) and his young son Martin on his Can-Am-engined powerboat . . .*

BELOW *. . . and off-roading with his Range Rover and a Yamaha.* (Both Phipps Photographic)

ABOVE *Back to business – Denny with his Can-Am McLaren at a Goodwood test.*

BELOW LEFT *Six-times TT winner Jim Redman explains a corner to me on the Isle of Man TT course.* (Mike Woollett)

BELOW RIGHT *Business and pleasure – at the drawing-board with Tyrrell designer Derek Gardner . . .*

ABOVE *Impromptu but invaluable Gulf publicity – the famous photo of the drivers on the roof of the Gulf motorhome at Clermont Ferrand. From left to right: McLaren, Hulme, Hill, Moser, Siffert, Stewart, two unidentified, Rindt, Elford, Beltoise, Ickx and Amon.*

BELOW LEFT *Motor racing history – with Maurice and René Dreyfus (right), when the latter's racing autobiography was launched in New York in 1983. René won the Monaco GP in 1930.*

BELOW RIGHT *With Len Southward and the engine of the 1915 Indianapolis Stutz at the Southward Museum in New Zealand.*

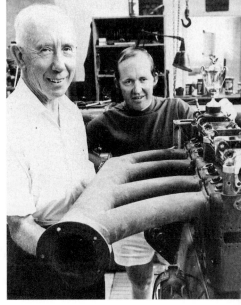

Historic drives – with Allan Bramwell's Cooper 500 and Manx Norton at Ruapuna, New Zealand, and aboard the Norton. (Both Euan Sarginson)

ABOVE *Track-testing the aero-engined Stanton Special, which held the New Zealand Land Speed record . . .* (Euan Sarginson)

BELOW *. . . and at the wheel of Eddie Hall's TT Bentley at Briggs Cunningham's museum in California.*

ABOVE *Track-testing at Ruapuna – Gavin Bain's 375MM Ferrari sports-racer . . .* (Harry Ruffell)

BELOW *. . . and a Tojeiro Jaguar sports-racer.*

BOTTOM *With Dick Crosthwaite about to do a lap of the Monaco circuit in a Bugatti on the morning of the Grand Prix!*

ABOVE *At Hockenheim in the H16 I bought from a German museum. Left to right: BRM mechanic Allan Challis, Innes Ireland and Denis Jenkinson.*

BELOW *Sharing a joke with McLaren Formula 1 driver John Watson.* (Nigel Snowdon)

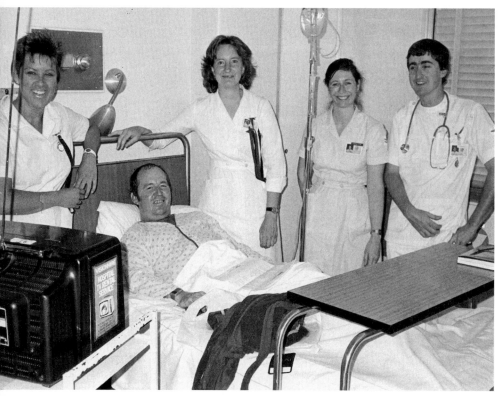

ABOVE *Off the track – in the Royal Adelaide Hospital missing the first Australian Grand Prix in Adelaide in 1985, struck down by a mysterious throat disease . . .*

BELOW *. . . and Jenks 'covering' the 1990 Canadian Grand Prix over lunch from the comfort of my hotel room in Montreal!*

ABOVE *New Zealand champions (left to right): Ross Jensen, Ron Frost, Roly Levis, Denny Hulme, Syd Jensen, Angus Hyslop and Jim Palmer.*

BELOW *James Hunt at The Barley Mow with his Austin A35 Countryman.*

ABOVE *'Grandad' Charles Mortimer with a road test XJS Jaguar outside The Barley Mow. He worked with me in my rare motoring book business.*

BELOW LEFT *In my element amongst the stock in The Barley Mow barn.*

BELOW RIGHT *Legendary Barley Mow landlord John Woodiwiss (right) with Colin Black (aka The Mole).*

ABOVE *Test-driving the 1922 TT Sunbeam in New Zealand.*

BELOW *Barley Mow lunchtime, left to right: Mike Hallowes, Nick Mason of the Pink Floyd, John Cooper, ESY, trad jazz band leader Chris Barber, McLaren F1 designers Gordon Murray and Peter Stevens.*

ABOVE *Ron Dennis, Patty McLaren and myself outside The Barley Mow at the 1995 launch of the re-published book I wrote on Bruce McLaren after his death.* (Dave Kenwood)

BELOW *My daughter Selina with her own fun book, that she wrote and illustrated.*

ABOVE That *meeting . . . Maurice Hamilton (left) and Nigel Roebuck with Nigel Mansell at Milwaukee.*

BELOW *With Ferrari world champions Phil Hill (left) and John Surtees at Albert Park for the 1996 Australian Grand Prix. Hill won the title in 1961, Surtees in 1964.*

ABOVE *'Our Gang' – Maurice Hamilton (left), Alan Henry and Nigel Roebuck at Albert Park in 1996.*

BELOW *A set-up photograph on Brighton beach for an* Autocar *book review feature. Yes, it beats working!*

THE PEOPLE YOU MEET

During his career in long-distance races Redman would win the 1,000 kms race at Spa four times, Nurburgring, Daytona, Sebring and Brands Hatch twice, and once at Watkins Glen, Monza and the Targa Florio. At the end of 1970 he had had enough and announced his retirement, planning to live in South Africa, but in the time it took his furniture to arrive by boat, he had changed his mind. John Wyer had already signed Derek Bell as Redman's replacement to race the Gulf-Porsche 917s, but as Bell had never done the Targa Florio, Brian was asked back for a one-off race in a new small Porsche 908/3.

When he first saw the car in the German factory he asked where the rest of the car was. 'You could sit in the seat and reach out and touch both front wheels. There was nothing in front of the driver but an oil cooler. It looked like something I didn't want to have any part of, but then they told me it had been 20 seconds a lap faster round the old 'Ring than the previous 908 . . .'

Jo Siffert crashed the car during the final practice the night before the race, but it had been repaired for Redman to do the start.

'I remember one of the mechanics saying to me, "Herr Redman, if you are going to crash the car, do not crash it on the right side." The fuel tanks were on the right-hand side.'

When Redman started, the tanks were brimful. 'I was approaching a downhill corner and thinking this was Richard's corner [Attwood had crashed there the year before] when I turned the wheel and nothing happened. It wouldn't turn. The car went straight across the corner, hit a concrete pole and exploded. It didn't crash and catch fire, Eoin, it just went WHOOOMPH!

'It was like sitting in the centre of a firestorm. I was wearing an open-face helmet and I shut my eyes tight, held my breath, crashed open the buckle of the safety harness and dived out, ablaze from head to toe. I was rolling on the road trying to put the flames out, but as soon as I put them out they would blaze up again because they were soaked with fuel. I can remember hearing someone screaming, but it must have been me because there wasn't anyone else there . . .'

The helicopter took 45 minutes to arrive and the team was told that Brian had been taken to a different hospital from the one in which he found himself, with his burned face swollen so that his eyes were closed and he was effectively blind. It was midnight by the time Richard Attwood and Pedro Rodriguez found him and spirited him back to the hotel and on to a jet chartered by Porsche and Gulf to get him back to a specialist hospital in Britain. He made a complete recovery but always wore the burn scars as a reminder.

Now tell me that racing drivers get paid too much money . . .

Tom Wheatcroft is one of those larger-than-life characters. You can't really believe the stories you hear about him until you actually meet him. We first met him on the Tasman Series. I had heard about this cheerful Englishman who had flown out to follow the races, so I tracked him down and arranged for him to have team pit tickets. Years later I discovered that Tom had built his business literally from nothing. He had been a tank driver in the war and they were based near Spa in Belgium when word came through that the German Army had surrendered. War was over. Tom's commander suggested they go down to a stand of trees where a German unit was dug in, and tell them about the change in play.

The Germans weren't ready for surrender and a direct hit in the driver's eye-slot put a blinded Wheatcroft in hospital. He was there for days convinced that he had lost his sight in a ridiculous incident that should never have happened. In the bed next to him was another blinded soldier who had a wife and family at home and was terrified at the prospect of his return to civilian life as a blind man. To his amazement Tom's sight eventually began to return, and after a complete recovery he was demobbed. The first thing he did in Civvy Street was to put his entire accumulated army pay into the blinded soldier's bank account leaving no identification.

Tom was and is quite simply the ultimate motor racing enthusiast. The difference between him and us is that he has worked to create a building empire that has made him a millionaire several times over, so he has the wherewithal to indulge himself and his hobby. The first racing car he bought was a Grand Prix Ferrari in Australia, but it was only when it arrived in Britain that he found out it had been fitted with a Chevrolet V8 engine in place of the pure-bred Italian V12. That was Lesson Number One.

You would have to say that Tom learned quickly. He employed experts to vet his 'wish list' from then on, and as his collection of Grand Prix cars grew it became clear that he needed somewhere to house them. He lived in the Leicester area near the famous pre-war Donington Park track and had watched races there as a lad. Like Brooklands, the Donington track had been taken over for war purposes, and it seemed unlikely ever to be used again. Tom bought the whole facility, built a new museum for his cars, then set about getting permissions to rebuild the circuit for international racing.

I think Tom thought that if he had a track with such a history, rebuilt to comply with all modern requirements, he could stage a Grand Prix, but that was far too simplistic. That was a builder's way of looking at it. It was reasonable. It made sense. But it didn't take into account the politics of modern motor racing. Bernie Ecclestone was and is the Tsar of everything he surveys in Formula 1, and never mind that his FIA title is to do with marketing, while Max Mosley is President. I have never been in any doubt that Ecclestone's word is law. Period.

The new Donington track and Wheatcroft's Grand Prix aspirations for it surfaced around the time that Silverstone had wrested itself out of the arrangement where Brands Hatch had the GP one year and

Silverstone the next. Silverstone now had the GP contract on a long-term basis, and there seemed no way that Tom would get his race, even though he tried long and hard through the courts. Eventually a Grand Prix came his way, even though it was a European Grand Prix in 1993. It was won in the wet in such fantastic style by Ayrton Senna in the McLaren that Tom must have thought the wait was worth it, and if another GP never came his way he could be content with having staged the race of an era won by a man literally driving out of his skin. Senna's McLaren was not competitive, but the rain would be the equaliser.

When the light went green Prost made a good start, taking his Williams into the lead from team-mate Hill. Richard Williams captures the scene brilliantly in his book *The Death of Ayrton Senna*, a description that ranks in journalistic terms with Senna's lap that day in Donington. Senna started poorly dropping from fourth to fifth, but he launched himself into a chase that would go down in history. He passed Schumacher, then Wendlinger.

'Coming up behind Hill's Williams, the two cars throwing up thin streamers of fine spray, Senna positioned himself again to the inside as they approached the Old Hairpin, a right-hander. Here, close to the spot at which Tazio Nuvolari's Auto Union had hit and killed a stag in practice for the 1938 race, the Brazilian claimed another victim, with the sudden conclusiveness of his inside pass astonishing Hill, who lacked the wherewithal to resist. But the Englishman was then in the box seat to watch through the spray as Senna screamed down the back straight, preparing the next incident in this tumultuous mini-drama.

'Prost, despite enjoying the advantage of being able to see where he was going, could do nothing to hold back Senna's advance. By the time they reached the Esses, the start of the circuit's final loop, the McLaren was on the tail of the leader's Williams. When they reached the Melbourne Hairpin, a panoramic 180-degree job, Senna took the inside, again off the racing line, but delayed his braking long enough to gain possession of the corner. Both cars wavered and twitched, but only one gave in. It was Prost, who knew what the cost would be if he disputed Senna's right to take the corner. Senna knew that Prost knew. And knew that Prost would let him go.

'Up above the pits in the press room, where correspondents follow the race on TV monitors, experienced people were looking at each other with awe in their eyes. History had just been made. In 1 min 35.843 sec, Ayrton Senna had written another paragraph in the story of motor racing. Something, it seemed clear, to rank with Fangio at the Nurburgring. Which meant the greatest of all time.'

Magic prose for a magic lap.

Fangio's amazing win driving a 250F Maserati in the 1957 German Grand Prix was a one-race summation of an incredible career for the

five-times world champion. It was his last season. The Maserati was
out-gunned by the Ferraris of Mike Hawthorn and Peter Collins, but
Fangio decided to make a one-stop strategy for fuel and tyres so that
he could start the race lighter in weight than the Ferraris. It was his
only chance. Things unfolded according to plan until the pit stop that
went totally awry and Fangio came out late, annoyed and charging.
The Nurburgring was always a leveller, a track so complex and
difficult that a maestro like Fangio could make it work for him. The
gap to the Ferraris dropped, and soon they were in sight. Fangio
'kerbed' every corner, only in those days at the Nurburgring there
were no kerbs, only grass infield. Fangio made the most of it.

I heard the story first-hand from trad jazz bandleader Chris Barber
who had gone to the race as a junior member of Horace Gould's
team. Gould had stopped out on the circuit with his 250F Maserati
and the team had the tow-car and trailer loaded and ready at the end
of the pit lane to go out and collect him as soon as the race ended.

'Every corner was strewn with clipped grass as though a gang-
mower had gone through. Fangio must have taken a short cut on
every corner on that last lap!'

Did they have a problem finding the Maserati on the long lap?

'Oh, no. He told us where he would stop . . .'

In those days the starting money relied on the driver actually
starting the race. Where he stopped was down to him. With no
chance of winning or placing it made more sense for a privateer like
Gould to take the money and stop.

Carroll Shelby, winner at Le Mans in 1959 driving with Roy
Salvadori in an Aston Martin, is captivating company. I went to
Switzerland for the 25th anniversary of the Ancien Pilotes Association,
arriving a day early and venturing into the bar. Shelby was there in
deep conversation with a television crew. Or so I thought. He spotted
me and shouted, 'Where the *hell* you bin? I been waiting for hours!'
And he hauled himself away from the TV people and whispered,
'Let's get the hell outa here.'

It turned out he was bored stiff and was anxious to be rescued by
anyone. We went to an Italian restaurant for dinner and as the wine
started to reach a serious rate of flow, Carroll's stories got better and
better. I asked if he had ever driven in the Mille Miglia. He hadn't but
he had done a recce for Aston Martin in 1954 with George Eyston.
Eyston was the only one of the pre-war World Land Speed Record-
holders (he held the record in 1937 and 1938 with his Thunderbolt)
who lived to a ripe old age. I remember meeting him at a lunch to
celebrate the 50th anniversary of Castrol. The cigars had come around
and I had forgotten to get mine cut. I saw Sir George puffing away on
the other side of the table so I walked around and asked respectfully
if I could borrow his cutter. He grabbed my cigar and started slicing
the end off it with his thumbnail.

'*God* gave me my cutter, young man,' he said as he handed my cigar back, perfectly sliced at the end. I've copied him ever since and told the story every time cigars are lit after dinner.

Eyston was setting up the pit-stop arrangements for the Aston Martin team. 'He had towels, he had hot water, he had mouthwash, he had *everything* arranged for the drivers.' Eyston was an Englishman Shelby admired. 'We were staying in this hotel right across from the train station in Florence. We couldn't get two rooms so George had a cot put in his room for me. We had been riding around the Mille Miglia course all that day in the Lagonda shooting-brake and he was tired. We got to bed about 10.30 or 11 and the announcements were coming over the loudspeakers in the train station about every 10 minutes. George didn't think much about it, but at about 12.30 they were still going on announcing the arrival and departure of each train and finally George was layin' over there in the bed, and he was a very even-tempered old man – if there were *ever* a perfect English gentleman it was George Eyston.

'Finally he starts mumblin' every time they announced a train and eventually he goes over to the window and starts yellin' back at them.' Shelby hoots with laughter at the memory. '"Shut that bloody thing down – it's 2 o'clock in the morning!" Honest to Christ, I swear on my mother's grave I'm not exaggerating. He'd lay down for about 15 minutes and every time they'd make another announcement he'd start mumblin', "Bloody impudent bastids . . ." And then finally they stopped the announcements about 4 o'clock. I *laffed* at him! I told John Wyer the next day and I thought John Wyer was goin' to pee in his pants!'

The Detroit Grand Prix was always my favourite, mainly because we always stayed in the Westin Hotel, which was in the centre of the street circuit and your room was never more than a 5-minute walk from the track. If it started to rain you strolled indoors, took the elevator to your floor and watched the proceedings in comfort. I met Paul Newman in a Westin Hotel lift. It was like a scene from one of his movies. The lift was empty when I walked in and pressed the button for the 27th floor, and as the doors were about to close, Newman stepped in. I was accidentally given a presence with one of the great men in Hollywood and a total motor racing enthusiast. I couldn't think of a thing to say. I gabbled something about the weather and what time was his practice session. I couldn't even remember what car he was racing. I was probably the sort of person he least liked to meet in public – someone who knew who he was, but not what he did . . . I fled to my room mortified and wrote most of that week's *Autocar* column about my mortification in the company of the Hollywood legend.

During every Detroit GP weekend Ford hosted a mammoth cocktail party at the Henry Ford Museum in nearby Dearborn. The museum covers much more than just motoring and is a fascinating place. I had met up with Edsel Ford, a good friend of Jackie Stewart, and we were chatting when his father, Henry Ford II, arrived. Henry was a big man with a commanding presence and a huge unlit cigar. There were 'No Smoking' signs everywhere.

'D'you suppose it's OK to light this up in here?' asked Henry II.

'Go ahead, Dad,' said Edsel. 'It's your place . . .'

Years before on a flight from Australia to London the plane stopped at Karachi around shaving time in the morning and I headed for the men's room with my razor. The room was being renovated and there was only one wash basin in use. The American and I arrived at the same time for the same purpose. I waved him on to shave and he did the same to me. Then he said, 'What the hell – let's share it.'

So we shaved in the same basin and shared the same mirror. You can't really get much closer than that to a total stranger. When we had both finished he asked if I would join him for a drink at the bar. After the first drink someone asked for his autograph, into the second drink and there was a small queue forming for the autograph of my shaving and drinking buddy.

'Excuse me,' I asked quietly between fans, 'but who are you?'

'Stewart Granger,' he replied . . .

Phil Hill raced for Bruce McLaren's team in the 1965 Tasman Series, and the American, world champion in 1961 with Ferrari, was able to unwind in the relaxed atmosphere. We were staying in the quiet Occidental Hotel in Christchurch not far from the centre of the city, a hotel where farmers and their wives would lunch on a visit from the country. Phil was late for lunch so we started without him and the dining room was quiet apart from genteel conversation and the rattle of cutlery. Suddenly the door burst open and Phil strode in. We asked where he had been.

'Where have I been? I've been arrested!'

The rattle of cutlery became a clatter as everyone in the room dropped knives and forks and listened, aghast. It turned out that an American tourist had been robbed of his luggage, which contained a number of $20 notes, and banks had been alerted. Phil had strolled into the shopping area and had paused at a bank to change some $20 notes. The girl behind the counter had taken the notes and fled. Some time passed and Phil had started to become impatient. The police had been called and Phil was being stalled. Phil had eventually snapped and grabbed the notes from the startled bank girl, who had been trying to make stalling excuses, and had strode from the bank. A few yards up the footpath he became aware of two people behind him, and one tapped him on the shoulder. He turned, expecting to find an autograph hunter, but instead found two policemen with a squad car cruising slowly behind them.

Phil was asked to accompany them to the station and as he was bundled into the back of the car, the driver said, 'Who is he?'

'He *says* he's Phil Hill the racing driver,' replied one of the policemen.

Silence. The other cop remarked on Phil's expensive chronograph wristwatch and asked how he had come by it.

'I was presented with it when I won the Le Mans 24-hour race in France,' said Phil.

'So it will be engraved?' asked the cop.

'Of *course* it's engraved,' Phil snapped, wrenching the watch from his wrist and shoving it at the policeman.

The back was unmarked, something that happens I suppose when you've won so many races and so many watches. It merely served to confirm the suspicions of the constabulary and Phil was taken in for questioning. By the time he had established that he was who he said he was, we had started lunch and the whole startled dining room thoroughly enjoyed his description of his morning shopping in Christchurch.

CHAPTER EIGHT

Book-dealing

IT WAS A hot soporific afternoon in the hangar salon at Christies, South Kensington. It was a long sale of motoring and aviation art and books, and those who weren't bidding were drowsing. There was a pause in the auction and I happened into conversation with the chap sitting beside me. He wore a dark blue pin-stripe suit and had been bidding astutely, buying expensively but carefully. I asked why he was buying these items, and he said because he regarded them as a good investment. I asked what he did for a living and he said he was a stockbroker in the City. I was buying old motor racing books for reference, but he was buying them as an investment. Maybe I was doing something wrong. We couldn't both be right and he was the one wearing a pin-stripe suit. I was probably wearing jeans and a sweater.

On the train from Waterloo to East Horsley I decided I would start dealing in old motoring books, but I didn't want to be a dealer in old books – I wanted to promote them as investments the way my saleroom neighbour in the pin-stripe suit did. There had to be a trading name that didn't sound like musty old books on motoring. Something about broking sounded right. Book broking. That was when the title Eoin Young's Specialist Book Broking Service was coined in 1978. It didn't really mean a lot, but it looked and sounded right. You might not pay a lot for an old book, but you would get your cheque-book out if it was an investment.

I knew motoring book dealers like Charles Mortimer who lived over the hill from me at Ewhurst and I knew Frank Stroud at Chaters in Isleworth, the same Frank Stroud whom I had visited in 1961 when his shop was in Chiswick and spent half a day there and three quid on books. I didn't need customers like me. I didn't want walk-in customers at all if I could help it. The business would be strictly mail order. In fact, that was a luxury that came after I had proved that trying to sell motoring books to passing customers from a shop in a Surrey village simply didn't work. There were too many customers like I had been in 1961 who looked upon a good browse as a relaxing way to spend the afternoon. I wanted them to spend money, not the afternoon.

If I was to be a bookseller I needed stock, so I paid a visit to Charles Mortimer, a superb character who had raced motor cycles and cars at Brooklands before the war and tracks like Silverstone after it, who had been a dealer in vintage cars and who now sold old motoring books and memorabilia. It was fair to say that he was the doyen of the trade with a genius for making the best of a deal whether he was selling or buying, always leaving his victim thinking what an extraordinarily fair chap he was. It was a valuable knack and Charles made the most of it. I knew customers who positively enjoyed having a cup of tea and a biscuit after Charles had relieved them of the contents of their wallet with their eager consent. *Such* a nice man.

It was accepted that Charles's prices were higher than most dealers, but his sources of supply and the quality of his books were always beyond question. If word got round that Charles had enjoyed a good 'buy', the collectors would beat a path to his door and reckon themselves fortunate if they were able to beat their collecting rivals to the choicest items in Charles's fresh stock.

Frank Stroud was different. I think he had been dealing in books longer than Charles, but he ran a High Street bookshop selling new books as well as old, reckoning that each side attracted trade for the other. Buyers of new books often wanted to weed out their library and sell old books to finance new purchases, while collectors of old books often found new titles they needed. I was going to say that Frank's prices were fairer than Charles's, but who could define fair when Charles couldn't keep up with the demands of his customers for rarer and more expensive old books?

I needed books to stock my first list, so I pulled duplicate titles from my own reference shelves, then visited Charles for some of his rarer and more expensive titles that would look good in my new list. There was no point in pricing them the same as Charles, so I tactfully negotiated a discount in view of the amount I was spending, then doubled all his prices. I reasoned that my customers wouldn't regard bargain books as investments. *Expensive* books must be investments. Blue chip collectors' items.

My first list in 1978 was a yellow card folder describing 26 titles. I tried to match the books offered to the potential customers, so I included the 1930s trio of MG racing books by Barre Lyndon (*Circuit Dust*, *Combat* and *Grand Prix*), thinking that they might appeal to a wealthy Japanese car collector I had met at the Japanese Grand Prix in 1976 and who had bought a supercharged 1933 K3 MG. It was like fishing with a very long line and only a few hooks, but it eventually worked. A telegram arrived two weeks after the book lists had been mailed. It was from Japan. It read: 'LIKE YOUR LIST. PLEASE SEND IT TO ME. MONEY FOLLOWS.'

My wife was very sceptical, and I was curious to see exactly what the telegram meant and which books he wanted. When the cheque arrived it was for the total of the 26 books listed as the basis for an instant motoring library. It also meant an instant profit and an instant problem. I was getting orders from other parts of the world and I had sold all my stock. Now I was visiting Charles Mortimer and Chaters more often, chasing auction sales and advertising to buy books. This was getting serious, but it was also enormously enjoyable. It was the first time I had been involved in trade, as it were, and it became apparent that a brisk camaraderie existed among dealers and collectors.

In that first list I was offering the two volumes of Laurence Pomeroy's *Grand Prix Car*, with their superb fold-out technical drawings, as a pair for £70. In the 1993 catalogue I listed them at £250 each, and by 1996 they were £350 each, so perhaps the element of investment really did exist for those original customers. I had offered the Lyndon MG books at £16 each; in 1993 they were close to £100 each. My next catalogue was a double-fold six-sided item in the winter of 1978/79 listing 40 titles.

I think it may have been my more comprehensive 1980 offering, which emerged as a multi-page catalogue, that prompted the fatherly attention of Charles Mortimer. I think he had been gently amused at my first attempts at book-dealing, but now he honestly believed that I might be getting in too deep. With the very best of intentions he telephoned me and asked if he could come over for a chat. He had received the new catalogue the previous morning, he said, and had gone through it carefully. If there were 300 books listed, he reckoned five or six were under-priced, he agreed with the prices of perhaps ten, but the rest were so far over-priced by his reckoning that he thought I might be getting myself into trouble. I was impressed that Charles should take the trouble to point out what he saw as the error of my ways when he could so easily have sat back, puffing on his pipe, and watched me sink without trace along with my expensive books. As tactfully as I could, I pointed out that most of the more expensive titles in the list had already been sold.

'Well I'm buggered,' he said, and we changed the subject to the modern world of motor racing because he still had a healthy interest in the sport that had been his life. He was also a writer of some note with a comfortable style, and I still rate his *Brooklands and Beyond* memoirs as the best book ever written about the Surrey track. Six months later he sold his business to former Aston Martin and Lagonda sports car racer Eric Thompson, and settled into restless retirement

having given Eric an agreement that he would not set up a rival
business.

By now I was beset with the problem that every book-dealer
knows. Where to put the stock? I could no longer offer a detailed
catalogue with only one of each title in stock, because there would
always be one happy client and several complaining because the
book they had chosen was already sold. I therefore set out to buy
good copies of good books whenever they became available. I had
boxes of books in rented rooms, but it was expensive and impossible
to display or find the titles when I needed them. I rented wall space
for shelves in other people's shops in the village and gave them a
percentage of any of my books they sold, but this was never
satisfactory. I needed somewhere large, dry and cheap to rent, but
such property simply did not exist in Surrey, where large, dry, cheap
buildings were usually commandeered for the storage of vintage cars.

Then came the day when the postman who did handyman jobs in
his spare time said he was surprised that I wasn't interested in the
barn at the back of The Barley Mow. I said I didn't know what he
was talking about.

'Your wife said you wouldn't be interested in a barn because the
books had to be dry. I would have thought the pub barn would be
just what you need.'

I made discreet enquiries about The Barley Mow in the village and
was greeted with raised eyebrows at every mention. At this point I
was not exactly sure where The Barley Mow, the pub that would
become almost a second home and office, actually was. The landlord
was painted as a drinker of heroic performance and a character not in
the habit of entertaining fools gladly . . . indeed, not entertaining
fools *at all*! I was cautiously intrigued and paid him a visit. Did he
have a barn to rent? Who wanted to know? I did. Why? Because I
needed book storage.

The pub was quiet so he took me out the back and showed me a
large old barn with beautiful beams that had been used as a village
hall. It had a sprung floor and a small stage at one end, and central
heating linked to the pub's boiler had been installed some years
before. In short it was ideal. We agreed a rental, my wife and her
friends whitewashed the interior walls, I installed shelving and I was
in business. Having a built-in pub was an additional attraction for
customers, and having more customers was an attraction for the pub
landlord.

Having large premises also meant that I could make a more
comprehensive mess, and as I was away covering Formula 1 races
every second weekend during the summer, the business was
inevitably suffering. I needed someone who knew about old
motoring books and had the spare time to help me. Charles seemed
ideal. I invited him over to see the barn and over a drink in the bar

he agreed that helping me part-time would not infringe his no-trading agreement with Eric Thompson.

Charles was superb. By now we were well ensconced in The Barley Mow and he was known as Grandad by the regulars in a pub where everyone had to have a nickname. He was a compulsive list-maker and I would chide him that he made lists of the lists he had made, but I needed some sort of organisation and Charles was the ideal answer since he had excellent contacts on both sides of the business and would often bundle his boxer dog into his Mini and set off to the other side of England to view a collection of books I had been offered. It became accepted that he would come back with a collection of, say, 50 books and leave me to value them while he went into the pub for a pint after his travels. I would join him and he would ask me what value I would put on the total. If I said £300 he would more than likely chuckle, tap out his pipe and say he had bought them for £100 so why didn't we split the difference and call it square. I had made a profit, he had made a profit and the stock was increased by 50 good books.

I was always uncomfortable buying books from private customers because I felt that they thought I was ripping them off. I always was, to a degree, but that was the nature of the business. You wanted to buy the best for the least while maintaining a credibility that might lead to further purchases if your client was happy with the deal he had done. This was where Charles was so good with people of his generation because he could settle down for a comfortable chat, during which he would charm his way into a deal that I would never have dared suggest. It worked the other way, of course. There were always the sellers eager to rip *me* off, and since I was a dealer I was fair game.

Charles enjoyed entertaining customers in the barn because he had all the time in the world, whereas I usually had other things I could be doing. One customer told Charles that he was so pleased to find him at the barn instead of me 'because Eoin always makes me feel as though he wishes he were somewhere else . . .'

I felt comfortable in situations where the idea was to get the seller to name his price. If it was too high you could politely point this out and make preparations to leave, at which stage the price required would sometimes be adjusted downwards. If the price was what you hoped it might be, you paid it and the seller was either delighted or privately annoyed that he hadn't asked for more. If it was significantly less than you imagined it might be, you could afford to say in fairness that you felt the books were worth a little more than that, and this disarming display of largesse would often bring other, much more desirable, items out for consideration.

Getting the seller to name the price has always been my aim. I remember one classic example in Australia where old car brochures were so difficult to sell that one of the local dealers referred a customer to me when I was passing through his city. The customer arrived at my motel room after dinner one night with a carton packed with vintage car sales catalogues, a collection that I quite simply couldn't afford to entertain buying. I decided that I would sort out the catalogues that I would buy if I could afford them, the catalogues I would like to buy on a secondary basis and the remainder that were good but which would bulk the collection far beyond my budget. While I was sorting through the catalogues the customer was hoovering up my duty-free Scotch. I asked him how much he felt the catalogues were worth, bearing in mind that the local dealer had told him there was no market for them in Australia. He just grinned. I wasn't sure whether this was the Australian way of nailing me in a corner and forcing me to make an offer, or the early effects of the determined attack on my Scotch.

I had reckoned that the most I was prepared to pay for my number one stack, which included vintage Bentley catalogues and similar items, was £500. The second stack would be a good buy at £500, and if I could buy the third stack for £500 I would have had an incredible night. My problem was that I only had £500 to spend. I tried another tack to prompt a price, but he still grinned and wouldn't commit himself. Finally I said, 'Look, when you were coming up in the lift with the box of catalogues in your arms you must have been thinking, "If I can take this mug for such-and-such an amount I'll be well pleased." So how much were you thinking then?'

His eyes lit up. 'Oh,' he said. 'Eight hundred dollars!'

That was about £400 for the *lot*. I said I agreed his price and we shook hands. The grin had gone, to be replaced by a puzzled look. Did you forget something, I asked as I wrote a cheque for $800. Huh? You forgot to say 'Thank you'. 'Oh. Sorry. Yeah. Thanks mate.'

And he had another whisky and went out into the night, shaking his head in amazement at the deal he had just done. Two days later in Adelaide for the Grand Prix I sold one of the rarer catalogues for £300 to a collector who couldn't believe his good fortune in finding an example in such good condition.

'You just can't buy things like this in Australia these days.'

Every dealer has a repertoire of tales he tells over lunches before auctions or when dealers get together. An art dealer in London once phoned me to say that he had bought the entire archive of original cartoons by Gilchick, an artist who placed much of his work in *Punch* magazine in the 1920s and '30s. He covered every form of sport, and while the dealer could easily find customers for golf and cricket, he was offering me the motoring cartoons. He brought them down for inspection, he told me his price, we discussed it and I bought the lot.

They were wonderful. I had a selection mounted and framed and

hung them in the barn, priced at £300 each, which I felt was cheap
for original motoring art with guaranteed provenance as presented
while still earning a useful profit. A new dealer was visiting the barn,
was intrigued by my new display of Gilchicks and asked if I would
give him a discount if he bought several. Ever eager to please, I
agreed. He bought six and wrote me a cheque.

Later that afternoon he was on the telephone and it was apparent
that he was not now as happy as he had been when he left the
barn. He had shown his proud new buy to a friend who ran an art
gallery, and his friend had said you could buy cartoons like this for
£30 all day long, never mind £300. I offered to buy every motoring
cartoon his friend could find at £30, but this was to no avail. His
friend had said that nobody would pay £300 for a Gilchick cartoon.
I pointed out, as reasonably as I could manage, that this was
obviously nonsense, because he just had, and he had told me he
was a dealer . . . Moments like that are so rare that they deserve
preservation.

I enjoy buying and I enjoy selling, but I prefer to buy from dealers
where the price is established. Ken Ball, the long-established book
dealer in Brighton and former book publisher, maintains that the only
way he can buy at book fairs or autojumbles now is if a dealer has
made a mistake and priced the book too low. Experience is the only
guide and no good dealer ever makes the same mistake twice. The
market has to be judged as precisely as a trout fisherman judges a
river. Aim the prices too high and they won't sell, price them too low
and the books will be snatched out of your hand.

Bargains have become harder to find in autojumbles in Britain
where the one-time seller who bought a stall to clear his attic was
like a goldfish dropped into a piranha tank. Autojumbles usually
open at 8 am for sellers to set up their stand and the public are
admitted from 10 am, by which time the bloody foam in the piranha
tank has settled, the goldfish has gone home amazed that his stock
sold so fast, and the general tide of public buyers flow around the
stalls. If the goldfish came back he might be surprised to see some of
his books offered at higher prices, but then again they would
probably already have been sold. There is no hint of malpractice here
because the goldfish has cleared his attic *and* been paid for all those
books his wife wanted to take to the tip, while the piranhas have
enjoyed an early-morning assist in covering the costs of their stand
plus their travel expenses and their lunch.

My local autojumble in Dorking Halls is a splendid affair. I used to
take a stall, but latterly I have concentrated more on buying than
selling. Some years ago I was offered a collection of old motor racing
books and went to view, but the collection turned out to be a dozen
'standards' in average condition, frankly not worth a discussion on
price or the trip to view. I asked if there might be other motoring

items I could look at. Was I interested in car handbooks? I said that I really wasn't, but I would have a look at them since I was there. The lady opened a wardrobe absolutely crammed with pre-war handbooks. But that doesn't fully describe what was on offer. It was a ceiling-height walk-in wardrobe and the handbooks were stacked six deep. There were hundreds and hundreds. I spent hours pulling them all out and looked like a chimney sweep when I had finished. There were a few for rare marques, most were for more ordinary cars, but all were in good condition and all would have some value. Now I broke my own rule and bought into something I knew nothing about. Always a mistake.

I took a stand at Dorking and set out these masses of handbooks marked at prices I thought would guarantee instant sales. By the end of the day I had sold perhaps three, and then only after an argument. I said to my friend Chris Birch, who was helping on the stand, that I thought we should do a runner and leave all these dusty old handbooks to the hall cleaners. He said I should offer them as a job lot to other dealers first. There was no interest except from one who came to inspect them, then said he couldn't afford them. I protested that we hadn't discussed a price. He suggested that whatever price I named would be too high for him. So make me an offer, I said. I think jokingly he said something like £20 and when I accepted he said he would have to check with his wife first. He came back almost at a run and pushed a browser away from tables announcing that he had just taken over the entire stock. Object lesson: never meddle in things you know nothing about.

Old tinplate toy cars are always being touted in newspaper and magazine articles as high-price collectors' items, and when I was in Christchurch in New Zealand a few years ago I found an antique shop with display cases crammed with tinplates from the 1920s to the '50s, all from a recent local auction. On the scent of a major killing, I asked the proprietor to work out a friendly price on his whole stock of tinplate toys. We agreed, and he packed them for airfreighting back to Britain. On my return I was talking to the incredibly enthusiastic Manchester dealer Les Wilson, who said that he was moving into a new area, dealing in tinplate toys. Did I have a deal for him! As soon as the packages arrived from New Zealand, I invited Les down to feast his eyes on my acquisitions. He inspected each one carefully and I could see a handsome profit on the horizon, until he put the last one down, looked at me and said, 'Eoin, these are fookin' *roobish*!' Another object lesson: don't deal in tinplate toys.

The Dorking autojumble sometimes serves me well, as can any autojumble you care to visit. On one occasion I had done several laps of the stands as dealers were setting up and was on the point of leaving when I noticed a late-comer trundling in with a trolley piled with cartons and Ferrari sales catalogues in one box. I followed him to his table and on the wall behind he had already displayed a huge original poster for the 1957 Monaco Grand Prix mounted on hardboard. I asked how much he wanted for it.

'D'you like it?' he asked. 'I got it for nothing from the Automobile Club in Monaco the day after the race.'

I said that since we had established how much he had paid for it, how much did he want for it.

'I think it's worth 50 quid,' he said, and I agreed with him.

Christies sent a van down the following day to collect some lots already listed for their Monaco auction in a few weeks, and I persuaded them to add the mounted poster. It sold for £1,100.

It also goes the other way. When the P3 Alfa Romeo that Tazio Nuvolari drove to win the 1935 German Grand Prix at the Nurburgring was being offered for sale by Christies at Monaco, I had advance knowledge because the car was owned by Bill Clark in New Zealand. The P3 was reckoned to break all sales records, so I thought perhaps there might be money to be made on the back of it. To this end I commissioned a pedal car model of the P3 to be made by craftsmen in New Zealand, but as it was supposed to be a secret project I couldn't tell them why or push them too hard for completion until it became apparent that the pedal car might miss the auction. It arrived by air in London, went straight to Christies bonded store, and was sent direct to Monaco for the auction. I think I had paid £2,000 for it, and it was in the catalogue with a reserve that would see a profit, but when I arrived in Monaco on the day of the sale, James Knight, now with Brooks Auction house, took me to one side and said, 'We've seen the pedal car and we don't like it.'

I'd also seen the pedal car and I didn't like it. And I owned it! Without specific instructions and assuming that if it was a pedal car it would require a cockpit that a junior Nuvolari could sit in, they had revised the proportions accordingly – and accordingly it looked nothing like the lithe lines of the actual full-size car that sold for just short of £2 million. I told James to sell it for whatever they could get, and sat with my head in my hands when the lot came up. The bids faltered at a few hundred pounds and I could see myself taking a long cold bath, but for some unfathomable reason two bidders felt obliged to own the pedal car and it lurched up beyond £2,000 and j-u-s-t covered costs. Object lesson No 3: no more pedal cars.

Auctions are an important source of supply for a collector or dealer, but it is important as a beginner not to be intimidated. When I decided to become a dealer the major auction houses in London usually had an 'expert' running the motoring side. Some were experts, some weren't. Some thought they were. Their auctions were best because there were always bargains to be found among lots where 'sleepers' had been missed, gems tucked away in a box of dross. Viewing is usually as important as the sale itself. Never take the catalogue at face value. Assume you know more than the auctioneer, which these days can often be true if you happen to be a specialised collector in your particular field. The auctioneer cannot possibly hope to have your detailed knowledge. He may have a good general knowledge of motoring collectibles, but you will usually know more about your chosen sliver of the market.

At one viewing before a Christies sale I sifted through a large carton of old Rolls-Royce photographs and, while I wasn't particularly interested, I asked if there were more in this lot. Oh yes, another *17* cartons like that in the basement. On this knowledge I bought the complete photographic archive of an important Rolls-Royce historian, while others thought they were bidding for one box. After the sale there was a furore when the word leaked out. I was paying at the desk when an irate Rolls-Royce collector stormed to the front of the queue saying he demanded to know who held bidding paddle number so-and-so. My paddle. I knew the collector who was ranting beside me, and I told him it was my number.

'Don't joke with me now, Eoin. This is *serious*.'

When he realised I wasn't joking he turned his wrath on me. 'Did you know there were 18 boxes in that lot when you bought it?'

I said I did.

'Well, *how* did you know?' he said, as though there was some insider dealing going on here.

'Because I asked at the viewing and I was told. Didn't you ask?'

Collapse of stout party.

At another sale there was a lot loosely described as Ferrari magazines and memorabilia. I recognised it as the remains of a collection of Ferrari material of which the important lots had been in a previous sale. This was presumably a box that the 'expert' didn't rate. It included an album of postcards, most of which were the rare postcards published by Ferrari to use in response to driver fan mail. The early ones were black and white, the later ones in colour. Some were worth several hundred pounds each to specialist collectors abroad, but the cards were not generally collected in Britain. I bought the lot well inside what I had budgeted, and when I came to sort out the box I realised that the old Italian newspapers used to line the box were actually reporting the Targa Florio race when Enzo Ferrari drove there in the 1920s.

Telling tales against auction houses is a popular pastime at dealer lunches since something of a them-and-us situation exists and there are as many tales of auctioneers taking bids off the window-cleaner or the back wall to pump the prices up as there are of dealer-rings designed to keep prices down . . . They still talk of the Phillips sale when a lot was described as various early copies of *Motor Sport* magazine. I tracked down the lot in a suitcase under a table and the lock was jammed. As we discovered later, each dealer found the lock jammed and made sure it was jammed again when he shut the case. Because in the suitcase were the rare first issues of the *Brooklands Gazette*, which became *Motor Sport* after a couple of years. Each dealer thought it was his secret.

The lot was estimated at £60–£80. The auctioneer started tentatively at £40 and suddenly a dealer shouted, '£400!' Another dealer shouted, '£600!', and the auctioneer's jaw dropped as he gaped around the saleroom. Another dealer bid £1,000 and the flabbergasted auctioneer had only called for an opening bid of £40. Ken Ball bid £1,200 and asked the auctioneer, 'Are you running this sale or are we?' I think the lot finally sold to another dealer for over £2,000. The in-house 'expert' came running down the aisle to ask anxiously what everyone had been bidding for . . .

I like autographs and books or photographs that have been signed. A motoring book autographed by the author or a racing driver becomes unique, or at least extremely rare, although there are cases – *Wallsmacker* by 1930s Indycar driver Peter De Paolo comes to mind – where the *un*signed copy is rarer because the author signed so many!

Years ago in a Christies sale there was an album of racing driver autographs that had obviously been carefully compiled in the 1930s and well indexed. All the major racing driver signatures were there including Nuvolari, but I was unable to find the Nuvolari signature and drew this to the attention of the auctioneer. The absence of Nuvolari's autograph was mentioned when the lot came up and the album subsequently fetched less than it would have done. Later, by the wildest outside chance there was a message on my answer machine to phone a collector who had retired to Portugal and had some books to sell. I returned the call, chatted for a while, then he said that his neighbour sent his regards – Mort Morris-Goodall. It had been Mort's autograph album that Christies had sold that afternoon, so I said to tell Mort that his album had sold short because we couldn't find the Nuvolari autograph. I could hear the expletives from the other balcony. It turned out that Tazio had specially drawn his tortoise emblem as his signature, something he only did for friends or acquaintances – an extreme rarity, and it had gone unnoticed!

Dealing internationally is enormously entertaining, with the language barrier actually improving the transaction. Some years ago an Italian collector was anxious to buy some of the more expensive books in my catalogue, so we arranged to meet at the Grand Prix. I would bring the items he wanted and he would bring items of similar value for trade. He arrived with a briefcase like an Aladdin's Cave. Each item I looked at was better than the one before, and it looked as though any form of trade that might be suggested was going to be an embarrassment, and I was anxious to distance myself from it. The Italian spoke no English, so I asked Denis Jenkinson if he would translate.

'He thinks you're not happy with what he has offered in trade,' said Jenks.

I said it was just that I couldn't decide which items to take in trade.

'He wants you to take it *all* in trade for the books you've brought down.'

It was one of those deals arranged in heaven and it had fallen into my lap. Included were a number of original Nuvolari items. I showed these to top Italian motor racing journalist Pino Allievi who looked through the Nuvolari documents, opened his briefcase, threw me his chequebook and said, 'Write what number you like . . !' I didn't because I prefer his friendship.

I deal with Schroder & Weise in Hanover, a Paris dealer we know as 'Le Catastrophe', Mario Acquati in the Monza Autodromo, who knows that the way to my wallet is through his fridge (he keeps white wine in it), Gavin Bain's Fazazz emporium in Christchurch, New Zealand, Fred Vogel in Sydney, Australia, and Walter Miller's sprawling operation in Syracuse, upstate New York.

Paris is where some superb early motor racing material appears, which is only natural since racing started in France. In an ephemera shop I found a newspaper supplement for the 1895 Paris–Bordeaux race. I realised that it was early and important, but until I checked my reference books I didn't realise that it was the *first* motor race, and I sold it for £1,500 to an overseas collector, only to have another offering more if I could get it back for him. I couldn't. Obviously I had under-priced it. In fact I had priced it as high as I dared, which just goes to show that some collectors know no limits to the price of acquisition.

One morning I arrived at Le Catastrophe's shop in Paris to find Ken Ball already combing his shelves for motoring books, so I obeyed unwritten dealer law and didn't move in on his patch. I asked Le Catastrophe if he had other material, and he took me out the back to show me a small mountain of pre-1910 aviation material he had bought at a country auction in France. I was marginally interested in aviation, and this was obviously extremely early and therefore rare, so I asked him to price the entire collection. He said he couldn't. I pointed out that it would save him listing and cataloguing all the items if he worked out what he had paid, added his profit to the total and named that as his price. He did and I bought the small mountain. It made up most of an aviation sale in London and all made money. Why do we call him Le Catastrophe? Because his shop always looks as though an anti-personnel bomb has just gone off in it. Rather like mine, in fact . . .

Five years after moving into the barn we were in need of more space. Charles Mortimer had moved to Cornwall and his place was ably taken by Aubrey Parnell, who had recently retired from the National Trust and was looking for, as he put it, 'something to keep me off the golf course and in gin'. He soon found that he could combine his interests with a talent for bringing a form of organisation to my business. He knew nothing about motoring or books, but nothing was too much trouble. A former Royal Marine, he was at his best when he was in command. His nickname in The Barley Mow was 'The General'. I went briefly into partnership with Chris Birch, a local taxi driver, who had discovered a local shop for rent, and Aubrey handled the move and the setting up of the shop on the other side of the village close to Effingham Junction. The retail shop didn't work out, but our mail order base is still behind the shop.

I regard books signed by author or subject as unique and therefore valuable additions to collectors' libraries. I once visited a classic car show in Barcelona on the way back from a championship rally in Spain and was having a communication problem with a dealer selling old motoring books and memorabilia. He spoke Spanish and I didn't. I didn't have a business card and was trying to find a way of convincing him that I was a dealer, or at least someone to whom he should be offering a discount. I spotted a copy of *The Men*, a book I had written with Barrie Gill in 1967, and I picked it up to show him my name listed in the foreword. The book fell open and I realised that it contained the signatures of Bruce McLaren and Colin Chapman on the flyleaf. I forgot my attempt to impress and immediately set about buying the book.

How much was it? Too much. The first figure mentioned is *always* too much, and also I couldn't convert his peseta figure to pounds in my head. I asked him to convert it into American dollars. He muttered something I probably didn't want to hear in Spanish and produced a dollar price. I said that was too expensive as well, and he pointed out that the book had signatures. Yes, I could see that, but only one or two. No, no, no – there were *many* signatures. There were, too. There were chapter profiles of some 20 Grand Prix drivers and *every* driver had signed his chapter during a Spanish Grand Prix at Barcelona! Suddenly the price became extremely reasonable, and within a day I had sold the book for a ten-fold profit!

A week later I bought and sold a copy of Innes Ireland's book *Motor Racing Today*, a fairly ordinary book but made special because it had been signed by a number of Grand Prix drivers at the Oulton Park F1 Gold Cup in 1963. I listed the signatures, found an original programme for the event to check the names and realised that every driver listed in the programme had signed the book – with the exception of Texan Jim Hall – and there was one signature I couldn't identify. Jim was the most affable of drivers and I couldn't understand how whoever had gathered the signatures had missed his. Perhaps he wasn't there? I checked a report of the race and discovered that Hall's entry had been taken over by English driver Mike Beckwith – the signature I couldn't identify! The book had therefore been signed by *every* driver in the race and was sold with the programme as an incredibly expensive unique collectors' piece.

Limited edition books are obvious investments because their numbers are by definition restricted. Some books become collectable because they are published in small numbers. The biography of Piers Courage is an example. After Piers's death in Frank Williams's De Tomaso in the 1970 Dutch Grand Prix, a book on his life was published for family distribution only. I have never seen a copy or heard of one being offered for sale.

An earlier motor racing biography was a rarity for a different reason. There was an edition in English of the Bernd Rosemeyer autobiography *Mein Mann Der Rennfahrer*, written by his widow and published in German after his death during an Auto Union record run in 1938. Lord Howe had written the foreword for the English edition and had been sent a copy in appreciation. After Howe's death some of the books from his library were offered in a Christies auction, and an astute collector, realising the importance of the Rosemeyer book, paid over the odds to buy it. It was thought that the entire stock of the English edition had been destroyed by fire deliberately or by accident in a warehouse in the lead-up to war. This was generally recognised as being a one-off, a unique collectors' item, but as I was putting the finishing touches to the writing of this book I had a letter from a German collector who advised that he too had a copy of the English edition of the Rosemeyer book in his collection, bought from a second-hand bookshop in Zurich in 1960!

Motor racing art is so subjective that I always advise collectors to buy a picture because they like it rather than as an investment. Or perhaps as well as. That way, if you fail to realise a profit as an investment the picture is still something to enjoy for its original visual appeal.

Artists like Frederick Gordon-Crosby and Bryan De Grineau worked for *Autocar* and *The Motor* respectively before the war, and their art is highly rated today. It wasn't always that way. When I first started writing for *Autocar* they were wrapping bundles of magazines in Crosby original cutaway drawings, then regarded as scrap paper! Peter Garnier, Sports Editor and later Editor of the magazine, was the saviour of the Crosby art. He rescued as much original material as he could and had it framed and stored. He wrote a biography of Gordon-Crosby using the colour art as illustration, and this has become a valuable collector's reference tome in its own right. Garnier told how Gordon-Crosby had taken his own life during the war, depressed after the death of his son Peter. He was somewhat surprised after the publication of the book to get a letter from a Michael Gordon-Crosby in New Zealand, a son that Garnier hadn't known about when he wrote the book!

A quantity of original Crosby art came on the market following the purchase of the *Autocar* title by Haymarket Publishing, and it was offered at a Brooks Monaco auction. Usually a quantity of art like this tends to depress the market, but at Monaco the market acted with its usual unpredictability. An Australian collector asked what I thought some of the Crosby art would make. I suggested £1,500 a picture, which he thought a trifle high. He was as amazed as I was when they sold for £15,000.

I once bought a large De Grineau drawing of MGs being tested, driven around *inside* the factory at Abingdon. The chap I bought it from said that I would be able to sell it to an unmarried MG enthusiast. I was curious as to what the marital status had to do with the customer profile.

'Simple,' he said. 'No wife would allow a picture like that on the wall!'

Pat Nevin took over from De Grineau on *The Motor* a few years before the war and was able to tell what life was like as an artist covering races. He grew up in Northern Ireland and went to the Tourist Trophy races at Newtownards as a lad, sketching portraits of the drivers during practice and shyly presenting them on the day of the race. Years later, after the death of TT Bentley driver E. R. (Eddie) Hall at his home in Monaco, his widow Joan brought out a delicate portrait of Eddie in his early days.

'It's my favourite portrait,' she said proudly.

I offered to tell her who had drawn the picture, when and where and how Eddie came to get it. Joan was amazed, but Nevin had told me the story only a few weeks before!

Before Pat Nevin died early in 1995 he asked that his photographer friend, Maurice Rowe, scatter his ashes on the banking at Brooklands.

A little knowledge can sometimes be valuable rather than dangerous. I was once poking around in a box of motoring art in a well-known dealer's London emporium when I came upon several un-signed pencil sketches. I recognised them immediately as the working drawings that Terence Cuneo had featured below his famous painting of Woolf Barnato's 'fastback' Bentley racing the Blue Train. I was on slightly shaky ground here because I knew the importance of the art and these expert dealers apparently didn't. What was the provenance of the art? They had bought the drawings at a country auction. Also included was the working sketch of a locomotive for a British Rail poster. We agreed a swap with a Targa Florio bronze I had bought in New York, and I made contact with Cuneo, whose studio was only a few miles from Horsley, to write a profile feature on him and use the artwork as illustration.

Cuneo was a fascinating man, who had painted only a few motoring subjects, most of them for a Rootes Group calendar. I sent him a copy of Garnier's book on Gordon-Crosby, and when I visited him again to have him check what I had written, he asked if there

was anything he could do for me in return for the Crosby book. I
suggested that he might sign the working drawings I had brought
with me. He was amazed. He said he had been searching for the
locomotive artwork and couldn't imagine what had happened to the
Bentley artwork supporting the Blue Train picture he had painted in
1970. I assured him that the items had been bought legally through a
country auction, hoping that the story I had been told was true. I was
relieved a few weeks later when I saw the drawings illustrated in an
advertisement for a West Country dealer showing art that they had
sold during the year. Cuneo died at the age of 88 as this book was
being completed.

Automobilia has various specialist areas. Laurence Edscer deals in
badges and posters, and as our fields don't clash we often travel
together. Ted Walker buys collections of motor racing negatives and
sells prints, so the three of us share sales pitches at various events.

My only venture into 'hardware' happened some years ago when I
was buying a collection of books from a man who was moving to a
smaller house – the usual story – and he asked if I also bought old
car parts as he was clearing his garage. The vintage cars had gone but
the bits remained. I looked around at the aged parts hanging around
the walls and suggested other dealers who might be interested. He
pointed to a box of old mascots and asked how much I thought they
might be worth. I confessed I had no idea. He said that he had been
offered £60 for the box and its contents. I said I thought it was
probably worth twice that. Would I pay a hundred? It was a gamble
but I had done a good deal on the books and my budget would stand
it.

Back home I emptied the box and poked through the various bent
and rusty badges and bonnet mascots. One looked vaguely familiar,
like a leaping Jaguar mascot but with adzed flanks as though it had
been chiselled rather than cast. I checked in a mascot reference book
and identified it as a rather rare pre-war French version of the Jaguar
mascot. I think it made around £800 at auction. The other 'find' in the
box was a large crystal bird like a falcon. I figured that this might
have been a French Lalique mascot, but it didn't feature in the mascot
reference book. I showed it to a mascot dealer and he shrugged, said
he thought it was too large for a mascot and suggested I put it into a
London art deco auction. It was a Red Ashay ornament and made
£550. So much for a no-knowledge gamble on a box of bits.

Of course there are the boxes that you buy on spec that turn out to
be someone else's rubbish, but they aren't so much fun to write
about . . .

Kenneth Ball has said that the only way we can make money from
buying books from other dealers is if they make a mistake. But there
are mistakes and mistakes. Often it depends on your knowledge
being greater in a specialist area, like my enthusiasm for buying items

signed by racing personalities. Sometimes it depends on the degree of profit another dealer feels he wants to make on a particular item. If he bought an unusual motor racing book, one in a foreign language, perhaps, for say £50 at a country book fair, he might decide to take a handsome profit and mark it up to £500 at a specialist autojumble where serious collectors could be expected. Now, if *you* have a customer who would happily pay £1,500 for the book, you will buy it and sell it on immediately, won't you? So who has made the mistake? The dealer with the stand at the country book fair probably bought the book in a job lot and it owed him a fiver so he is amazed and delighted to sell it to some mug for 50. He'll go home and tell his wife about it. No mistake, just a handsome profit. The dealer who takes it to the specialist autojumble and marks it up tenfold hoping a mug will pay out for it is equally amazed and delighted when you buy it after a token haggle. His wife will be helping on the stand with him, entertaining good customers with a glass of wine. They'll open a better bottle for themselves on the strength of the sale. No mistake, just a handsome profit. And then *you* fax your customer in a foreign country and offer it at £1,500, and he fuses his fax machine getting back to you with his Visa number before someone else gets it. No mistake here either, just a handsome profit. And when he gets the book, your foreign customer will be phoning his friends to come and see the book that he 'stole' from his tame dealer in England. *Everyone* is happy in the chain. No mistakes.

But I know what Kenneth Ball means. He was one of the earliest dealers on the motoring book scene when the collecting world was smaller and prices were lower. There were fewer dealers and fewer customers. The prices of rare old motoring books have increased in parallel with the price of rare old cars. When car prices dipped a few years ago, book prices stalled. When the car market picked up again, the book market gathered speed again as well.

CHAPTER NINE

Motor racing public relations

LUNCH IS PROBABLY what I do best, and while smart young men in suits and ties may demand princely ransoms for more comprehensive programmes of public relations, they are still aiming for the same end result as a relaxed chat over lunch. Perhaps because all the top-dollar PR men are too busy earning and talking to top brass they don't have the time to relax with the press people they started out to woo. They tend to miss what they originally regarded as their goal – looking after journalists and providing them with information when required rather than trying to ram it down their throats with a plastic veneer of insincerity.

My weekly 'Diary' column is essentially chat and gossip, all the background tales that don't fit a straight race report and would otherwise be lost for ever. It also means that because I don't write a straight race report, I don't have to be hanging on drivers' coat-tails, and I don't have to bother myself overmuch with the minutiae of qualifying times or write to a deadline on Sunday night. I can combine pleasure with pleasure and make sure the right people are in the right place for lunch.

I started on the PR trail with the Gulf Oil Corporation in 1967. Gulf sponsored the McLaren team in Can-Am and Formula 1 and later at Indianapolis, but my introduction actually came through John Wyer, who was first to gain Gulf sponsorship for endurance sports car racing with his Ford GT40s, Mirages and eventually the fearsome Porsche 917s.

I am sure that Gulf was involved in racing purely on the personal whim of the Executive Vice-President, Grady Davis, who loved sports car racing and thought that investing millions of Gulf Oil dollars sponsoring his chosen sport was perfectly reasonable. Grady was a great character, feared within the company as something of a tyrant, but he was a pussycat at the race tracks, an absorbed racing enthusiast. He flew to most of the races in North America in one of the Corporation's executive jets, and there were occasions when he would ask me how I was getting back home to England. I'd tell him I was catching the red-eye from, say, Los Angeles to London, and he would suggest that I put my bags in his jet for the flight back to Pittsburgh headquarters. I could catch a flight home from there. The catch to this offer was always that I had to play gin rummy with him and drink the driest dry Martinis you can imagine. My problem was that I didn't like playing cards and I liked dry Martinis even less. This didn't faze Grady. When I protested that he always won money from me and I couldn't afford to keep on losing, he would drawl, 'Stick it on your expenses . . .'

I'm sure the only reason I was given the job was that I appeared to know about racing, I knew most of the people involved and I could write about it. No one in the Gulf Oil Corporation knew the faintest thing about racing – or wanted to! Paul Sheldon, the head of PR, knew the oil business inside out, but racing was totally foreign to him.

'You wanna title?' he boomed the day I met him. 'Make one up.'

So I did. I had embossed business cards made that said I was Director of Gulf Motor Racing Press Relations. I had an office in the Gulf building in Pittsburgh that I seldom visited, and when I did I was regarded in some awe because I reported direct to Grady – their boss's boss – flew in his jet and on occasion stayed at his home. One weekend he showed me his collection of hunting rifles and guns kept under lock and key, then produced an automatic handgun from a bedside table. I asked what he shot with that.

'People,' he replied with alarming succinctness, then added, 'I mean intruders . . .'

I remember one lunch with PR Director Sheldon and some of his friends in similar businesses. One of them asked if I had ever written any fiction.

'Sure he does,' grinned Sheldon. 'Every time he makes out his expenses!'

Gulf had a hospitality motorhome that went to all the races, and if it wasn't the first such press hospitality unit for a sponsor it was certainly one of the first. We also had a purpose-built hospitality unit for Gulf at European races. This had a viewing area on the roof with internal ladder access through a trapdoor. The safety rails around the rooftop area had Gulf advertising banners around them so that corporate guest safety doubled as an advertising hoarding, the sort of ad hoc advertising that Bernie Ecclestone would ban instantly in today's F1 paddock.

Once we were at Clermont Ferrand for a French Grand Prix and Jackie Stewart asked if he could use the motorhome for a meeting of the Grand Prix Drivers' Association in the days when all the drivers got together regularly to discuss matters of the day. Usually safety. I pointed out that this would mean Gulf losing valuable time with their press guests, but I offered the facility on condition that the drivers would climb the ladder for a photo shoot when the meeting was over. It was nigh on impossible to get all the drivers together for a photograph under normal circumstances because of clashing sponsors and team rivalry, but Jackie agreed and I had the bank across from the trailer thick with photographers. The drivers eventually came out on the roof and hundreds of photographs were taken of this unique presentation of drivers – all leaning over a Gulf banner they hadn't realised was there . . .

This may have been the same French Grand Prix when journalist Mike Doodson had taken on the job as Formula 1 PR for the John Player tobacco company, then sponsoring Lotus. I was staying at a small hotel on the outskirts of Clermont Ferrand, which was, in fact, an excellent restaurant with a few rooms above. Nick Brittan was doing PR for STP and we tended to travel together. He was writing a column for *Autosport* and doing STP PR while I was writing a column for *Autocar* and doing Gulf, so we were kindred spirits. I had been his best man and he had been mine, so we were something of an unholy alliance.

We were enjoying an after-practice tipple in a small room off the main reception when we heard Mike Doodson's best French arranging a large dinner for John Player, stressing how important the occasion was with top brass from that company and Lotus attending as well as the Fleet Street journalists. We waited until he had gone, then asked Madame what had been organised because we had arranged for the specialist press to dine with us that evening and we decided to get some mileage from the dinner at Dood's expense.

Madame provided us with blank menu cards and we concocted a spoof menu to be given to the sponsors, team and press guests while Dood had the only 'straight' menu. Our special version started with Fagash Soup and got worse with a closing line about the smoking of cigarettes being dangerous to your health.

Nick and I thought this was a wizard wheeze until Dood arrived breathless half an hour before his guests were due, to say he had to drive to the airport to collect an urgent parcel for Team Lotus and might be a few minutes late. Could we greet his guests for him and sit them at their table? Now it seemed that we were being accomplices before the fact, but our guests arrived and so did Dood's John Player brass and press guests, and we all sat at our separate tables with the usual badinage being flung around. Dood eventually returned, still breathless, and asked for menus. As instructed, Madame gave the spoof menus to the guests and the straight menu to Dood. The journalists started to titter, thinking it was a spoof menu arranged by John Player, but the John Player people were beginning to colour as they read down the menu wondering what the *hell* was going on. Only Dood was reading his menu serenely, oblivious to the mayhem that was brewing at his first corporate press dinner. We had briefed our guests as to what was happening, so we had a grandstand view of something like a real-life sitcom. The Players people were persuaded that everyone thought it was a jolly good joke, but Dood was livid, certain that we had perpetrated this dastardly trick simply to sabotage his public relations debut. Mindless nonsense looking back on it, but wonderful entertainment at the time.

The Can-Am scene was more sponsor-orientated, but in fact the wooing of journalists was then in its infancy. An American champagne company had signed exclusive rights on the series so that their bubbly would be sprayed by the winner. A PR man was appointed who drove to every race across the US in a station-wagon loaded with champagne and instructions to host a sponsor party at each race. By mid-season the poor guy was throwing a party in his motel room every weekend, but nobody was going because the champagne was so awful!

When Tom Wheatcroft had completed his Grand Prix museum at Donington he asked if I would handle the promotion of the opening ceremony, and we tried to think of a racing personality who would be appropriate to perform the opening ceremony. We decided that Raymond Mays, father of ERA and BRM, would be ideal, and he accepted. It was while I was researching Mays's career that I stumbled upon the fact that it was exactly 50 years since he raced his Brescia Bugattis named Cordon Bleu and Cordon Rouge. He had been dining after a successful hill-climb and ordered Cordon Rouge champagne. He was a romantic and decided that the stylish G. H. Mumm label on the bottle would make an excellent name for his Bugatti, so it became christened 'Cordon Rouge'. The champagne makers sent him cases of their product. Thus encouraged, Ray named his other Brescia 'Cordon Bleu', wrote to the cognac makers informing them of this, and they also sent him cases of their product.

I contacted the London office of the modern G. H. Mumm distributors and suggested that they might capitalise on the half-century of their association with Mays's Bugattis by sponsoring the opening of the Donington museum. The PR manager thought it a capital idea, and extended the project to cover vintage events during that summer. Ray was asked to take part in a television interview the day before the museum was to be opened. The main question was how he regarded the modern Grand Prix cars covered with sponsors' decals when in his day it had all been different and cars raced in national colours. I suggested to Ray that he point out that, in fact, he was the first man to race with commercial sponsorship through G. H. Mumm.

The first take was long and Ray paraded the champagne plug like a seasoned pro. Mere money couldn't have bought the time it took. Then the director stepped in and said that the take was fine but it was too long. Could Ray say his piece in half the time. It looked as though the plug was going down the drain, but Ray rose to the occasion, abandoned his lead-in, delivered the plug on its own and everyone thought it was fine. It went out unedited the following evening and the man from G. H. Mumm was over the moon.

I suggested borrowing a Rolls-Royce Corniche convertible to use as a picnic table excuse for more Mumm bubbly at a Silverstone race. The Rolls was in the press car park, the sun was shining and the top was down. It was the ideal setting for a top-drawer picnic. Unfortunately and unaccountably it started to *snow* heavily and the picnickers fled, leaving me to try and raise the hood. It refused to budge and I had visions of driving home a Rolls Royce full of snow, but I remembered something that I had read in the handbook about using the wheelbrace to wind a nut on the hood-frame if the power erecting mechanism failed. I thus wound the top up manually and resolved to raise the matter with the man from Avis. (I had hired the Roller for the exorbitant sum of £25 a day!)

'You *did* have the selector in reverse, didn't you, sir?'

Sir hadn't thought of that. He knew how to wind the hood up with the wheelbrace but not something simple like having the selector in reverse, to guard against accidentally raising the hood while the car was moving. Major embarrassment.

The Can-Am series was a breeze because the Gulf-sponsored McLarens were so dominant in the late seasons of the 1960s and early '70s, but there were mechanical hiccups from time to time. It may have been the first race of the 1969 season at Mosport Park in Canada and CBC TV had announced their intention to make a half-hour programme on the team. This was what PR was all about, and I was determined to make sure that everyone co-operated. They were shooting driver interviews with the Gulf livery on the motorhome in the background. Bruce came out first and was his usual affable self, answering all the questions carefully and cheerfully. Then it was Denny's turn. I was standing behind the cameraman and beside the soundman. To this day I can't remember the first question the interviewer asked. It was something like, 'Don't you get frightened out there in such a powerful car.'

Denny turned on him and shouted to me, 'Eoin, tell this dopey c— to stop asking such stupid f—ing questions,' and stormed back into the motorhome, slamming the door behind him. The soundman beside me looked as though he had been deafened by the swearwords in his headphones. The interviewer looked as though he was going to burst into tears. Now he knew why the American press had christened Denny 'The Bear'. I went into the motorhome to find Hulme sprawled on the settee, tittering with delight.

'What did you think of that, then?' I said. 'Denis, for Christ's sake, you're ruining this whole f—ing programme!'

He rewarded me with that big grin and said, 'Aw, c'mon, I was just gettin' his attention . . .'

And he went back outside, clapped a big arm across the interviewer's shoulders and settled into what was probably one of the best TV pieces he ever did.

On the Gulf Can-Am and Indycar trail I tried to find a different human interest press release story relating to the team and the drivers, mentioning the sponsor and the upcoming race in such a way that it would be included for topicality and the piece could be run in its entirety. These features went through the Gulf PR system to newspapers and magazines throughout North America. One of our best results was a piece on how the drivers coped with travel during the season. Hulme said he always preferred to stay at Holiday Inns 'because I always know where the towel hangs when I come out of the shower with soap in my eyes . . .' America liked that. Here was a foreign celebrity who had something nice to say about their pre-packaged way of living. Every reader knew about Holiday Inns and they had *all* come out of the shower with soap in their eyes. And now they had taken on board that the McLaren team was sponsored by Gulf, the same oil company that had gas stations in their town, on the corner of the next block.

The McLaren team steam-rollered the Can-Am scene in the formative years, but when you read the results dispassionately some of their wins were lucky ones as the Gulf-orange cars on occasion crossed the line with engines on the point of expiry, suspensions or transmissions on their last legs, or damage from off-course excursions in the closing laps. Their superiority may have been, in some measure, as a result of minimal opposition. At one point, I am sure, the Americans decided that it simply wasn't worth mounting opposition because the McLaren team were *so* dominant. Whatever shape they were in, one of the pair was nearly always there at the finish and nearly always in front.

I remember one classic moment at the Mid Ohio track when Peter Revson was comfortably out in front in the McLaren and the win was little more than a formality. I typed out the Gulf press release detailing Revson's crushing victory for the Gulf-McLaren team and how this was Revson's so-and-so win and the team's umpteenth since the series started. The usual stuff. I commandeered the press room photocopier and copies of my deathless prose were spewing out into the rack when there was a noise like a dustbin full of nuts and bolts rolling down metal stairs. It was Revson going past the press box window billowing smoke from an engine that was reducing itself to the sum of its component parts before our very eyes. This seemed to render my press releases rather surplus to immediate requirement, so I tore up all the copies, threw them in the bin and went back to the motorhome to change arrangements from a victory party to a wake.

We were well advanced on the wake when Revson arrived with a face like thunder. You would expect him to be unhappy having had victory snatched from his grasp, but he was *livid*! With me. He was brandishing a pristine copy of my somewhat over-optimistic press release and demanding to know if I had been responsible. I confessed all. He had it fixed in his mind that I had obviously written this mid-race while his engine was still in strong shape and that somehow the advance notice of his win had spooked the motor and was the direct cause of its demise. My mistake was to have left the original of the release in the photo copier where it had been discovered and dozens of copies had been distributed to guffawing journalists in the press room and rival teams in the paddock. Revvie really did have a sense of humour burn-out that afternoon . . .

The Le Mans 24-hour race in 1969 was another nail-biting finish, but of a different type. The Gulf hospitality unit was in the paddock behind the pits and from the roof you could see the final chicane. A press release at the end of a 24-hour race is normally a formality because the actual *race* has normally been finished for hours and the survivors are stroking home to the traditional 4 o'clock finish. The 1969 race was different. As the count-down began in the closing stages the GT40 Ford driven by Jacky Ickx and Jackie Oliver (Gulf's 'Pair of Jacks' I called them in awful PR-ese) were leading the Herrmann/Larousse Porsche 908 on one lap and the Porsche was leading the next. I had the press release on hold as I ran up and down the ladder to the viewing platform like a jack-in-the-box. One lap the GT40 would be in front, the next time round the Porsche would be just ahead. This went on lap after lap in the closing stages, but eventually Ickx stole a margin and led across the line in one of the closest finishes in the history of the 24-hour race – with the exception of the orchestrated 'dead heat' Ford fiasco when the McLaren/Amon Ford finished yards ahead of the Hulme/Ruby Ford in 1966.

Life with the Wyer team at Le Mans was made special because John Wyer always booked the entire team into the Hotel de France at La Chartre-sur-le-Loir about an hour from the track but worth the drive for the relaxed atmosphere in the little village square. Wyer had been staying there for years since his days with the Aston Martin team. His nickname in the team – but certainly not to his face – was 'Deathray', because of his venomous glare if things were going badly. A

dressing-down from Wyer was something seldom forgotten. I have
seen a driver in tears after John had abused him for crashing a team
car. He certainly had a way with words that aptly described people
and situations and left no one in doubt as to their place in his
estimation at that moment. I was in the pits when Wyer was told that
one his rival team managers was in hospital. 'Oh?' he replied.
'Nothing trivial, I trust . . .'

The pilot who landed the chartered Gulf plane at Heathrow instead
of Gatwick certainly remembered his mistake for some time
afterwards. As the aircraft was positioning for its final approach I
casually asked Wyer how we would go about getting our cars from
Gatwick. He looked across at me as though I was being particularly
obtuse.

'Young, you will go to the car park and get your car in the normal
manner.'

I pointed out that we were about to land at Heathrow, and he was
thunderstuck.

And yet he could be the gentlest of gentlemen and wonderful
company, a dedicated team manager and a master tactician in
endurance races. He delivered a string of race wins for Ford and later
took over the Porsche team to win for them as well when the famed
Teutonic efficiency had proved unable to match the pace or guile of
the Wyer-managed Fords.

Gulf withdrew their sponsorship at the end of the 1973 season and
I was making arrangements to concentrate solely on journalism when
Ken Tyrrell phoned. 'Gulf is out of racing,' he said, which I thought
was rather stating the obvious and didn't require a phone call. 'You're
out of a job,' he continued. I said that might appear to be the case
but . . .

'Do you want to work for Elf?' he asked, cutting me off in mid-
sentence.

I said I didn't know.

'I asked you a question,' he said with a degree of irritation. 'Do you
want to do the same job for Elf?'

I said that I would be interested.

'Good,' he said. 'Come down to the office and pick up your air
tickets. I've booked you on an early flight to Paris in the morning and
you've got an appointment with François Guiter at 11 o'clock.'

He had made the arrangements before he had asked me. I gathered
later that since Jackie Stewart had retired at the end of the 1973
season, Guiter felt the team might need someone to make sure the
British press stayed interested in it. With Jackie on board they hadn't
needed a PR man because Stewart was quite capable of handling the
press as well as winning world championships.

There were some hectic highlights of life with the Elf-Tyrrell team.
For the first Grand Prix round the streets of Long Beach in 1976 we

had been booked into a hotel that sounded like something of a coup because we were told it was just beside the pits and walking distance from the paddock. In fact, it *was* the pits! It had seen better days and was now a peeling refuge for Californian pensioners. A card on the noticeboard in the lobby read 'Burial Crypt Drawer for Sale. Cheap for Cash'. I was travelling with the racing artist, Michael Turner, and we checked in having just arrived, exhausted, off the London flight. The following morning I was about to go down to breakfast when the door-handle came off in my hand and I was an instant prisoner. The telephone didn't work and I had to break down the door to get out of my own room! The Tyrrell mechanics were breakfasting downstairs and were all grumbling about the hotel. I asked which room Jody Scheckter was in.

'Oh, he took one look at the place and cancelled,' said chief mechanic Roger Hill. 'Here's his phone number.'

I called the number, discovered that it was the Imperial 400 Motel nearby, and re-booked the whole team there. I didn't even know where it was, but if Jody had decided it was better than this one, we should be there too. Ken and Norah Tyrrell arrived from London that evening and discovered that I had re-arranged the team bookings; he was *very* angry. I had an authentic Tyrrell froth-job down the phone (Ken was renowned for his spit-flecked rages when suitably aroused). I wasn't aware that he had paid a sizeable deposit at the original hotel, and he was determined to stay there. The next morning he booked in at the Imperial 400 and the other hostelry was never mentioned again . . .

For the 1976 Japanese Grand Prix the Elf-Tyrrell team was booked in at the Western-style Mount Fuji Hotel – Western as opposed to Japanese with wooden pillows and raw fish for breakfast. I had a twin room and at the last minute Hugh McIllvaney from the *Observer* arrived to cover James Hunt's chances of winning the championship. There wasn't a hotel bed to be had within miles of the track, so I offered Hugh my spare bed. Hugh was and is one of the top sporting journalists in Britain, a doughty Scot whose capacity for his native tipple is legendary, and I greeted my new room-mate rather warily. I enjoy a Scotch too, but not to the art-form that Innes Ireland and McIllvaney had raised the pursuit.

I had always maintained that Innes was my least favourite neighbour on a long-haul flight. By the time I had supped enough to want to settle down and sleep, Innes wanted to fight someone. Anyone. Innes – who won the first Grand Prix for Lotus in 1961 – had made an amazing transition from racing driver to racing journalist as Sports Editor of *Autocar*, but he retained his roistering spirit when his piece had been written. I imagined Hughie would be the same, but rather to my amazement he refused to touch a drop while he worked on his Hunt feature. Was this the Scottish drinking machine of which legends had been told? Had the legends lied? No.

When his feature had been written and phoned to his Fleet Street office, Hugh launched himself into the booze as though his country's export reputation depended on it. I never saw him after the race, but his bags were packed and sitting ready in the room when I came back after dinner. Hugh was upstairs partying with the drivers and mechanics, delighted that a long and harrowing season was over and that Hunt – certainly no stranger to partying! – had won the title.

The first bus for the long drive to the airport was due to leave at 4 am and Hugh was due to be on it. From time to time I woke during the night, but his bags were still there. Had he forgotten about the flight? I hoped not. I woke again to the sound of heavy breathing and realised that a far-from-sober Hugh was standing over my bed, windmilling his fists inches from my face and saying over and over again, 'What did I ever do to you, Eoin Young? Why won't you talk to me?'

I pointed out as carefully and reasonably as I could that I wasn't talking to him because a) I didn't know he had returned, and b) I was asleep. Vaguely mollified, he made effusive farewells and launched off down the corridor with his bags.

I fell asleep again but in moments the phone was ringing. It was the front desk. The Japanese manager was doing his best to get his tongue round 'McIllvaney', and it appeared that Hugh was wanting to settle his bill with $50 travellers cheques. I assured the manager that this would be OK.

'No, no,' he persisted, 'Mr McIllvaney wants to pay his bill with *one* $50 travellers cheque.'

I said I would settle Hugh's bill, and finally slept for the rest of what was left of the night. Hugh paid me back in England over a splendid lunch. Fine man. The next lunch we had together was after James's memorial service in London in 1993.

Life with Elf was great while François Guiter was in charge. He was a lot like John Wyer in that no one was in doubt who was Le Chef when he was around. He was a big man and he had been in the French Resistance as a frogman during the war. I remember one party around the swimming pool at the Ille Rousse in Bandol when Tyrrell in schoolboy mode pushed Guiter into the pool fully clothed in suit and tie. I hadn't heard the frogman stories and I could see my job going out the window as my French boss struggled half-drowned to the edge of the pool. But the big man went in like a porpoise. Scarcely a ripple as he turned the playful push into a polished dive.

Guiter was the man behind the resurgence of young French drivers in Formula 1. He put the French Elf oil company sponsorship behind promising young drivers in racing schools and the lower formulae, and if they had ability he made Formula 1 opportunities appear.

François Cevert was a Tyrrell driver from the Elf ranks, and so was Patrick Depailler. Dave and Pam Wilkie ran the Elf hospitality motorhome for years and it became the focal point of the Grand Prix paddock. One 'met at Elf' for lunch as a matter of course.

The worst assignment I had for Elf happened the morning François Guiter phoned from the South of France and said that an English journalist had been badly injured in a road accident near the Paul Ricard track after an Elf press presentation, and could I bring his wife down to be at the hospital with him. In fact, it was New Zealand journalist Murray Taylor who had been passenger in a car driven by another journalist who had been killed instantly when they ran under the back of a mobile crane. This was a bizarre advantage because the driver was able to raise the vehicle on its bracing legs and lift it off the wrecked car so that the ambulance crew could save Murray. It was impossible to book a commercial flight so I arranged to charter a small plane, which seemed to take for ever on the trip to Toulouse. Murray's wife Glenice, also a New Zealander, made the trip bravely considering that she didn't know the extent of her husband's injuries. I didn't really know her and it was years later that she told me that she had brought a Harold Robbins book she was reading and had thought it a trifle raunchy. When she realised I was reading the book as well, she was so embarrassed that she slipped her copy under the seat of the plane and left it there!

When we were ushered into the intensive care ward, I nearly fainted at the sight of Murray's injuries, but Glenice simply went to his bedside, held his hand and whispered encouragement to him. One brave lady. He looked as though he had been beaten with baseball bats, his head swollen huge with serious cuts and bruises.

We drove to the hotel where the Tyrrell team happened to be staying for testing at the track. They had heard the news, and Ken made a place for Glenice beside him at his table. I thought this was Uncle Ken being kind and doing his best to cheer up the poor girl after her ordeal. The meal progressed and they chatted, but soon it became apparent that Glenice was beginning to colour and get angry, loudly defending her corner. This didn't seem to be in any script I knew for comforting young ladies in their moment of distress. She said later that she realised Ken had deliberately led her into an argument to make her respond the way she did – and she felt so much better for it! Murray recovered to run a Formula 3 team in Europe and the Taylors now live in Auckland where Murray works with a public relations company linked with motoring, motor racing and international yacht racing.

Elf was heavily involved in the North Sea oilfields and bought a chain of petrol stations in Britain. They launched a nationwide poll to find out how Elf was perceived by the British and an interesting point emerged. The French were delighted that a significant percentage of people associated Elf with the name of a car. This, said the French PR people, proved that their sponsorship of the Tyrrell Formula 1 team was paying off handsomely. The public now obviously believed that the Tyrrell F1 car was called an Elf. It didn't seem the moment to explain to the French management that some years earlier there had been a popular small car on the market called a Riley Elf . . .

François Guiter was a consummate politician and he worked closely with Bernie Ecclestone on the overall racing scene. It was Guiter, an enthusiastic photographer in his spare time, who pioneered and financed on-car cameras in Formula 1. The first films were fairly awful, fuzzy and jumpy, and only made during practice, but they persevered to the point where on-car cameras, now providing amazing footage during telecasts of GPs, helped with the development of video technology.

Guiter was reaching retirement age and grooming his replacements, but, apart from the splendid anglophile Jacques de la Beraudiere, who left to join a London auction house, they had none of Guiter's political poise or his enthusiasm for motor racing. Guiter's successor gave the impression that he had taken the position because it was fashionable to be at the races, a politically advantageous move within the company. My services were dispensed with as soon as he was able to do so, and the Elf motorhome became more and more a French haven. I can't say I was unhappy to learn that he had been dropped in disgrace after the embarrassing premature public announcement of a delicate corporate matter in Formula 1 that had not been finally agreed by all parties and cleared for release.

I later worked with Ford, hosting a lunch table at their Formula 1 motorhome, after I had flown to a French Grand Prix in the Ford plane and discussed the Ford Formula 1 involvement on the way back with Competitions Director Michael Kranefuss. He was proud of their new motorhome and I asked what he regarded was its main purpose. It served as a team base for management and catered for the team and press. Did he know any of the press who availed themselves of the hospitality? Er, well, a few. I suggested that the Ford investment might be better spent in catering for key members of the press rather than offering an open house for anyone who wandered past. He agreed, offered me the job as host and eventually the Ford motorhome became one of the 'in' places for lunch in the paddock – a sort of Barley Mow on Tour – with the added advantage that if Ford had an announcement or any of the team wanted to indulge in some mild lobbying, all they had to do was join a table.

The team motorhomes are an important extension of the sponsor's public relations programme and the operating staff become key figures even though their job role may be defined as driver and cook. Some find the dual role impossible to fill and perform their hospitality role with scant grace, while others become adept members of the PR team. Stuart and Di Spires are excellent examples, now hosting the Ford motorhome and serving smiles and a full English breakfast on chilly early mornings at circuits all round Europe. They have become known as 'Mum and Dad'. A sincere smile is, after all, the most effective – and the cheapest – form of public relations.

CHAPTER TEN

The
Gang of Five

AT ONE STAGE, when our travels took us to most of the races as a loose group and we travelled on the same flights, shared hire cars, stayed in the same hotels and ate together in the evenings, Denis Jenkinson called us the 'Famous Five': himself, Alan Henry, Maurice Hamilton, Nigel Roebuck and me. Later, when Jenks wasn't going to as many races, the 'Famous Four' become known as 'The Cartel' by some journalists who could never figure out how to join our group. There was nothing sinister involved, no secret handshakes, no jealous guarding of information, although it's true to say that the gossip was usually traded freely by the time the wine waiter had been summoned for the second or third time.

The puzzling aspect of our 'club' was that it didn't have to feature motor racing on the conversational menu. One particular incident underlines this. I suppose it's difficult for us to appreciate or to remember what it's like *not* to be on the inside of racing, having been there for so long. We have privileged access, but we have come to take it for granted. Before the Ecclestone regime announced that the regular press could have permanent credentials, a sort of FIA identification credit card to hang round your neck, we had to write to every race organiser, plead for press passes, then on arrival trek to wherever the race office was – usually in the city centre and as far as possible from the track – and plead all over again to get the pass we needed.

One year we were in Madrid before the Spanish Grand Prix at Jarama, and a tall Australian lad, who had recognised me from my column photograph and figured he could claim some sort of Anzac affiliation, asked if he could beg a ride to the track. I explained that there was a group of us but that we could probably squeeze him in. I introduced him to the others, all of whom were obviously well known to him as names, and when we got to Jenks the poor chap went into some sort of worship mode. He would be able to tell all his mates back home that he had Actually Spoken to DSJ, Shaken Hands with the Great Man.

We squeezed in together and a mile from the track we stopped at a cafe for coffee. And a brandy. And another coffee. And another brandy. By now it was late morning and we were close enough to the track to hear the first cars going out to practice. The Australian began nervously checking his watch and glancing from one to the other of us to see who would make the first move for the circuit. Then someone ordered another coffee. This was all too much for him. He seemed to have been hijacked by a group that he had imagined ate, slept and drank motor racing, yet he had been an hour in our company and motor racing had not been mentioned *once*. And now the cars were obviously wailing around the track, and the press corps seemed to be disregarding this commencement. Eventually we paid the bill, drove to the track and set off to chronicle the weekend's activity, leaving the Australian to re-evaluate the approach of the mainstream motor racing press . . .

I suppose we're an odd assortment who all grew up in different parts of the world wishing we could *be* Jenks and enjoy his gypsy existence, never imagining that we would get to know him and be accepted as a member of his gang. It was an honour he didn't bestow to many. Your telephone number was either written on Jenks's kitchen wall or it wasn't. Simple as that. I suppose Jenks is a loner and always has been, a man with friends in all the different areas of motor sport and life and all compartmentalised: a world of his own.

Home is a gamekeeper's cottage tucked away in the woods of rural Hampshire. The kitchen wall beside the telephone is a handwritten record, a sort of vertical message board. Telephone numbers. And if someone said something that amused him, he would write the quote on the wall to chuckle about afterwards. Motor cycles and old cars vie for space and attention inside and outside the house. For years his famous white E-Type Jaguar, the car he had driven thousands of miles in long summers to races across Europe, sat on blocks with its rear brakes frozen. At one time Jenks had a penchant for 'Aunty' Rovers bought cheaply for local transport. When one failed it was pushed into the hedge and replaced by another. They are still there.

I doubt if Jenks has ever thrown anything away. He has rooms crammed with all the paperwork generated from races and cars since he first became involved. Corridors are walled with magazines. I can only imagine the clumps of Ferrari and Maserati catalogues and racing car documentation that must be deep in some of those piles, acquired casually in the course of what he regarded as normal visits to Modena. If we had been along we would have been looking for hems to touch. Jenks must find it hard to believe that I actively seek the paperwork he has stacked, virtually insulating his walls, to sell to collectors who seek it even more actively!

He was fascinated when I first started dealing and came with me when I took a stand at an autojumble. I hadn't thought to wonder what he was bringing, and he had barely unpacked a pile of very early copies of the Porsche magazine *Christophorus* when dealers had swept them away. Jenks said he thought 20p each would have been too much! Today one copy would sell for £200 . . .

If we accept that racing drivers come from a different drawer from the rest of the human race, you must also appreciate that in the world of motor racing writing, Jenks has a drawer to himself. He was always an iconoclast, always a breaker of idols, never one to be impressed by reputations he hadn't nurtured or bestowed on others himself. If he took a shine to a driver – and he had the highest regard for men like Stirling Moss, Jimmy Clark, Gilles Villeneuve and Ayrton Senna – that driver would spend the rest of his career deified in Jenks's notebook. You couldn't apply to join. Jenks did the selecting.

He had the huge advantage of having been there and done it before the rest of us were out of school. We all read and re-read (and *still* re-read) his report of sitting alongside Moss when he won the 1955 Mille Miglia for Mercedes. Talk about the right hand of God. Jenks had raced motorcycles and ridden as sidecar passenger for Eric Oliver when he was winning world titles on a Norton in the late 1940s, so he started from a base of no fear. He respected talent and he could sit alongside and assist with no worries about his partner's abilities. They shared responsibilities. He and Stirling spent days going over the route of the 1,000-mile race and Jenks compiled his famous 'loo roll' of route notes wound on to a pair of spools and read through a window in a tailor-made box. The box is willed to Alan Henry!

We reckoned that Moss chose Jenks for the Mille Miglia ride because he had a proven record of being at home under competitive pressure, wasn't afraid of speed and wouldn't be over-awed by the situation. He was also small and light. They made each other famous during that long day in 1955. Forty years later, in a special demonstration drive at the Goodwood Festival of Speed, Moss and Jenks rode again for the first time in the very car they threw around Italy. Jenks was in tears. We could only imagine how he felt, because we had never been there and were never likely to be in any situation remotely similar to that piece of history-making.

Racing has changed totally, even in the years I have been involved, so Jenks must feel that his world has also changed completely. I sympathise with him, but he saw the best of it and for that I will always envy him.

I didn't appreciate quite how much racing and Jenks had changed until the morning of a Grand Prix in Montreal a few years ago. The race is staged on an island in the middle of the St Lawrence river, which means that access and parking is a major problem. Because the television coverage is in English, hours long and detailed, I made it a habit to watch the race on TV at the hotel. It was raining. I informed the others at breakfast that I wasn't going to the race. What a surprise, they said. I was working on a feature in my room mid-morning when there was a tap on the door. I assumed it was the maid to do the room. It was Jenks.

'I feel awful,' he said, tugging at his beard. 'I'm not going to the track. Can you bring me a set of results?'

I told him I wasn't going either and why didn't he join me for lunch. We watched the race together on TV over a splendid room service lunch and a bottle of wine and I took some photographs of this rather extraordinary occasion. I could imagine me skiving off for the race afternoon, but *not* Jenks. When the photographs were printed I was embarrassed that Jenks might be embarrassed. Not at all. He sent one of them to his car club magazines!

One of Roebuck's after-lunch tales in new company (old company has heard all these stories before) is of sitting a few feet from the track at Montreal just after a slow corner before the pits where the cars come out on full noise and acceleration. We had enjoyed a rather good lunch at Elf and a few laps into the race Roebuck asked me a question. No reply. He asked again, thinking I hadn't heard because of the shattering noise around us. Then he realised the awful truth that I had nodded off. Well, it *was* a warmish afternoon . . .

Alan Henry and I both worked in banks and both became bored by it, both became infected by the motor racing bug and lured away to a world as far removed from banking as it is possible to be. Henry, Roebuck and myself all began by telling an editor that a report of a race was, in our modest opinion, crap, and that we could do a better job. Being invited to do so, we did.

Alan's nickname is 'Bruin' because he's a big chap, but big and comfortable like an overstuffed sofa rather than big and aggressive. He is marvellous company. For years over dinners in one country or another we would implore him to write the way he talked. He tended to be a tad pompous because he thought his work required a measure of formality. He enjoys the ability to cut his cloth to suit the particular garment he is making, thus when he is writing a book it becomes a historical document and demands a measure of respect, but now his weekly column in *Autocar*, a page ahead of mine, has become the first item I seek in the magazine because I know he'll be writing the way he speaks. I love it, but I can imagine that some of the people he writes about aren't quite as receptive to the way he weaves some of his words.

Nick Brittan started such a weekly column of outspoken comment in *Autosport*, and I remember Ken Tyrrell telling him that he *loved* some of the things Nick wrote about other people and *hated* what he wrote about him!

The Henry bookshelf must be overloaded – with books he has written himself. His output is prodigious by any measuring. We joke with him about a week going by and no new book announced, but to be fair there have been new books by Henry appearing in bookshops that I never even knew he was writing!

Alan arrived in motor racing a driver-generation after I did, and he talks of getting to know a young Niki Lauda early in his career. 'Back in 1972 there were those who questioned whether Herr Lauda could drive a pig up a passage on the strength of his performances in the hopeless March 721X. I wasn't one of them, of course, having decisively concluded that he was world championship material on the weighty evidence that he once stayed overnight in my parents' house. My mother later considered putting a commemorative plaque on the bedhead.'

AH advanced his career alongside James Hunt as well as Lauda, the new generation as they then were. Hunt always called him 'Hens' and Alan could and did tell hair-raising tales of the escapades the circus got up to on the South American Formula 2 series.

Many of us in the writing game have had a particularly close association with a driver, and when that driver is killed your world collapses. You feel grief perhaps greater than at a death in a further corner of your own family. It happens once and then you don't let it happen again. With Alan it was Tom Pryce, and the poor guy suffered the appalling twist of fate that led him to be standing on the bank at Kyalami that stopped the dead-man trip of Pryce's Shadow, the Welshman having been killed instantly when a marshal ran across the track in front of him and he was struck in the face with the marshal's fire extinguisher. The car carried on for the length of the straight in an eerie way, following the line of the track the way a riderless horse will stay with the field. At the first right-hander it ploughed straight ahead across the path of Laffite's Ligier, slamming the bank where Alan was standing.

Compounding the calamity in South Africa, Maurice Hamilton was standing with Alan on the outside of the corner on what I think may have been his first race abroad while he was working with me. I was standing on the inside of the corner, being a cautious sort of chap, and I waited as the huge dust cloud settled to see whether any of the journalists and photographers on the bank had been hurt. Mercifully they hadn't.

Maurice was introduced to motor racing by his father Paddy in Northern Ireland, who took him to his first race – the TT at Dundrod – when he was seven. Paddy was one of those fathers we all wish we'd had if we couldn't have our own. I remember Maurice telling me how, when he was a lad, his father told him, 'I don't care how much you drink, son, just remember to act sober . . .'

Paddy had a flash of white hair and a ready wit. He was a man who liked a drink and who enjoyed 'the crack' around the circuits. (I have to explain to readers other than Irish that 'crack' is a word that covers good conversation, good chat. I had to have Maurice explain it to me.) Paddy had a flourishing building business in Northern Ireland and he was anxious that Maurice should join the family firm and take over on his retirement. But Maurice was bitten by the racing bug for which his father would have to take responsibility, however much he might regret it. The Hamiltons, *père et fils*, went to Monaco for the 1973 Grand Prix and Maurice was determined to use the race as his entrée to the world of writing.

There was no point, he reasoned, in writing a report of the race because it was being well covered already, so he determined to write a personal colour piece on what the race was like from the spectator's viewpoint, something that couldn't and still can't be written once you're 'on the inside'. You lose the perspective of the paying punter once you have a press pass. Fate had it that he took his first piece to *Competition Car*, a short-lived monthly with an office in Kingston-upon-Thames. Maurice left his copy with a secretary who promised that the editor would read it and he said he would call a few days later.

Maurice remembers the day that changed his life. 'I went into the office and there's this little fellow in a leather jacket wandering about. I asked him if I could speak to the editor, please, Mr Nigel Roebuck? And he said, "Yes, that's me."' Roebuck had liked the piece and had already arranged to use it. The rest wasn't quite history. Hamilton's problems were only just beginning. He knew now that he could write and he knew writing about motor racing was what he wanted to do, but how to begin making it a career?

Traditionally there have been few openings for budding motor racing writers because prime jobs on motor sport magazines tend to be jealously guarded by the present incumbents. Most have risen to the post fuelled by enthusiasm. I can't think of any in the mainstream racing press who have had formal training in journalism; they make up for this by their ability to communicate their enthusiasm to their readers in an acceptable fashion. The 'Fleet Street' brigade, by contrast, nearly all have training in journalism, and what they may lack in inside knowledge of a complex sport, they make up for in professionalism.

Maurice Hamilton says we met at the Nurburgring in 1976 when I was working with Elf and we had Jackie Stewart taking journalists for laps of the old 'Ring. Roebuck had introduced us (maybe this 'Cartel' thing is tighter than I thought!) and I put Maurice in the car beside Jackie. He wrote a piece that was so good that I offered to send copies of it to my syndicated magazines. Five published it and

Maurice told Gerry Donaldson in an interview for his book *Grand Prix People* that I had refused to take a commission on his payments from the magazines. I don't remember that bit. Bad for my reputation. Alan Henry says I offered him a similar deal when he first started, but on less favourable terms!

This led to Maurice coming to work for me, but not before a meeting with his father in London. It was as though I'd asked for Maurice's hand in marriage. I don't think I was fully aware of the gravity of the fact that Maurice had finally told his father that he wouldn't be following him into the family building business, preferring his chances in trying to follow his star in motor racing.

His father and mother came over for a dinner in London and Paddy took me aside and asked what I really thought of Maurice's chances. I'm sure he wanted me to say that Maurice was groping at career straws so that he could have one more try at keeping him in the family company. But I told him that Maurice had that important combination of modesty and ability that would take him a long way in motor racing writing. Paddy accepted that and gave Maurice his blessing. He hasn't looked back.

Maurice writes for the *Observer* and Alan writes for the *Guardian* as well as being Grand Prix Editor of *Autocar*. Maurice enjoys a rapport with the mechanics in most teams, and his books with photographer Jon Nicholson on Damon Hill after his first full season in Formula 1, and *Pole Position*, which tells the story of the 1995 F1 season through the eyes of the Williams team members, are both modern racing classics. After the success of the book on Damon, he was asked, to his surprise, to work with sprinter Linford Christie on his autobiography. It was a new world for Hamilton and it involved travel to Australia and the USA where Christie was training and competing. Maurice must have been less than impressed when his only credit in the book was a passing mention of his Christian name in Christie's foreword.

Writers can be touchy about things like that; we like credit where it is due. I know how Maurice felt. In 1967 I was asked by another writer to help him out with a book he was writing on racing drivers. Each chapter was a driver profile. It amounted to my writing nearly half the book and I was promised cover billing, my name with the other writer's on the cover. That appeased my professional vanity and made the work worthwhile. But when the book came out my name was not on the cover and only passing credit in the foreword was given for the chapters I had written. I never fell into that trap again.

Roebuck has always been Roebuck, seldom Nigel, unless you need a favour, in which case he has already spotted the ploy and it doesn't work. Nigel and Maurice may suffer from not suffering fools gladly, if at all, whereas I think Alan and I tend to count up what other assets this particular fool may have before advising him of his shortcomings.

Jenks will simply ignore the fool, consigning him to a limbo somewhere beyond his consideration.

Roebuck hangs his hat on a variety of pegs and refuses to be shaken.

'I'm fairly nakedly biased,' he says. 'But I don't think I'm devious about it.'

Certainly not. Roebuck's colours are clearly nailed to the mast of whatever subject he chooses to go after in his weekly 'Fifth Column' page in *Autosport*, which is a must-read for every red-blooded enthusiast around the world – as well as those inside the world of motor sport, who respect him as a man who says what he thinks and to hell with accepted convention. It's the Tyrrell/Brittan syndrome. They love to read it when Roebuck is lambasting someone who doubtless deserves the approbation, but they hate it when his spotlight happens to fall on their own shortcomings.

Jean Behra was Roebuck's first hero and remains a hero on a personal pedestal along with Mario Andretti, Gilles Villeneuve and Alain Prost, modern drivers with whom he enjoyed a valuable rapport.

Roebuck's break came when he read a race report in the American monthly *Car & Driver* and wrote to the editor acquainting him with the inadequacy of the piece.

'It's totally out of character for me to do something like that, but I told them they couldn't afford to be without me any longer.'

I have to agree with this being out of character, because Roebuck has always struck me as being almost diffident, short of stature, and dedicated to his work. That said, he is not a good chap to be at odds with. Fools, as I mentioned earlier, are certainly not suffered. The American magazine wrote back, perhaps intrigued by his outspokenness, and commissioned him to cover the 1971 Spanish Grand Prix at Barcelona. Thus the first race he ever covered as a commissioned journalist was a Grand Prix, a fact that still amazes when you consider the difficulty of getting started today, as then. A case of ability and opportunity getting together and fusing into one of the best motor racing writers in the business today.

Roebuck and I share an enthusiasm for wine, although he will say that in his case it's quality and in my case it's quantity. He really is a wine buff with a temperature-controlled cellar at home and a cottage in France where he retires from time to time to work uninterrupted and to get closer to both of his enthusiasms. He lives near me in Surrey and most Wednesdays we meet for bangers and mash at The Barley Mow. This is actually quite a strange arrangement in a competitive business – competitive in that you're as good as your last column and you can't afford to be seen to be losing touch. His weekly page in *Autosport* is fairly similar to my 'Diary' page in *Autocar*, yet we can spend a couple of hours over lunch each

Wednesday and I don't think we have *ever* clashed when the magazines come out, although we may have often covered the same subject from spiritedly and diametrically opposed viewpoints.

There was one occasion when a Roebuck exploit *was* my column. Elf and Renault had invited a group to the Paul Ricard circuit in the south of France to actually *drive* the current turbocharged Renault Formula 1 car! The whole thing looked enormously complicated, leaving aside the danger aspect of the operation. Few of the journalists managed a clean start without stalling, and it became apparent that embarrassment was more of a consideration than the possible danger of conducting 1,000 horsepower up the straight. Renault had hired the nearby airfield for the runs. I kept rearranging my place towards the back of the queue, reckoning that rain or a wreck would curtail activities before it came to my turn.

Roebuck was strapped in and stormed off with some aplomb, I thought enviously, but then there was a rush of revs and the Renault was spinning wildly into the weeds on the edge of the runway. I was among the first to reach the hapless 'Buck, and the way he tells the story, full of compassion, I leaned down into the cockpit and said, 'Thanks for that – you've just written my column for me . . .'

Perhaps his public school education (Giggleswick in Yorkshire for eight years) encourages Roebuck's enthusiasm for school food like bangers and mash. Certainly it is responsible for my favourite Roebuck story, one that he tells so well, but will probably never write. When he was a prep schoolboy in short pants, Castrol published achievements books at the end of the year, and included a coupon to fill in if you wanted lubricant advice for your car. You noted your name and address and your car.

'I can't imagine why I wrote "Rolls-Royce". It would have been more in keeping for me to have written "Ferrari".'

He put his address as the name of the house at school, but not the name of the school. There must have been cross-referencing between the oil company and the car-makers, and if a prospect seemed suitable there would be a follow-up. Rolls-Royce obviously thought RR-owner Nigel S. Roebuck with a country house address might be considering a new model.

'I was standing in the milk queue one morning when the headmaster plucked me out of the line and told me that there was someone to see me. I was introduced to a gentleman in a suit who said he was from Rolls-Royce, and they had a demonstration car for me to try. They had obviously realised their mistake, but decided to make the best of it, and I was taken for a drive around local roads before being delivered back to school.'

And what happened then?

'I was flogged . . .'

It was also Roebuck who lost his hire car in Florida. In a shopping mall car park. It's something I always dread doing and he did it. He realised he had no idea where he had parked the car when all the car parks looked the same and by then he couldn't remember what make it was, let alone simple things like colour or registration number. So how did he solve the problem? This is the clever bit. I would probably have phoned the hire company and told them the car had been stolen. But Roebuck brought some of his famous lateral thought into play, took a taxi back to his motel, waited until darkness when the shopping mall had closed, took another taxi back – and his car was sitting just where he had left it, the *only* car alone in the huge car park . . .

One driver who, by his very nature, crossed 'The Cartel' was Nigel Mansell. To a man we would applaud his abilities on the track, but be less than impressed by the way he conducted himself outside the car. We felt, and this view was shared by Williams designer Patrick Head, that the world would be a better place if we could find a way of hermetically sealing Mansell in the cockpit for the entire race weekend. Only when he emerged from the car did he find endless ways of denigrating the reputation he had forged every time he went out in the car. Quick, he was; charismatic he wasn't. At a race weekend he was a man without charm, without the understanding of what was required to be part of a team.

The Fleet Street journalists were committed to obsequiousness because their editors demanded a morning serving of Mansell quotes for their readers every second weekend over breakfast; we were in the fortunate position of being able to make up our own minds. For much of the 1992 season we had managed to avoid an audience with the Great Man during the summer that would bring him the world championship, and this extended to 1993 when he was racing and, against all our predictions, winning in Indycars.

Roebuck, Maurice and I went to the Indycar race at Milwaukee the weekend after Indianapolis and before the Canadian Grand Prix at Montreal. Once again we had managed to spend the weekend avoiding the Great Man, but as we waited in the pit lane to cross the track and climb to the top of the grandstand to watch the race, our Nemesis made his appearance. We had been waiting for American journalist Gordon Kirby, who was talking to one of the Indycar drivers. Roebuck and Maurice had their backs to the pits and I was facing them when Mansell appeared from behind the pits on a course where he couldn't avoid us even if he had chosen so to do. I watched him as he came up behind Maurice and said, 'Oooh, I could have 'ad your wallet then, Maurice,' and clapped him on the shoulder like an old mate he hadn't seen for a long time. The latter was true. I pre-empted the situation by leaning forward and shaking Mansell by the hand, which left the others with no option but to do the same while I stepped back and took photographs of the momentous occasion.

When Mansell had gone, Roebuck, consumed with mock indignation, turned on me as if it was all my fault. 'You are an unprincipled bastard,' he snapped. I thought it was wonderful and had the film processed as soon as I was able. Roebuck demanded the negatives, which, if memory serves correct, I handed over because I had already printed several copies. One was mounted, framed and hung in pride of place in The Barley Mow where it was seen by the various members of the Formula 1 fraternity who passed through during visits to the nearby Tyrrell team headquarters.

Somehow word of the famous fraternisation photograph had reached Prost, and Alain decided to play along. At the next race, while still in the car, he spotted Roebuck and beckoned him over. There was no love lost between Mansell and Prost, whom Mansell accused of playing politics to ruin his (Mansell's) chances at Ferrari.

According to Roebuck, a grinning Prost said, 'I 'ave 'eard about the photograph in the pub of you and your friend . . . so now you 'ave a choice. You can be my friend or 'is . . .'

I then took the precaution of taking the picture to the Grand Prix at Silverstone and having Prost sign it. He wrote, 'To my mate, Nige!' with suitable Gallic ambiguity, and it was re-hung in the pub to Roebuck's theatrical discomfort.

If motor racing and the people in it have changed radically from the time I covered my first Grand Prix at Rheims in 1961, so has the means of writing about it. Maurice Hamilton wrote his reports longhand for years but I never did, mainly because my handwriting is so appalling that most of the time I can't read it myself! My ever-present notebook is in no danger of being stolen. Having said that, it was once. For years I used a Rolls-Royce leather diary cover, which I thought was a pretty classy way of carrying my notebook.

Jenks had pioneered the idea of covering the Grand Prix at Monza from the original tiny press stand at the top of the grandstand just under the roof. From there we had a bird's eye view of the cars being wheeled out on to the grid with all the razzmatazz, then the attacking action at the start, all the noise of the cars and the *Tifosi* and those hectic wheel-to-wheel nose-to-tail slipstreaming battles before the 'safety' chicanes slowed the lap speeds, broke up the slipstreamers and spoiled it all. We somehow had an involvement with what was going on, despite our altitude. Then they installed a television set so that we could see what was going on beyond our sight. Then we were confined to the huge new air-conditioned press room above the pits.

The trick was to leave our place in the grandstand just before the end of the race to fight our way through the tunnel under the start-finish line. If you waited until the end, you were resigned to waiting for an hour or so for the crowd to drift away. I had battled through the tunnel and emerged into the pit lane to be told by the *Daily Mail* journalist that Jody Scheckter's road car had been stolen from the car park. This was a great story for my column, and I went to pluck my notebook from the top pocket of my shirt, only to realise that someone had already done it for me! In the gloomy tunnel, my notebook in its Rolls-Royce leather cover obviously looked too much like a wallet for a light-fingered thief who was obviously wondering now what language the notes were written in . . . A report of double theft appeared in the *Daily Mail* sports diary the following morning.

I covered the Tasman races for *Motoring News* in the late 1950s and early 1960s, telephoning the results and airmailing the full report. I wrote the centre spread report each week for £10 and I thought I was being handsomely rewarded. It wasn't until I came to Britain that I realised I wasn't. But just having your reports used was a triumph considering how many would-be motor racing journalists were desperate for the opportunity that I had gained by geography. I was there and they weren't.

Getting a contract to cover races meant an easier task when it came to getting a press pass. Just getting a pass at a track like Monaco was a good deal more stressful than writing about the race. There was always the chance that the lady in charge of the press desk had argued with her husband over breakfast and was making life as difficult as possible for everyone else that day. To try and ease the credential situation for bona fide journalists, Bernard Cahier, one of the sport's senior photo-journalists, organised the International Racing Press Association with a leather armband carrying the bearer's photograph. The FIA eventually took over and issued an annual pass, which did away with the queue at the organiser's office in each country.

I taught myself two-finger typing while I was working in the bank in Timaru, and I can type faster than most people in the press room. I worked my way through several Olympia Traveller portable typewriters before the word processor arrived to strike terror into the army of computer-illiterate journalists in the press room. Paul Treudthardt, then with Associated Press, had one of the first, a huge affair with a bubble screen, and I remember watching him using it at a Belgian Grand Prix at Zolder. For most of the first practice day the words 'Practice for the Belgian Grand Prix took place today despite the looming threat of . . .' hung eerily on the screen. I forget what the threat was, but I was impressed that it didn't need paper to be written on.

In his 'Memory Lane' piece in the 45th anniversary issue of *Autosport* in August 1995, Nigel Roebuck recalled how Jenks had processed his famous report of the 1955 Mille Miglia. 'He did it in longhand, on many sheets of paper, which he then popped into a mailbox in a dusty Italian hamlet. The story was at least 20,000 words (! – my exclamation mark), and he had, of course, no copy. 'Never gave it a thought,' he says. Fortunately for all of us – not least Jenks – the classic piece of motor racing literature arrived intact, but the thought of its journey makes me shiver still. Thirty years on, a jammed fax machine was the biggest fear, and nowadays it is the vagaries of electronic mail.

'About the only aspect of race reporting that hasn't changed,' wrote Roebuck, 'is that you still have to go to an airport, fly somewhere, collect a hire car and drive it to a circuit. Once there, you still need a notebook and a tape recorder. Those things apart, a press man who retired when I began, in 1971, would barely recognise the job now.'

The fax machine was the wonder of the age for me and still is. I could type my column, print it, feed it into the fax and it would reappear in magazine offices in different parts of the world. Then the laptop word processor revolutionised the press room. The idea of learning a totally new system filled me with dread, but once I had mastered the Tandy 200 I seriously wondered how I had ever coped with a regular typewriter. It seems an age ago that adding copy in the middle of a typewritten paragraph was just too complicated and messy. With a word processor it's the work of a moment. It doesn't necessarily make you a better writer, but at least it's easier to be a bad one.

The Tandy 200 was known as the Land Rover of Laptops because it was simple, strong and reliable. Its shortcoming was a lack of memory capacity, but this could be extended and you still see the occasional robust Tandy in press rooms, demanding a second glance the way you look twice at a classic car in a modern car park.

I have never been able to cope with the complexity of computers. They fill me with dread. The only thing certain is that if you make a mistake it's *your* fault. Which reminds me of Jeff Hutchinson who had one of the early Data General word processors when that computer company sponsored the Tyrrell team. Jeff was in the press room at Spa, beating the computer with his fists Basil Fawlty-style and shrieking abuse to the effect that the f—ing thing couldn't spell. He had been running his copy past the spell-checker and it stubbornly refused to clear a word that Jeff had used. I mentioned, as tactfully as I could, that Jeff had spelled the word incorrectly in the first place. A fully enraged Hutchinson was legendary in press rooms around the world. He swung round at me and shouted, 'But I *always* spell it that way!'

Nigel Mansell has made his point that journalists should never be in a position to criticise racing drivers because they can have no first-hand knowledge of what it is really like out there. Eddie Irvine, in the spotlight at the Nurburgring after the announcement that he would be switching from Jordan to Ferrari in 1996, was asked whether he was worried about the piranha proclivities of the Italian press where Ferrari team drivers were concerned.

'I don't pay any attention to the press at all, to be honest. There's no point. I don't know a journalist who knows anything about motor racing, so there's not much point in listening to them.'

The packed press room sat silent, each journalist from a dozen different countries sitting there with an 'Is he talking about me?' expression. My ebullient colleague Mr Henry weighed in with a spirited response in his *Autocar* column the following Wednesday.

'This [Irvine's comment] confirmed my view that I've met few racing drivers who know anything about personal PR. Don't get me wrong; I've been around too long to lose any sleep over whether some stroppy customer with a crash helmet speaks to me or not.'

Everyone with Castrol R in their nostrils read *Motor Sport* and regarded it as the bible. If it was in *Motor Sport* it must be true. Generations of schoolboys grew to be grown-up schoolboys believing every word if it was written by Jenks or The Bod (*Motor Sport* editor William Boddy). In 1992 Maurice Hamilton and I featured as racing drivers in a double-page spread! It was a How Not To Do It, tongue firmly in cheek piece but it put us down in history, if history is made by appearing between the traditionally green covers of *Motor Sport*.

Harry Calton at Ford had suggested that we might like to do a sprint at Goodwood. We would drive a Ford Escort RS2000 guest car in a championship that ran all summer in rallies, hill-climbs, economy runs and autotests. Series organiser Stuart McCrudden phoned to ask if we might be free the Friday before the sprint. Why? Testing, he says. *Testing!* And I thought we were skiving off for an afternoon at glorious Goodwood thrashing Mr Ford's motorcar. Testing . . . Roebuck fell about, hooting with laughter.

'Testing! What are you doing Friday? Testing! Good God, I never thought I'd see the day . . .'

Peter Gethin runs a performance driving school at Goodwood and one of his instructors took us round. It was like tuition day at Gleneagles for Jackie Stewart's Grand Prix mechanics' clay pigeon shooting weekend. An expert showed you how to do it and you went out and did it your way. You hit one and you had no idea why. You missed the next one and you had no idea why. At least at Goodwood there were school signs to show apexes and braking points. A piece of cake. Not a very large piece, admittedly, but reassuring.

Sunday, and the markers were gone. Someone had torn up the instructions. We were in trouble. I couldn't believe how busy it was in the RS2000 cockpit and how boring it looked from the outside. It certainly felt fast, hanging on to the edge of control, but the cars are so quiet on the outside that they didn't look or sound exciting. I always seemed to arrive at the famous Goodwood chicane faster than I had intended and I was braking, grabbing something lower than I was in by way of gears, and scrambling through in a thunderous slide and screaming engine. Must watch Maurice through there, I thought. He looked as though he was going shopping. He told me I did too. I asked our works engineer Paul Wilson what the form was for starting.

'Six thousand and dump the clutch,' he advised.

I did just that. Clouds of tyre smoke and an amazing start, 4.5 seconds faster than Maurice in practice. Excellent! Obviously I had an aptitude that I had previously imagined was lacking. This was pride preceding a fall. I pretended to commiserate with Maurice. Maurice was hard to find.

Then I am being clamped into the six-point harness and waiting for the first official run. This time I'm really going to give it some stick. There's a corner or two that don't seem to be quite in the same place as I'd remembered from previous laps. Basically I'm battling a medley of what I imagine to be the right lines and apexes and an armful of missed and wrong-slotted gears. I'm 5 seconds *slower*. Maurice is faster. Now he wants to talk about, 'Which gear are you in through St Mary's?' and 'How fast are you going through the left-hand kink and how many revs are you getting?'

We decide that we must be talking about two totally different circuits and I sink into the desolation of the 5 missing seconds. The 5 I've lost are far worse than the 5 I thought I had over Maurice. No wonder Formula 1 stars are like bears with a sore head on race weekend. This stuff is mind-damaging. You don't know you've got an ego until its gets dented.

I knew Ford would have a hospitality motorhome at Goodwood, and as we were 'works drivers' it had the makings of a good day. I had taken the precaution of bringing some wine in case Ford stocks ran low. They were low, all right. They didn't have *any*. Maybe this is another reason why I've changed my mind about being a racing driver. When you're a works driver, you're not allowed to drink at work. I thought I might have a surreptitious paper cup of red with my lunch when some chap cocks an eye at it and says, 'I hope that's Ribena.' I asked who wanted to know and he says, 'Me. I'm the RAC Steward of the meeting.' Of course it was Ribena. I was a racing driver. Who did he think I was – a motor racing journalist?

Formula 1 today is so intensely competitive, so hugely expensive, that teams become like warring nations, with fierce loyalties. You are either in the team or you are not. If you are not a friend you automatically become a foe and not to be trusted. As journalists we are generally grouped as everyone's foe and trusted in short measure, fed with team and sponsor propaganda. Sometimes there are pleasant personal touches that make it almost worthwhile being around race tracks for the past 35 years. Tyrrell design director Harvey Postlethwaite was taking me around the Tyrrell factory during the winter off-season and we came to a 'NO ENTRY' door. Harvey ushered me in.

'This is the new car. You shouldn't really see it, but I suppose you're "family" so it's OK.'

He probably hadn't heard the story of my visiting a much smaller Tyrrell factory one warm summer afternoon in 1970. The double doors to one of the buildings were open so I wandered over to chat to the mechanics. I wasn't aware of any nervousness but after I had been to see Ken Tyrrell I noticed that the double doors had been firmly shut. I had happened upon the top-secret new Tyrrell Formula 1 car without realising it, my minimal technical awareness not taking it on board that the car the mechanics were preparing was not, in fact, one of the off-the-shelf March 701 cars the Tyrrell team had been fielding that season, but the very first Tyrrell car!

Williams designer Patrick Head probably didn't realise that he had made my day when, after the memorial service in London for Duncan Hamilton, Le Mans winner in 1953, Patrick introduced me to his mother, saying, 'This is Eoin Young, mother. I always think of him as a gentleman journalist . . .' Makes it all worthwhile, somehow.

CHAPTER ELEVEN

Chris Amon

THE BRUCE & DENNY Show on the Can-Am sportscar series in North America could easily have been the Bruce & Chrissie Show. Chris Amon was always the nearly-man, gifted with huge natural talent but a complete inability to channel it to his advantage for any length of time. Bruce was always keen to give fellow New Zealanders a chance and Amon had all the attributes Bruce liked in his countrymen – quick, quiet and dedicated. Chris thought later that he probably enjoyed testing as much as he enjoyed racing, and as such he would have been McLaren's ideal partner if he hadn't been lured away by Ferrari with an offer he couldn't refuse in 1967. He was a member of the original McLaren team but he missed out on the glory years. Amon was like the fifth Beatle.

We shared various escapades in the 1960s, but by 1976 he had run out of enthusiasm and gone home to the farm. Years later we sat at his bar late into the night fortified only by a tot or two of medicinal whisky as he talked of his racing days.

He was 18 in 1962 and racing a 250F Maserati when he was first spotted on the New Zealand circuits by Reg Parnell. A year later he was in a Cooper on the Tasman Series and Parnell had seen enough to sign him to drive in his Formula 1 team in 1963.

'A telegram eventually arrived saying "PLEASE BE IN ENGLAND BY GOOD FRIDAY". That was ten days away but fortunately I'd had the foresight to get a passport. I arrived on the Friday evening, had a quick seat fitting, went to a local hotel and was picked up the next morning at 7 o'clock for the drive to Goodwood. By 10 o'clock I was in the car practising in the 1.5-litre Formula 1 Lola-Climax. The first Formula 1 race I saw, I was in! I finished fifth.

'It had rained a bit before the start and Reg had been telling someone about this bright young prospect from New Zealand. They had wattle screens at the chicane and Reg was just saying "And here he comes now" when I demolished them right in front of him. There was no damage and I kept on going, but his "bright young prospect" had got it a bit wrong.

'I knew Bruce and Denny then, but not very well. People forget that I was three or four years behind them. Bruce and I had talked on a couple of occasions but we had no real contact. I certainly didn't know him very well. I probably hadn't met Denny at all by then. Denny didn't socialise a lot and the same could be said for Bruce then, I suppose.'

Chris had studied motor racing from his school days and was looking forward to his first Grand Prix at Monaco where he was teamed in Parnell Lolas with Maurice Trintignant, who had won the race in 1955 and 1958.

'Trint's engine blew in the last practice session and we had no spare, so Reg told me I'd have to give Trint my car and watch the race because they had to get the starting money.'

Chris had a huge accident at Monza – he broke ribs but was lucky to survive the crash. A few weeks later Parnell sent a Lola with a 2.5-litre and a couple of mechanics to the Tasman Series for Chris.

'It was an awful car with loads of chassis flex and I still wasn't totally recovered from my Monza accident. I had driven to Auckland for the Grand Prix but when I arrived at the race office the secretary said, "Are you OK? You've heard, have you?" I didn't know what she was talking about. Reg Parnell had died suddenly in England. It was absolutely shattering news for me because he'd looked after me like a father and I'm sure we would have gone a long way together. He had already done a deal with Lotus to buy two of the ex-works monocoque Lotus 25s, and because he was great mates with Wally Hassan and Harry Spears at Coventry-Climax we were in line for good engines in 1964. We were going to have the best cars with the best engines!'

Reg's son Tim took over the team for 1964, but Reg was an impossible act to follow. It was very much an Old Boy network in those days and while Reg Parnell might have been able to open doors all the way to the top, Tim quite simply didn't have the experience. He had been dropped in the deep end.

'Tim was on a steep learning curve with a very small budget. The deal with Coventry-Climax died with Reg and we had to use BRM engines. Mike Hailwood had driven a couple of races in 1963 and we were to team together in 1964. That year Mike and I lived together in a flat in Ditton Road, Surbiton. I'd lived in Surbiton the year before in a bedsitter. I lived there at first because you told me that's where I should live.'

He laughed, remembering those days.

'When I first arrived in England I think Reg asked Bruce to organise something for me and he asked you to organise something for me . . .

My first visit to The Gloucester Arms was probably the night after I got back from that first Goodwood meeting. You and Wally Willmott said to come down for a beer. So I went down for a beer. I'd never drunk English beer before and I had four pints and I was violently ill when I got back to the bedsitter.

'Tim was running an older Lotus 24 for Peter Revson, so Revson moved in with us at Ditton Road. I think he came to stay the night and he stayed for the year! Tony Maggs was there off and on. And Bruce Harre, who was a McLaren mechanic. And Bruce Abernethy who was supposed to be my manager.'

Abernethy had been a champion speedway rider in New Zealand and he bought the charred wreckage of Phil Hill's Cooper that had burned out in the Austrian Grand Prix at Zeltweg. I can remember the chassis standing in the entrance hall at Ditton Road while Abernethy decided on the next stage of the rebuild.

Late in 1964 Chris set the wheels in motion to join McLaren. 'Tim's thing was going nowhere as far as I was concerned and I think he'd decided he didn't really need me for 1965 because Mike [Hailwood] was paying for half the team and BRM said if he ran Dick Attwood they would give him free engines. It coincided with the arrival of Firestone on the racing scene with Bruce and the deal with Peter Agg for Elva to build customer Can-Am cars. They wanted Bruce to run their Elva 2-litre sports car as well, and that's when Bruce approached me to drive the small car.'

Firestone testing in 1965 had become an important source of income for the McLaren team, and as Bruce became busier with the development of his Can-Am cars, Chris was drafted in to test drive. His dedication to a job most drivers try to avoid would lead directly to his drive with Ferrari. He had driven a GT40 Ford for Carroll Shelby at Le Mans in 1964 with Jochen Neerpasch and he was also driving Fords in 1965 when he was asked to drive the Ford GTX – nicknamed 'Big Ed' ('Big Edsel', a reference to the 1950s US Ford sedan of the same name that was a spectacular market failure) – which was an open 'spyder' version of the GT40 with an automatic transmission. For reasons never properly explained, this top-secret project for the tiny McLaren company, still based in their original Feltham workshop, was always claimed as a totally in-house US Ford effort. We had it cordoned off at the end of the workshop, but it was all the work of Gary Knutson and Howden Ganley. Why Ford wanted to claim total credit has always puzzled me because it was an abject failure, too heavy and too slow without enough power to benefit from the two-speed torque converter transmission.

'I drove it in the 1965 Can-Am series and it was a bloody disaster. It didn't go worth a damn. We had done a lot of testing with the Ferguson system in a McLaren Can-Am chassis and it used to blow engines on a regular basis. The engine was doing a lot of running at the bottom end of the rev range because of the torque convertor, and it was detonating, breaking cranks, firing rods out the side of the block. Whatever the Ford GTX had in it was either their own or an adaptation of the Ferguson system. But the car was bloody hopeless. At Riverside it was way off the pace and the Ford hierarchy told Bruce they thought I was the problem. Bruce was *really* irate about that, but they said they wanted Johnny Rutherford to have a few laps in it. If I was off the pace, Johnny was *way* off the pace. We soldiered on with it and the last race we did was in Nassau for the Speed Week.

'Bruce and I were entered in the Formula Vee race in works Beach Vees, but he was late arriving so I drove his car in one heat and mine in the other. There were 80 entries! I had the engine taken out of his car and put in mine before he arrived for the Sunday race. I disappeared at the start and won while he extricated himself from the pack to finish second. I won $10,000 for that. Bloody good money then, but McLaren director Teddy Mayer fronted up and said he wanted half. I said, "Hang on, I wasn't driving for you, I was driving it for this guy Beach." But Teddy said they'd paid my expenses to get there and drive it and the Ford thing, so I lost half my prize money . . ."'

Amon was on a Formula 1 promise with McLaren in 1966, but the programme floundered with the Indianapolis quad-cam Ford engine reduced to 3-litres at huge cost and complication, and then the Serenissima V8 as a stop-gap. Most of Amon's driving was for John Frankenheimer driving the McLaren-built camera car during the making of the movie *Grand Prix*.

Chris did Daytona and Le Mans for Ford. The 1966 Le Mans pairing with Bruce went down in racing history. 'Before Bruce got in the car for the last hour or so they told him that if things stayed as they were, they were going to arrange a winning dead heat with the Hulme/Miles Ford. Bruce and Ken Miles were told before they got in for the last stint. Denny and I were told when we got out. Then the organisers decided they weren't going to wear a dead heat, but if you look at the finish on film, Bruce made absolutely sure that it was no dead heat because he crossed the line two or three lengths ahead of Miles. The Le Mans organisers decided that as we'd started one position back from the Hulme/Miles car, we had covered more distance anyway, which was true, but coming out of that last corner Bruce made bloody sure he was in front! Ken Miles was quite upset about it, but Denny never said much that I can remember. There was no particular acrimony.'

Amon's dedication and technical ability during his Firestone testing put his name in the frame at Ferrari for 1967. He had shared the winning Ferrari at the Daytona 24-hours and the Monza 1,000 kms with Lorenzo Bandini. Bandini died when his Ferrari crashed and caught fire in the Monaco Grand Prix.

'I wanted to win Le Mans in '67 for him. He was tremendously helpful to me when I first went to Ferrari. I think it was in his nature. I knew him to say hello to when he was out on the Tasman Series, but he really didn't speak much English at that point.

'It was like going into a hornet's nest at Ferrari because there were four drivers for the two Formula 1 cars. Bandini had helped Surtees inadvertently to win the championship in '64 when he punted Graham's BRM up the back, but although Graham and the others thought it was deliberate, I doubt that it was . . . I'd raced against him. He didn't have any ulterior motives. He was just a genuinely nice guy. He was the only one in the team who really felt secure. He was more experienced and probably a notch above Mike Parkes.

'I could speak Italian, but badly. I was only there three or four months before Bandini died after the Monaco crash. He was speaking more English than I was speaking Italian. I started living in Modena from August '67, then my Italian improved a bit. It had to! At Le Mans in '67 I wanted to do well for Bandini and because Bruce and I had won the year before, but it was the year of Foyt and Gurney and the army of Mark IV Fords. We were running well up in our open P4 Ferrari around midnight when I got a puncture just after the pits and I had to try and drive the full lap with a flat rear. The problem was that the rear upright extended below the rim. I was going slowly down the straight – well, I say slowly but you're never going as slowly as you think. I was probably doing 80–100 mph in a shower of sparks. I thought the sparks were from the rim but I was actually grinding the magnesium upright down.

'We carried a ridiculous little spare so I decided I should try and change the wheel. I got my torch out and found a wheel hammer and a jack of some sort. The first problem was that the torch battery was flat so I took the wheel hammer, made a blind swipe at the knock-off and the head flew off the hammer and bounced into a ditch. All this was on the side of the Mulsanne Straight with the others going past at 200-plus! Here I was crawling around in a ditch in the middle of the night trying to find the head off this bloody hammer. I couldn't find it so I thought I'd try to carry on driving it back, but the tyre shredded and knocked a fuel line off and the whole lot went WHOOOMPH!

'I stood up in the cockpit and steered as long as I could, then baled out over the side. The car carried on, careering down a ditch and causing a bit of consternation because it stopped beside some Gendarmes who were running around with fire extinguishers but couldn't find the driver. Me. I was about 100 yards back up the track, walking towards them!

'I had a pilot flying my Twin Commanche and the next day we landed wheels-up at Fairoaks. I watched the propeller blades curl up and I had the door up and was standing on the wing while the thing was still bowling down the airstrip. It was simply reactions from the night before . . .

'Ferrari didn't go to Le Mans in 1968, and in 1969 the 312P coupé wouldn't start and I was nearly last away and coming up through the tail-enders when John Woolfe lost his Porsche 917 coming through White House corner right in front of me. He went round, hit the bank and the thing just blew apart, a ball of flame and pieces everywhere. The fuel tank came across the road and went right under my Ferrari. Everything was on fire and I was doing 170 mph with a tank full of someone else's burning fuel jammed under my car!

'It took a long time to stop but I never waited for it to stop. I couldn't see what the hell I was doing. I had my belts undone but this car had doors that opened forwards and I was trying to force it open, but as soon as I got it open the flames were coming straight in. I waited for what seemed like an eternity for the thing to slow down. I launched myself out when it was still going quite fast and Frank Gardner nearly ran me over in the road. He said he saw someone sail out of the ball of flame in front of him, while the car careered to the side of the road and burned itself out while I walked back to the pits. I was quite OK but it was a horrific shunt.

'I got on very well with Enzo Ferrari, but as I said when I arrived it was a hornet's nest with four drivers and two cars. After Bandini died he ran three cars at the Dutch and Belgian GPs for Parkes, Scarfiotti and me. Parkes had a huge accident in Belgium and by then it was too much for Scarfiotti and he pulled out. After that we ran only one car. I perhaps never had to experience the pressure within the team, and at 23 I was also younger than most drivers had been at Ferrari.

'Enzo never went to the races but he seemed quite fatherly towards me. He was a funny guy. He never discussed the races much. He'd talk about anything *but* the races. He was always very interested in his driver's romantic affairs. He was really bloody good to me. I got him into the Tasman Series but he really only did it as a favour to me. He only built a car for the Can-Am series because I wanted to do it.

'It was a very special thing for me to be at Ferrari because I'd always been a great student of motor racing history. One of the things that disappointed me was that all the old cars weren't around. There was a storage shed out the back with lots of bits of cars and I found D50 Lancia engines, the twin-cylinder GP engine and lots of old V12s. I used to spend hours there just poking around, but I wished the cars had been there too. I was always conscious of everything that had gone on there before, the history of the place. I used to pinch myself when I woke up in the morning. It was very special.

'I did a *lot* of driving, a helluva lot of testing in Formula 1, Formula 2 and sports cars. I'd be at Modena testing four or five days a week.

'It was a *huge* mistake to leave Ferrari but I'd got very disillusioned.

The new flat-12 engine was very quick but it kept breaking crankshafts. March Engineering had approached me several times and I liked the idea of getting a Cosworth engine. I really felt that my two main competitors were Stewart and Rindt and I wanted equal equipment to them, equal engines, and this was the motivation for me to move. But talk about out of the frying-pan into the fire . . .'

Amon never got to grips with Indianapolis. 'I often wished I'd stuck to the Indy thing. If I could have started the race at Indianapolis I would have probably quite enjoyed it. My first year was 1967 with George Bryant's team in what was basically the 1964 car that BRP [the British Racing Partnership] had built for Indy with Ford engines. They were off the pace but I wasn't going too badly. I never got as far as qualifying because a rear upright broke half-way round the first turn, I had a huge spin and brushed the wall. It took them several days to fix it.

'I had these two old mechanics on the team and what they didn't know about the Speedway wasn't worth knowing. I kept saying that there was something wrong with the car after they'd repaired it and it was losing me 10 mph. They said it wasn't the car, it must be me. I told Bryant to put someone else in the car to try it and he told them the same thing, so they took the monocoque apart and found a fractured pick-up point inside. So I never had a chance to qualify.

'I went to Indy with the McLaren team in 1970 but the car wasn't very good. It was quite a spooky thing to drive. Denny had been quite badly burned early in the month of May while testing and this didn't help because he was the only one who had a reasonable amount of miles in the car. I was struggling to run much faster than I'd been running three years before in the Bryant car.

'It was easy to get put off by the place, easy to get involved with other people's accidents, which was an aspect I didn't like. I was also having a difficult time with Formula 1 politics at March, so my attitude probably wasn't what it might have been. The McLaren wasn't set up, I didn't know how to set it up for the Speedway, and nobody in the team did. If I'd gone there with an experienced team and a good car, I would probably have liked Indy.

'We had to go back for the Grand Prix at Monaco. The plane out of Chicago was around 6 pm Thursday evening and the flight out of Indy was 4 pm. I ran a few laps but I was thinking more about getting to the airport and I was doing laps around 160 mph. Then I went out again and ran ten laps at 169–170 mph, which was right on the pace and I felt that I'd finally mastered the thing – the car *and* the Speedway. But when we came back from Monaco the following Tuesday I couldn't get back within 6 or 7 mph of those speeds. I don't know whether they'd left the car the same or not, or whether Teddy [Mayer] had been playing with it, but I couldn't get back on the pace.

'It was nothing to do with the speed because I went to the Belgian GP at Spa two weeks later and my fastest lap round there was 152 mph, which was only about 6 mph slower than I'd been averaging around Indy – and there was a hairpin at Spa!'

Chris was famous for the chaotic state of his personal organisation. 'I've been criticised for my decision-making, but you've got to remember that I was pretty young when I was having to make them. I might have done better if I'd started a few years later, but having started so young, by the time I was 32 or 33 I'd had enough and I was of an age that I could start doing something else; if I'd been 40 when I stopped it would have almost been too late to start another career. So my racing was almost a university thing, then I went on to do what I was supposed to do, running the farm. I still had the motivation to do something else whereas Denny didn't have that motivation to do anything else and inevitably he got bored and went back to racing. I never wanted to do that. There are times when I miss racing and I wonder about having a few laps in something, but I would never want to go back to that way of life.'

I wondered whether Chris would have enjoyed his racing more if he had been winning. His lack of luck was legendary.

'In any sport confidence is a huge factor. In 1968 and 1969, when I came out here with the Ferraris on the Tasman Series and started winning races, it got easier and easier to win then because my confidence level was up. I never had that level of confidence in Formula 1. I was running against the same people I ran against in Formula 1 but my Tasman car was competitive – it wasn't any better, but it was as good as the competition – whereas in Formula 1 it never was. The Matras were quite good in Formula 1 but the engines weren't. Matra had huge potential but they couldn't keep engines together. It was a good car. And the money was good, more than £1,000 a week, the most I'd been paid. It probably wasn't as much as Stewart was getting, but it was a lot. I got disillusioned after the 1972 season when Matra pulled out.'

He was involved with various projects that staggered and failed, including a Formula 1 car of his own, and late in 1975 he accepted a drive with the small Ensign team.

'I really subconsciously began to think that whatever I did was going to be a can of worms, and that's when I started to lose interest. I drove for Ensign in 1976 for two reasons – for personal enjoyment and because I didn't want to go out on a total down-note. Mo Nunn was running on a tight budget, we had engines that were three or four years old, but it was nice to be able to qualify in the top six and run in the top three or four. I found it quite easy to do that, but it ceased being fun because the thing fell apart all the time. By that time I was wishing I could have turned up in the morning, practised, qualified, raced in the afternoon and gone home again. It was all the standing around and the bullshit. It was starting to get to me. The glamour had gone. It was purely a job. It was time to get out.

'I enjoyed my time at Ferrari best. The Matra years were good too, but Ferrari was probably better because I was much more involved with the team, living in Modena, at the factory nearly every day, eating with the team. I really lived with them and felt very much a part of it, whereas with Matra it was a bit more remote. Ferrari got criticised for their temperamental behaviour but they were a dream to work with compared to March. I had a couple of good mechanics at March, and Robin Herd and I got on all right, but when he was with Max Mosley it was different. Even at Ensign there was a lot of niggling, financially induced because Mo was struggling all the time. I always felt there was less politics at Ferrari than in any of the teams I drove for.'

Amon is always bracketed with Bruce McLaren and Denny Hulme because they were all New Zealanders and were all racing in Formula 1 at the same time, but Chris never felt that they were an item.

'I didn't really see much of Bruce and Denny. I always felt that Bruce was disappointed when I left at the end of 1966 and went to Ferrari. I felt that we lost something there, but he was always quite friendly. I'd told Bruce that I really couldn't resist the offer from Ferrari and I think he half-way understood, but I think he was also disappointed. We lost something personal after that. It would have been great to have driven for the McLaren team in Formula 1, and I think that was Bruce's plan for me, but I think I made quite the right decision because in 1967 he was only running a 2-litre BRM and it wasn't until 1968 that he started to get it together in Formula 1. And by that time I was well established at Ferrari.'

I wondered whether he and Denny became closer after Bruce's death.

'Not really. I mean, we always used to have a chat at each race, but when I think back to 1968–69 the McLaren operation was a fairly closed shop and when you were out of it you were *really* out of it. But Bruce couldn't have been too peeved about me leaving because he asked me to do the Indy thing with him in 1970. But I wasn't a great personal mate of Denny's. From 1967 until 1972–73 I hardly lived in England anyway, and even then I still had a place in Switzerland, so I didn't have much of a chance of mixing with Bruce and Denny socially.'

The chance of a fatal accident was always present when Chris was racing. 'Apart from the shock of Jimmy's death in 1968, I think it made a lot of drivers uneasy because he was the acknowledged master and appeared to be infallible. It made everyone think, "Christ, if it can happen to him, it can happen to everyone." That year of 1968 was horrific with a driver being killed on about the 7th of each month. Jimmy on 7 April, Mike Spence on 7 May, Scarfiotti on 8 June,

Jo Schlesser on 7 July. On the seventh day of the month you weren't that keen to go out in the car . . . I'm not a greatly superstitious person but it was horrific.

'Bruce's death in 1970 was absolutely shattering. I'd spent most of the month of May with him at Indianapolis. But I've got to say quite honestly that none of those deaths made me want to stop racing. I think of necessity you build up a sort of hard buffer in your subconscious. If you didn't, you couldn't carry on racing.

'I don't class Denny's death as an accident, but it didn't make it any easier to accept. Well, I suppose it *did* really. I was happier that Denny died of natural causes. If he'd been killed I would have thought it such a tragic waste because he didn't *need* to be there. It was an insignificant race compared to what he'd done in the past.

'I was out mowing the lawn when Tish [Chris's wife] came out and said Denny had been killed at Bathurst. I carried on mowing the lawn for about 5 minutes because I couldn't get the message through, I was thinking what a huge waste and wondering what the hell had happened. Then the reports started coming through that it was a heart attack and not an accident, and I was almost relieved at that, but it was a huge shock, probably more of a shock in a way because by then my hard mental shield had dissolved a bit . . . because I wasn't involved any longer and nobody else I knew was . . .'

We had been talking about racing and the people we had known and it was now late into the night in Amon's farmhouse at Bulls in New Zealand, as far as you could get from Formula 1 but in a way encapsulating the entire period I had been in racing.

CHAPTER TWELVE

Bangers and Mash at The Barley Mow

BRICKS AND MORTAR don't make a pub. People make a pub. That quirky mix of personalities and prejudice, friendships and feuds, gossip and intrigue, together with the smell of beer and smoke that blends into the curious ambience of an English country pub, is found nowhere else in the world. The Barley Mow in West Horsley, Surrey, is like no other English pub in England, never mind the world.

It has gathered something of an international reputation as a motor racing watering hole since I realised that the barn behind it would be ideal as a base for my motoring book business. In fact, the Tyrrell team, off a country lane about a mile away, had used The Barley Mow from time to time, but it was not exactly a focal point for them.

John Woodiwiss, the landlord, *was* The Barley Mow, and if he had lived a few more months beyond his 60th birthday he would have been the longest-serving landlord of the public house since records had been kept. I liked to think he would have been ideally cast as the publican at Jamaica Inn, the pub that featured broodingly in Daphne du Maurier's novel.

It is difficult to convey accurately the appeal of The Barley Mow because any attribute described singly sounds alarmingly like a deterrent, the charm coming from the sum of its component parts. It is *so* different that Americans want to take it home as a change from their bars where you need a torch to count your change or see what you're drinking. New Zealanders succumb to the quaintness compared with their so-called taverns, which are more like the stand-up-and-down-a-bottle as featured in the movie *Once Were Warriors*.

The Barley Mow sits long and low back off a right-hand curve of The Street, so that coming from the Leatherhead–Guildford A246 Epsom Road (turn down at the garage owned by motor racers Bobby Bell and Martin Colvill) it's easy to miss. Denis Jenkinson nearly missed the turn in his Morris Minor on one of his early lunch visits and almost ran down one of the feisty elderly regulars known as The Brigadier. While Jenks was parking his car The Brig, who always walked to the pub, stormed in saying, 'Some bloody fellow nearly ran me down just then, and when I raised the matter with him, he said, "What's the matter? I missed you didn't I?"'

I hastily whispered to The Brig (aka Rodney Nicholas) that Jenks was actually quite famous in racing circles, having ridden with Stirling Moss when he won the Mille Miglia. When Jenks eventually arrived in the bar I introduced him around and The Brig greeted him a good deal more warmly than he had before.

'What's the matter with him?' Jenks muttered when we had moved around the corner of the bar. 'I nearly ran him over before, and he was *very* angry!'

The Barley Mow has been keeping husbands from their dinner for the past 400 years. St Mary's Church ran its own alehouse, The Red Lion, when a licence to keep another alehouse was lodged between 1568 and 1575, which could have been for what is now The Barley Mow. The central part of the building is the oldest and shows characteristics of a house built about 1500 or earlier. This is why the roof beams in the old section of the bar are very low. They are no problem for people of modest stature such as Roebuck, Jenks and myself, but some famous foreheads have been struck mighty blows on the low beams.

In the 17th century the pub was further modified when the back wall of the present lounge bar was rebuilt in brick to form a large inglenook fireplace. Inside the chimney breast, according to pub records, was a small chamber presumably used for smoking bacon. When the fireplace was removed after wartime bomb damage, it was thought that this may have been a priest-hole but, if it had been, the poor priest would have been half roasted in addition to being well-smoked. A hazel club was discovered in the chamber, blackened and rock solid, as it was the practice in those days to smoke timber and harden it for use as a weapon. John Woodiwiss remembers the club being in the pub when he took over in December 1967, but he thought he might have 'given it away to someone who was interested in it'. Woody never was much of a romantic.

In 1888 The Barley Mow was sold at auction together with the Queen's Head at East Clandon – the pair fetched £3,250 including their surrounding land. The sales catalogue describes The Barley Mow as consisting of a bar, bar-parlour, parlour, tap-room, cellar, kitchen, scullery, four bedrooms and a store room. The outbuildings consisted of a barn, which had formerly been a skittle alley and a malthouse before that, a four-stall stable, loose box, store room with loft, coach-house, a two-stall stable and a large garden with two sizeable meadows. The coach house had been converted from what was the original brewhouse.

The Barley Mow originally looked out over the village green, which has gradually been built over. The pub itself is listed as being of Special Architectural and Historical Interest and the huge chestnut tree in the forecourt is subject to a local Preservation Order. Mr Black always bets on when the last leaf will fall in the autumn and always loses.

Horsley is in fact spread over two villages. West Horsley is the older of the two, and East Horsley is a more modern development with parades of shops that grew up with the arrival of the London–Guildford railway line. Legend has it that after his execution, Sir Walter Raleigh's widow lived in West Horsley and kept his head in a bag by her bedside. On her death Sir Walter's head was said to have been buried in St Mary's Church.

I lived on the far side of East Horsley diametrically opposed to The Barley Mow, which may have been the reason that I never knew of its existence. However, having braved the famed belligerence of the landlord and rented the barn, it became my regular dallying place.

John Woodiwiss was a great character, a publican who subjected his customers to a continuous but calculated campaign of abuse. If you survived it you became a regular. If you didn't survive it, then it didn't matter that much to Woody anyway. It simply meant that you 'couldn't hack it' and you hadn't qualified to join the club.

When Nick Brittan, a seasoned campaigner when it came to drinking houses, first visited the pub, he came back to our house for dinner and Sandra asked him what he thought of The Barley Mow.

'It's the most amazing place,' he said. 'It's just like a gentleman's club where everybody calls each other Mister and the landlord tells everyone to eff off.'

That's pretty much the way it was and it didn't seem that unusual once you became accustomed to it. You only noticed the lack of the heavily spiced badinage when you went into just about any other pub in the country. Make that the world.

Woodiwiss had created his own world inside The Barley Mow and he made the rules. He once banned a turbaned Sikh from the bar because he said he didn't like people wearing hats in his pub. The outraged Indian made an official complaint about racial discrimination, Woody was taken to court and returned fined but unbowed. He just didn't like people wearing hats in his pub.

The Senior Regulars all had nicknames. Rodney Nicholas, as recounted, was The Brig (he was actually a Major), Aubrey Parnell, who worked for me, was always The General (because it was generally conceded that he looked and behaved like one), Charles Mortimer, who had originally worked with me in the barn, was Grandad (because he looked and behaved like one), Colin Black, formerly head of Unilever, was The Mole (because he looked like one). I was christened Ebenezer because it was popularly supposed that I was extremely careful with the money I made selling books. Mr Black always introduced me as Ebenezer, adding the footnote that 'his father is the chief Rabbi in Timaru, you know'.

This reputation for my carefulness with money always puzzles me because I consider myself something of a shopaholic with budgetary considerations along the lines of the Siamese motor racing prince, Bira. Bira, who raced ERAs pre-war, won the 1955 New Zealand Grand Prix in a 250F Maserati, then retired from racing. His affairs were managed by his royal cousin, Prince Chula, since Bira was somewhat haphazard about finances. It was said that if Chula promised his cousin £1,000 as a birthday present, Bira would dream up a variety of £1,000 items – then buy them all!

Aubrey Parnell was awarded the OBE for his services to the National Trust, and after his retirement he still served as a locum administrator while working for me. He loved his nickname of The General in the pub, but was sometimes embarrassed by it beyond The Barley Mow. As a matter of daily habit we would visit the bar of The Meridiana in East Horsley for a coffee or something a tad stronger before moving on for lunch at The Barley Mow.

The Meridiana is a full-scale Italian restaurant re-developed from the original Horsley Hotel, owned and staffed by Italians in the middle of the oh-so-Surrey village and of course staunch Ferrari fans. Tyrrell design director Harvey Postlethwaite is a popular visitor, having worked at Ferrari and being fluent in Italian. During one of his two stints at Ferrari, Harvey was being interviewed on Italian television, and one of the older Ferrari engineers, watching at his home, was nudged by his wife who said 'Listen to him! He speaks better Italian than you do!'

Aubrey was at the Meridiana bar late one morning when he was introduced as 'General Aubrey Parnell' to Horsley catholic priest Father John Sheahy. Father John, a popular Irish clergyman, was leaving when Aubrey drew him to one side and said, 'Father, I'm not really a General, you know.'

Father John smiled. 'I quite understand . . . security and all that . . .'

A Barley Mow regular always noted for 'going solo' and not buying a round is Stewart Macgregor, a Scot born in Tanganyika but educated at Dollar Academy in Scotland and from a long line of medical academics. MacGregor was Loudmouth in Barleyspeak, and at one stage, when he and the landlord had a noisy difference of opinion, he decided that we should form a splinter group and drink up the road at the King William IV pub. The first time we went there and ordered a drink at the bar, one of the 'Billy' regulars turned to his mate and said, 'Oh God, those Barley Mow wankers have arrived.'

The next day I phoned Chris Willows, PR boss at BMW, and asked him for half a dozen lapel pins. He was mystified at the request until I explained it . . .

Bearded printer Adam Taylor is 'Henry' because he looks like Henry VIII, solicitor Peter Scholes became 'PK' for Parrot Killer because he smashed an electronic Parrot that drove everyone crazy by repeating any conversation it heard. Roger Watson, the village baker, is known as 'Spot' from Spot the Jam, a reference to what is popularly perceived as a minimal amount of jam in his doughnuts. He now uses the slogan on his bakery vans . . . John Avery is known as 'Maestro' because he is a conductor and organist.

Woody liked the nicknames, mainly because he could never remember proper names. One lunchtime he sat there deep in thought and suddenly said to Valerie, 'What's what's-is-name's name?' Val told him immediately. Telepathy.

Valerie ran the kitchen and there was an eager following for her bangers and mash, regular English pub fare, but one that overseas visitors found unusually interesting. One magazine in New Zealand helped its readers by explaining that 'the dish consisted of fried sausages, mashed potatoes, baked beans and fried onions'.

New Zealand photographer Euan Sarginson visited the pub while he was holidaying in Britain, and I introduced him to Woody the first time we went in. The second time we went in, Woody said "Ullo, Hugo.' Euan was flabbergasted – Hugo was his father's name. But Woody thought Sarge's beard reminded him of Victor Hugo, so he was Hugo for the rest of his holiday.

Woodiwiss never drank beer. Vodka was his tipple. In heroic amounts when the spirit moved him. Which was fairly frequently. He served several different brands of beer, but when asked which he recommended he would likely as not say, 'None of them. Go up the road to the "Billy".' This was one of his ways of weeding out people who were liable to linger over a half pint and get in the way of his conversations with his regular 'club' members.

When I first went into the pub it was divided across the middle into a saloon bar (carpeted) and a public bar with a flagstone floor. Then the wall came down and the bar became one, but still with the carpet as the demarcation line. There was a strong contingent of builders, roofers, carpenters and labourers in what was later called Construction Corner who prized their right to be abused by the landlord. It didn't happen at other pubs and it was regarded as an official measure of appreciation.

One evening one of the labourers said to me, 'Do you know what I like best about this pub? It's that people like you talk to people like me . . .'

With Woody's death in May 1994 his legendary badinage and professional rudery was sadly missed. Brian Miller took over the bar, having recently retired from running his own pub nearby, and it was generally considered that if we couldn't have Woody, Miller was an OK replacement and he continued the Woodiwiss style of outrageousness.

I had always imagined that if I stopped covering every Grand Prix the journalistic side of my business would come unravelled, but I soon found that I was doing what many of the regular old hands on the Formula 1 treadmill wished they could do, but were unable to. To generate some column material over a race weekend when I didn't go to a race, I staged a Not The So-and-so Grand Prix Lunch and invited a group of racing people not directly involved in the race that weekend. The lunches soon became more entertaining than the Formula 1 races that were on television during that summer. Stirling Moss, Tony Brooks, John Cooper, Gordon Murray, Pink Floyd drummer Nick Mason, trad jazz man Chris Barber and others enjoyed the bangers and mash and the motor racing gossip. The lunches on Grand Prix Fridays worked so well that we staged some in the off-season, and James Hunt was a regular.

At one of these lunches James was sitting next to Ken Tyrrell, and Ken had been particularly annoyed at the savaging James had given one of the Tyrrell drivers in his BBC TV commentary with Murray Walker.

'Sometimes, James,' Ken said with a slight edge to his voice, 'it would pay you to keep your mouth shut.'

James beamed at him. 'Oh, I couldn't agree more, Ken. The problem is that the BBC pays me to keep it open . . .'

If one of the group had a special car we would take a group photograph around it after lunch. James had arrived in his Austin A35 Countryman, a tiny late-1950s estate car, which James, in his straitened financial situation, loved driving.

'You can get it on the limit so easily. If you drove a Porsche or a BMW to the same limit you'd be arrested!'

I asked James if he would care to bring the A35 round to the front of the pub, thinking he would demur, that it wasn't quite the wheels expected of a superstar. He was delighted and the group shot was taken with the A35 sitting in pride of place.

Denny Hulme visited the pub when he was in England and was surprised one lunchtime when a chap with a group of strangers at the bar came over and said, 'This is really an extraordinary coincidence but I've just been telling my friends that you look just like the racing driver Denis Hulme.' Denny gave him his big grin and said that's because he was.

At one stage *Autocar* ran a series of one-on-one interviews, which they ran under a special 'Bangers and Mash at The Barley Mow' logo like a pub sign. Ron Dennis, Harvey Postlethwaite, John Barnard, Patrick Head and Lord Hesketh all had the pub treatment. So did Indianapolis winners Bobby Rahal and Al Unser Jnr, brought down on different occasions by Roebuck's friend, American race reporter Gordon 'GK' Kirby.

When Haynes decided to re-publish *Bruce McLaren, The Man and his Racing Team*, the pub seemed an ideal venue for a launch. So on 2 June 1995 Patty McLaren, Ron Dennis, Howden Ganley and Tyler Alexander joined my table as the new and old McLaren team, together with Allan Dick, editor of the New Zealand *Driver* magazine. John Cooper and Ken Tyrrell were sitting together. Ron made a speech remembering Bruce as the man who gave his name to the team Ron now heads, then John Cooper and Ken Tyrrell said a few words about the quiet young man who had raced for their teams. Both were near tears with shaky speeches, and there were lumps in several throats. It was the most moving occasion the room had seen.

John Cooper told the story of the 1959 American Grand Prix, the final race of the season when the main contenders for the world title were Tony Brooks in a Ferrari and Jack Brabham in a Cooper. Brooks was sitting across the room at the lunch hearing the story of the championship he didn't win for the umpteenth time. Brabham didn't win the race either. Bruce McLaren did. But Brabham won the title.

The Barley Mow was a favourite lunchtime haunt for the burly bearded Tyrrell designer George Ryton, team manager Rupert Mainwaring and design head Harvey Postlethwaite. The subject one day was diets. George and Rupert had taken a wager on the amount of weight they could lose before the start of the season at Phoenix. That evening I was thinking I should lose a few ugly pounds and join them in their diet, but apart from muscling in, I couldn't see a diplomatic way of doing it. The next day Rupert said that they had found a new recruit for their diet. I asked who it was and he said, 'You.'

We each wrote a cheque for £500 and gave them to Harvey Postlethwaite to place in the Tyrrell safe. This was serious combat dieting with so much money at stake. I tried the diet meals available in supermarkets, but I could see how you could lose weight eating them – they tasted so awful that there was no way you could enjoy them. I stopped drinking. Well, nearly. I decided that I would have only one glass of wine a day and that with dinner in the evening. I found the biggest wine glass I could (naturally) and gradually watered it with a large bottle of mineral water so that it lasted through the meal, becoming weaker and weaker.

It seemed that the daily minimum number of calories a man should have was 1,500, for a woman 1,000. I decided to tailor my own diet and aim for a maximum of 1,200 calories. I shopped at Marks & Spencer for the ready-made meals that carried the 'Less Than 300 Calories' stickers. This probably wasn't in any of the accepted guides on controlled diets but it worked fine for me, the meals were great and I was shedding pounds with surprising ease.

After a fortnight George's robust shape didn't seem to be diminishing, and in the pub Brian Jackson asked him how many pounds he had lost.

'Five hundred,' said George on his way through to the restaurant . . .

The day the bet was made we had all weighed ourselves on Woody's bathroom scales, and to our joint surprise Rupert and I weighed exactly the same, so there could be no suggestion that either of us could cheat, although I'm certain we both must have explored the possibilities. I know I did and I'm *sure* Rupert would have. I never saw Rupert from the day of the weigh-in, but I had reports that he was working hard on his weight reduction. I was doing so well that I was being told to stop if I started feeling dizzy! You can't believe how appallingly righteous and fit you feel when you don't drink and you watch your weight instead of having other people watch it for you.

The date of the season-opening US Grand Prix at Phoenix and our diet deadline was drawing closer, but I had decided to go out to New Zealand instead of going to the race, so I phoned Rupert and suggested that we have our weigh-in before he left for Phoenix. This may have been the break Rupert was seeking. He said he was too busy in the lead-up to the race and we would have to do it *after* Phoenix. Did he know that I was going to New Zealand and wouldn't be back for weeks? I'd had enough of dieting by now and I had decided that I felt so good it was already worth my £500 wager, but I thought I should see it through if only to see how close I could run Rupert for the cash.

I wish I had had my camera ready to take a photo of the look on Rupert's face as I walked into the Tyrrell pit garage at Phoenix. It was a mix of shock and horror topped off with a measure of intense annoyance. We set up a pair of the scales the team used for weighing each corner of the car, and I stepped on, fairly certain that Rupert must weigh less since he had put so much effort into it. He was fairly certain about it as well. I forget what my weight was, but it all depended on whether Rupert weighed less. I was sure he would. He stepped on and he was a pound or so heavier. He couldn't believe it, and nor could I! He started stripping his shirt and taking his trainers off, but I pointed out that I could do that as well. Not to put too fine a point on it, Rupert had *lost*. I had lost 30 pounds weight and won 1,500 pounds cash.

I flew on to New Zealand for a few weeks and came back to claim my thousand pounds profit. George and Harvey thought it was a good deal funnier than Rupert, and I found out why at the British Grand Prix in July. At the Tyrrell motorhome I was introduced to Rupert's wife, and she gave me to understand that she definitely didn't think our diet competition was a matter for levity. It seems that Rupert had forgotten to tell her about the bet and the first she knew about it was when the bank statement arrived . . . Oops.

A group of Tyrrell team people arrived at The Barley Mow one lunchtime late in 1994 with a fair-haired young man I didn't recognise, but he seemed to have that confidence, that bounce in his step, that marked him out as a young racing driver. It happened to be a Wednesday when Nigel Roebuck was due in for lunch, so it probably wasn't the smartest thing the Tyrrell people could have done if they wanted their new young driver to stay a secret. They could have fooled me – they'd done it on a number of occasions – but when Roebuck arrived I whispered, 'Who's that blonde kid at the Tyrrell table? He looks as though he might be a driver.'

Roebuck glanced over and said, 'If you don't know, I'm not going to tell you.'

He had been in Japan for the GP and knew that it was the new young Finn Mika Salo who was driving for Lotus in the last races of the season, and Tyrrell were anxious to sign him for 1995. I weasled the name out of Roebuck and went over to introduce myself. He was politeness personified. The Tyrrell people looked slightly uncomfortable. What we didn't realise was that Salo went outside with his mobile phone and called his manager, Mike Greasley. 'Grease' told me later that Mika had said, 'I think I've blown it. The team have taken me to a pub and there are a couple of journalists there.'

Greasley had finished the conversation for his protégé: 'Don't tell me, the pub is The Barley Mow and the journalists were Young and Roebuck.'

Salo thought his manager must be psychic.

CHAPTER THIRTEEN

The Grand Prix generation chasm

IN THE LATE 1960s I wrote a monthly distillation of my weekly *Autocar* column for the American monthly *Road & Track*, and on the way to the Chrysler Grand Prix at Palm Springs recently, I visited the magazine for old time's sake. Laurence Edscer and I went to lunch with some of the old hands, Dennis Simanitis, Joe Rusz and Jonathan Thompson, and naturally talked about the way Formula 1 was today and the way it used to be when I was writing for them.

'One thing's for sure about Damon Hill,' said Thompson as we were driving back to the office. 'He isn't enjoying Formula 1 as much as his father did . . .

I thought that about summed it up in a sentence. Not so much a generation gap as a chasm.

I can't imagine Damon allowing himself to be in a position where he would crash off a table in a night club and stab the broken stem of a glass through his leg causing a wound severe enough that he needed hospital treatment. His father Graham was up on the table and running down it to get to the stripper on the stage when one of the tables collapsed. Were those the days? I think they were. It was one of the annual 'Filth Nights' organised by '50s racer Cliff Davis. They were always a sell-out. If you were able to get a ticket you counted yourself one of the racing establishment. The whole evening was in the worst possible taste and everyone loved it. The bread rolls where in the shape of a chap's wedding tackle. The strippers were *hideous* and they received rapturous applause.

I look at Formula 1 today and think how incredibly lucky I was to be around in the early 1960s. I'm not knocking modern Formula 1, I'm just saying that it is so totally different in every aspect that it defies comparison. The drivers of the 1960s look at Formula 1 today and they find it hard to take on board the blunt face of commercialism in the modern Grand Prix paddock, the huge transporters and motorhomes, several to each team, the amount that sponsors pay their teams, the size of the retainers paid to the top drivers, the size of the press corps, the enormity of the international television audience, the coverage in the daily press as well as the specialised magazines, the petty public bickering between the drivers, the questionable tactics on the track.

If you want to lay blame – or praise, depending on how you look at it – at the feet of one man, that one man is Bernard Charles Ecclestone. He has his critics, but I'm not one of them. Grand Prix racing is now the most popular action sport in the world, transcending the national boundaries of football, baseball, ice hockey and cricket. I have watched him from the days when he was Jochen Rindt's manager. Before that the trawler skipper's son had raced Cooper 500s, worked for the Gas Board, sold second-hand cars, managed GP driver Stuart Lewis-Evans, bought Connaught GP cars at the team's winding-up auction and campaigned them. There were a lot of downs in those days and now he is up. Up so high he's almost out of sight. He is reported to earn £30 million a year, and he still lives in London and pays British taxes. He is President of the Formula One Constructors Association and Director of Marketing for the FIA. The man who rates the top 500 richest men in Britain reckons Bernie earns a pound a second!

'I'm doing the job in the best way I can. So maybe I upset a few people on the way. Make a few people happy, make a few people unhappy, but that's how it is.'

Bernie may be rich beyond the imagination of the team managers that he has made rich beyond their own imaginations, but you will hear few complaints in the modern Formula 1 paddock. Performance is hugely rewarded. Ecclestone is said to have been the promoter who singlehandedly brought Formula 1 racing from the sports pages to the front pages, but I think he did it the other way round. In the 1960s the biggest Fleet Street dailies sent a man to a Grand Prix only to cover a crash. If it was a major accident it would be worth a front-page spread. If there was a crash-free weekend they would take a paragraph from their man at the track or simply list the results from the wire services. Now every major newspaper in Europe has a specialist writer at each race plus the main television coverage from each country. Four or five hundred media people crowd each race to the point where a one-on-one interview with a top driver has to be arranged well in advance with the team's media representative – if you are lucky! The majority have to make do with the press conferences.

All of the above have combined to create a situation where a top driver becomes a prisoner of his success to the point where he has to protect his private time, then earns a reputation as being big-headed and stand-offish. Some drivers didn't have to go that far out of their way to be big-headed.

Nigel Mansell came into Formula 1 with a *Boys Own Paper* hero background and somehow managed to turn it on himself. He had scrimped and saved and mortgaged his house to race, and broke his back and his neck on the way to his first Formula 1 drive with Lotus. And his battle was only just beginning. He had his champions in journalist Peter Windsor and team manager Peter Collins, but he would always say there were those who were implacably against him. Peter Warr, the Lotus team manager, is one who earns Mansell's major hate award. When Mansell left Lotus at the end of 1984, it was Warr who announced that Mansell would never win a Grand Prix 'as long as I have a hole in my arse.' Alan Henry observed in *Autocar* that, 'At that time, as I recall, he was not alone in advancing this somewhat colourful theory.'

Mansell was a fantastic driver, but as soon as he stepped out of the car he managed to regularly shoot himself in the foot. Both feet at times. He didn't seem to be able to help himself. He would drive an absolutely blinding race to win, then make some asinine comment in the press conference that had the journalists of the world shaking their heads in bewilderment at the way this man whom they had watched handling his car so brilliantly for two hours could handle himself so badly in a few minutes afterwards. The media didn't understand his clumsy attempts at humour, and in the end they didn't *want* to understand them. Aware that the tide was turning against him, and unwilling to believe it was anything *he* had done, Mansell would turn on the press.

In his book *My Autobiography* he says, 'Outside of the publicity you have to put up with, there are many levels of life and experience and although it's irritating, I don't ever let it put a large cloud over my life. In any case I have also had the pleasure of working with a great many professional journalists, who I am sure despair of the dross written by their low-life counterparts as much as we sportsmen and women do.'

In his review of the book, Henry writes, 'Understandably Nige has a pop or two at the press, asking what critical journalists know about driving Grand Prix cars at 200 mph. This is about as valid as saying art critics are useless because they can't slosh the Dulux with sufficient flair to make the potting shed look like the Sistine Chapel.'

Unless you are bigger than the game, you don't shout at the captain. Not if you expect to play again. He was hired to drive the 1995 McLaren-Mercedes in a move that appeared to make no sense to anyone with the exception of Mansell's bank manager. At the launch of the new car and the new team, Mansell kept saying that if the car went as well as it looked it was going to be a great season. The car was on display almost standing on its nose, which turned out to be the *only* angle from which it did look good.

Ron Dennis was endlessly on record during previous seasons as saying that he didn't understand Nigel Mansell and would never hire a driver he didn't understand. Somehow Ron had begun to understand. Nobody else could understand any part of the deal, and we speculated how long this shotgun marriage would last. The answer was not much longer than the honeymoon.

In his autobiography Mansell gets the boot in early: 'When you've won 31 Grands Prix, and two world titles, your tolerance threshold is that bit lower. You know straight away when you're in a bad car and you have a pretty good idea how much work needs to be done to make it competitive. I realised it [the new McLaren MP4/10B] was a bad car the first day I drove it in testing at Estoril.'

And later: 'When I joined McLaren, I really believed that the team was something special, but in fact they were no different from the other teams I had driven for – Williams, Ferrari and Lotus – in that they are not infallible and they make mistakes. There is no magic ingredient to get things right. It requires sheer determination and hard work and the right people making the right decisions regarding equipment to put on the car. What I found to my dismay was that some of the people in the McLaren team hadn't a clue what to do about the problems.'

In addition, the cockpit was too small for him. End of marriage. And with the publication of his autobiography the end of his career in racing.

Ron Dennis replied with wry diplomacy: 'It is sad that he [Mansell] should put not only myself and this company, but many other companies he has driven for, into a position where they have to make a choice as to whether to highlight his own weaknesses or let the moment pass. I believe that it is better to be bigger and more professional than he has obviously chosen to be, and it is better to let him have his say . . .'

The pit lane joke about Mansell being an ideal driver if there was a way of hermetically sealing him inside the car for the duration of the weekend wasn't a press quote. It came from his own team. I wonder whether this was why Mansell signally failed to give the credit due to his team and car when he had the best car and was on his way to winning the world championship. On the way back from the Hungarian Grand Prix, where Mansell clinched the title for Williams, I seemed to be the only journalist not applauding the new British champion. I didn't want to be hypocritical, so I wrote what I thought and sent it down the line by modem to *Autocar* to print that week. The next morning I phoned the editorial office to make sure the copy had arrived safely. They said if they'd known I was going to write a column like that they would have streamered it on the cover! That week it was the only word to suggest that perhaps the new king had no clothes. I reprint the column in part because within months the tide was turning and those who had stood highest and clapped loudest in Hungary were having second thoughts:

'I watched the fastest driver in the best car finish second to Ayrton Senna's McLaren in the Hungarian Grand Prix on Sunday and clinch the 1992 Driver's F1 World Championship. Which really says it all if you are of a cynical turn of mind.

'I reckon Nigel Mansell is the fastest driver in F1 today and his Williams-Renault is, by a country mile, the class car of the season. It's just that Nigel won't acknowledge the fact that that car is the major reason he is luxuriating in finally capturing the championship that has eluded him for so long.

'If you doubt that the Williams is the best car, I can only refer you to the fact that Mansell's team-mate Patrese simply sailed away into a huge lead before spinning.

'But I feel sorry for Mansell. Why, oh why, did he have to make a clown of himself and twist his Canon cap backwards when he was being interviewed by BBC television about becoming world champion? He demeans himself and the title. He is a man respected but not liked by his peers and he is currently painting himself into a corner within his team.

'To the public Mansell is a popular hero, the F1 equivalent of Gazza, and a similar army of fans are beginning to follow him if his Silverstone victory is anything to go by (when the crowds spilled over on to the track at the end of the race).

'At the wheel, Mansell is incredibly quick, a driver of immense bravery and self-taught skills, but he is without the essential finesse of a Senna or a Prost – in or out of the car.

'There is a parallel with Jackie Stewart and Jochen Rindt for readers whose memories stretch back to 1969 and 1970. Rindt was faster but Stewart was better, and yet they were neighbours in Switzerland and the best of friends off the track. So Grand Prix racing has changed since then and massive sponsorship has brought pressures Stewart or Rindt could never have dreamed of, but Mansell lacks innate charm. There are jokes about him surviving a charisma bypass and talk in the pit lane that he's the most, if not the first, unpopular world champion.

'James Hunt, the last British World Champion in 1976, endeared himself to few people outside his own gang by acting the public schoolboy hooligan and refusing to toe the sponsor's party line: sneakers with dinner jacket, that sort of thing. I never liked Hunt's antics, yet I wrote a book with him at the end of his title season and he is now an entertaining Barley Mow lunch guest.

'I can't see this happening with Mansell. Even Frank Williams said that he never had the same fond memories of Nigel during his first stint at Williams that he had for Alan Jones or Keke Rosberg. And here is the renegade back in the fold and winning the title.

'After winning race after race in the Lotus Type 72 in 1970, Rindt used to say that "a monkey could win in my car". The new champion loses points in my book by seldom apportioning credit where it is due.

'Perhaps I suffer from a generation gap. Comparisons with the past are seldom worth exploring, but my first full Formula 1 season was in 1962 when Graham Hill won the title. As Hill did at the time, there have been British champions since who carried the sport's crown with polished aplomb. May I hope that Nigel Mansell will try to emulate them?'

Mansell had the equipment to be a British champion in the Graham Hill mould: a moustache. What he lacked was the mechanism behind it. While Graham had the sparkle to be a personality, Nigel struggled to raise a titter from anyone who didn't wear big boots and drink pints of lager. Graham was a true 'Personality' in the BBC Sports Personality sense of the word. The sad postscript is that Nigel Mansell didn't measure up to the meaning of the award when he won it, and even more unfortunately, neither did Graham's son Damon. Don't get me wrong. I'm not tarring Damon with the Mansell brush. I'm saying that Damon is a nice guy but that's not enough. Maybe in today's high-dollar Formula 1 rat-race there is no way of pleasing everyone. Mansell went too far; Damon doesn't go far enough.

You can say it was easy for Graham and Jackie Stewart to wow the television audience with their antics in the 1960s because there wasn't the money about then and being serious hadn't become important, but to believe that is to miss the point entirely. In the 1960s Graham and Jackie were among the highest-paid racing drivers in the business, and their business was beating each other on the track, but there was still room in their routines for them to be people. You can look back and scoff at the difference between the money then and the money now, but in terms of the money then they were Schumachers and certainly not complaining about their remuneration.

But if you feel I am being unfair to Nigel Mansell, let him have the last word, again from his book: 'It annoys me when I read that I do not have the natural talent of a Senna or a Prost and that "I made myself" a great driver. Firstly you cannot run with, let alone consistently beat, guys like that unless you have as much talent and, secondly, I have the satisfaction of knowing that two of the sport's greatest figures, Colin Chapman of Lotus and Enzo Ferrari, both considered me to be one of the most talented drivers they had ever hired. Their opinions speak for themselves.'

Not a lot you can say about the man after that. Certainly the folks he quotes aren't in a position to query them.

Stuart Turner, the polished after-dinner speaker who masterminded the competition departments at BMC, Castrol and Ford in his time, told a joke at a British Racing Drivers' Club dinner about Jackie Stewart in the back of a London taxi.

'He could see that the taxi driver kept glancing at him in the mirror, recognising him as someone he should know, obviously with the name on the tip of his tongue but unable to remember it. This went on until they arrived outside Grosvenor House in Park Lane and Jackie paid the fare. Just as he was going up the steps, the taxi driver shouted out, "I've remembered who you are – you're Nigel Mansell!" Jackie spun on his heel and said firmly, "I am *not* Nigel Mansell." The taxi driver shouted back, "Bet you wish you were!"'

Perhaps the motor racing media are responsible for fanning embers of discontent into a roaring feud like the one that blazed between Damon Hill and Michael Schumacher in 1994 and 1995. Then there is the suggestion that perhaps Bernie Ecclestone was sitting back happily as the feud made news every second weekend. There were those who wondered whether Bernie, if not orchestrating the situation in the first place, was content with the results. When a decision on the continued clashes between Schumacher and Hill was demanded from the FIA, Max Mosley ruled that they should act like the adults they were supposed to be and basically they should sort it out themselves. The inference was that the FIA was responsible for a major international professional sport, not a nursery.

Juan Manuel Fangio represented all that was noble about Grand Prix racing, and when he died in 1995 the sport lost a statesman. He must have chuckled at some of the antics of the modern brigade of Grand Prix drivers. Ask any of the older generation of racing people who were honoured to meet Fangio and they all remember his eyes. They probably weren't able to chat other than through an interpreter because he spoke only Spanish, with enough Italian and German to cope with living and racing in those countries, but there was always his gentle smile and those deep eyes. Today all that has changed. If you aspire to success in racing, you have to speak English. In Fangio's day the focus of Grand Prix racing was continental with Alfa Romeo, Ferrari, Maserati, Lancia and Mercedes.

Tributes to the great man after his death mentioned the manner in which he left the fee section of his contract with Alfa Romeo blank because he regarded it as an honour to race for the company. This may come as a surprise to a generation brought up on world champions who demand millions for their signatures on contracts, but John Cooper remembers the no-fee days, saying that Jack Brabham drove for no retainer when he won the world championship in 1959. In 1960, when he won again, Cooper paid him nothing.

'The drivers got 50 per cent of the starting money and 40 per cent of the prize money. The mechanics got 10 per cent.'

Cooper remembered Fangio coming to Goodwood to drive the BRM V16 and being disappointed when the car failed, so John offered him a Cooper Bristol drive, which he accepted as something to do that afternoon. No managers, no contracts, no pack-drill.

One of the most famous racing photographs shows Fangio's 250F Maserati in a four-wheel drift in the downhill swoops after the pits at Rouen. Cooper recalls clambering down to a vantage point to get a photograph of this awesome sight. This was long before the days of the autofocus camera, and John was setting up his equipment for the shot when Fangio spotted him on the side of the track and waved in the middle of his trademark polished power drift.

'The great thing about him is that he won five world titles in four different cars and he never had a row with anyone.'

Stirling Moss remembered his old team-mate in his address at Fangio's memorial service in London. This was a serious Stirling speaking from the heart.

'We are here to remember *our* hero, *my* friend Juan Manuel Fangio of Balcarce. He was five times world champion, but he was much more than that – he was a very *special* man. My first memory of him was at Bari in June 1950. Lance Macklin and I were in Formula 2 HWMs in a Formula 1 race, underpowered cars but British Racing Green on the Continent. We were soon lapped by the Alfettas, and Nino Farina, a tough man at the best of times, cut me off and I had to brake. But he went too wide and I re-passed him at the exit. Fangio was following in another Alfetta, and when he passed me he looked across and gave me a smile as though to say, "That was a cheeky move – but I liked it!"

'I got to know Fangio well in 1955 when we were both driving for Mercedes. He allowed me to follow him, to study his style, his lines and his tactics. Team manager Neubauer wasn't keen on this. He was worried that we might crash. I saw Fangio's amazing stamina in the Argentine Grand Prix. He drove the 96 laps to win in terrible heat when every other car that finished was shared between two or even three drivers just to make it to the line.

'In 1956 in Cuba I experienced his kindness. We were checking in to the Lincoln Hotel when a Castro-ite appeared with a .45 automatic and said he was kidnapping us. Fangio said he would go with them but would they leave me because I was with my wife and it would spoil our holiday!

'In 1957 I witnessed his virtuosity at the 'Ring. He was in the 250F Maserati and had decided on a one-stop race. He stopped on the 12th lap of the 22-lap race with a 28-second lead, but he had problems in the pits and when he went out again he was 48 seconds down. He lowered the lap record *ten times* and passed Pete and Mike on the way to winning the race. He went on to win his fifth world championship that season, having driven four different makes. He started in 51 GPs and won 24 of them for an amazing win ratio of 47 per cent!

'I have written down a few words that may help to remind us of this remarkable man and some of his qualities.

'Humility. His father was a stone mason, he was a humble man who came from an ordinary background, yet he fitted in, in any company. Despite the international fame and stature he achieved he remained a modest man and was never egotistical or pompous.

'Respect. I have never known a person in any walk of life who commanded such respect. Maybe this mirrored the courtesy that he showed others. He treated all those he met, from the highest to the lowest, with equal dignity and importance. When he was talking to you, *you* were the only one who mattered.

'Kindness. He never said anything unkind about anyone, not his mechanics, not other competitors. Not even about his cars. But then it wasn't just his words. His actions spoke far louder. How many people, given a private audience with the Pope, would share such an honour with a little boy he had just met in Milan?

'Loyalty. He never forgot those who helped him. He remained devoted to his family, his friends and the town of Balcarce. His museum there bears testimony to this.

'Aura. He had an amazing presence, stature and dignity wherever he went – you could *feel* it around him.

'Simpatico. He was such a *gentle* man. You know, I was never able to speak to him – not even one sentence – in his language, nor did he to me, but we understood each other and there was great warmth between us.

'I think that helps to sum up the person we are here to remember, the man we all respected, the man I loved – Juan Manuel Fangio of Balcarce.'

James Hunt was the first driver I really disliked. It was, I suppose, a result of me being a member of the establishment, schooled in manners and diplomacy by Bruce McLaren, and if James specialised in anything apart from driving very fast, it was tweaking the nose of the establishment. He flatly refused to conform. He had surfed into Formula 1 on the foaming Hesketh champagne wave. The portly young Lord Hesketh had come up through the proper schools, so he knew *how* to behave. It amused him to see the outrage in the paddocks of the world when he arrived with his helicopters and Rolls-Royces.

James was his perfect driver. When the Hesketh team withdrew from Formula 1, James was ideally placed when Emerson Fittipaldi announced that he was leaving the McLaren team. Teddy Mayer was a member of the establishment brigade and James Hunt probably didn't come very high on his list of prospective drivers; it was rather as Nigel Mansell would come to McLaren 20 years later. Hunt's advantage was that he was the *only* available driver with any form, and Marlboro were happy to have him aboard. Mayer and Hunt rode an uneasy alliance that stormy season of 1976, which ended in Japan with an enraged Hunt shouting abuse at Mayer at the end of the race in which he had clinched the world championship. James was under the impression that Mayer had given him wrong pit-signals that lost him the championship – instead of winning it for him!

The Sunday after that wet race in Japan I was back in East Horsley when the telephone rang just before lunch. It was a publisher who said he had James Hunt in his office and wanted to know if I would be interested in writing a book with James on his championship. I said I wouldn't. Surprised, the publisher wanted to know why. I said I thought writing books was a chore, there wasn't enough money in it, and besides I didn't like James Hunt. There was a long pause, then the publisher said he thought he might be able to do something about the money. He offered £3,500. To me in 1976 that was a king's ransom. But there was a catch. The book had to be completed in two weeks and James would be at his home in Marbella during that fortnight. I asked him to phone back after lunch.

My wife Sandra agreed that it was worth me being away for 14 days to earn that much money. When the publisher phoned back for my decision I took a deep breath and said his fee wasn't high enough. He immediately increased it by £1,000 and I immediately accepted.

Daughter Selina seems to have inherited the idea that the first offer is never enough. She won a UK national competition for writing and illustrating a children's book. The prize was a cheque and a contract to publish her next book. She went up to London for a meeting with the publisher and when she came home I asked what she was being paid for the second book. She said they had offered £1,000. Thinking this was great for a teenager at the start of her writing career, I congratulated her. She looked puzzled. I asked what she had said.

'I told them I could make more money than that stacking shelves in Waitrose!'

And what did they say to that?

'They said come back and see us next week.'

She was offered £2,000 at the next meeting. Then she decided to get an agent to handle the financial side while she did the creating.

I flew to Malaga and James had booked me into the Marbella Club. We talked and taped in the mornings and I transcribed and wrote in the afternoon and into each evening. So much for the delights of Marbella. I never saw more than the walls of my room. To try and speed the process James arranged for an English secretary to transcribe the tapes. I told her I wanted to know exactly what James said, not what she thought he said. It was taking me an hour to transcribe a tape, but this poor girl had spent an entire morning on one tape and phoned in tears to say she had only transcribed two pages.

'What's the problem?' I asked, puzzled.

'He *never* completes a sentence. I have *no* idea what he's talking about.'

When I listened to a tape I was working on I realised she was right. I had been automatically finishing the sentences for him, the way I did with Bruce McLaren and Denny Hulme when I used to do their columns.

Seven days after signing the contract I was back in London with the completed manuscript. The deal had been one-third payment on signing the contract, one-third on delivery of manuscript and the final payment on publisher's acceptance. The book was completed so quickly that I had received all the money while my solicitor was still trying to unravel the contract. I told him not to bother. Then the problems arose.

David Benson of the *Daily Express* had written an instant book on Hunt's title season and 'our' publishers panicked. They took the decision not to go head-to-head against the other book, which had the backing of the newspaper, even though our book was by the champion himself. I had a funereal phone call from the publisher to say that they were desperately sorry but they were delaying publication until the following year. I was on a lump-sum deal without royalties, so it really wasn't my problem. I had done my bit. The book was now their problem.

Early in the New Year I had a phone call from Peter Hunt, James's brother and manager, saying that the book now had a new publisher and they wanted three more chapters to update it – a chapter on James's early life and a chapter after the Argentine and Brazilian GPs. No problem, I said. Fifteen hundred pounds each chapter and I'm your man.

There was a pause. Peter said, 'Eoin, I'm afraid your contract commits you to supplying copy to publisher's acceptance and the publisher wants three more chapters.'

I asked if he had a copy of the contract with my signature on it, and I could hear him rustling through files. 'I think my copy must be a working copy. It doesn't have any signatures on it,' he said. I told him if he could find a copy of the contract with my signature on it I would be happy to do the final three chapters for nothing, knowing full well that he wouldn't because I had never signed the contract in the first place. I'd just written the book in record time before the contract had been cleared by my legal man. At my suggestion, and with James's agreement, the book was titled *Against All Odds* and the final chapters were written by David Hodges.

Working with James on the book I had been able to see the other side of him, a serious side if there was such a thing, or at least a different side from the one he displayed when he was 'showing off', as my mother used to put it if I was misbehaving at home in the colonies.

We must have reached something of a personal accord because at the Belgian Grand Prix in 1979 I was lunching with guests at the Elf motorhome when an emissary from the Wolf team arrived to say that James Hunt wanted to talk to me. I suggested that he might tell James he was welcome to join us for lunch. The emissary looked nervous. James had said it was important. On the way to the motorhome I was wondering what I could have written that would have resulted in a private carpeting in the team motorhome. I was ushered through to the personal Hunt quarters and he was sitting at the table smoking and looking very serious.

'You're the only person I can trust in the paddock and what I am going to discuss with you is *extremely* confidential. I'm going to quit. I'm announcing my retirement from Formula 1 at Monaco and I want you to handle the arrangements.'

And this is from the driver I couldn't abide.

I said, 'Now James, hang on a minute. Can we pretend you never told me that and I'll leave now because I don't want any part in this.'

Eventually we agreed that I would come to his hotel that evening after dinner and he would tell me what he had in mind. Our usual evening on a race weekend was for 'The Cartel' to have dinner that would stretch into coffees and a liqueur or so. When I announced that I was slipping away straight after dinner they demanded to know where I was going and why. They said they would follow me. They didn't.

James, myself and his then girlfriend, Jane Birbeck, retired to their room so that James could go through all the reasons why he wanted to stop doing what he was best at. Jane's nickname was Hottie, an abbreviation of her original nickname bestowed by James, Hotloins. Having a dizzy blonde on board for this exercise didn't bode well, but Jane was a good deal more in command of the situation than James was. A very sensible, down-to-earth young lady. Dizzy she definitely wasn't. I came to wonder what she was doing with an off-the-wall cove like James.

Basically James was scared, but scared in a rational sort of way. He had weighed his chances of winning in the Wolf against the chances of having an accident trying to stay on the pace, and he had decided that the odds of hurting himself were increasing. I agreed that when a driver even starts to entertain thoughts like that, it's time to stop. But stopping at Monaco, I felt, was definitely a bad move. James's retirement announcement would inevitably get swept away in the euphoria of the race weekend and rate a sidebar mention alongside the sports report when he deserved better. But I still didn't want to be involved. I agreed not to breathe a word to anyone.

One afternoon Sandra came into my office to say that she had just heard on the news that James had retired. I feigned surprise. A few minutes later the phone rang. It was James. I said I'd heard that he'd retired. He laughed.

'It's a madhouse in here. There's a guy on the phone next door shouting down the line something about "Today he was the first journalist to learn that James Hunt was retiring".'

I asked if he'd mind if I told the story as it had unfolded from that day at Zolder, and he told me to go for it. It made a fine full-page *Autocar* column on a driver I had started out disliking intensely.

James settled down to get his motor racing kicks from commentating on BBC Television with Murray Walker. His confidence and ease at the microphone has been highlighted by the subsequent difficulties in replacing him as a foil for Murray.

Gilles Villeneuve might have been put on earth to drive a Ferrari Grand Prix car. He was a driver who made his own rules. He craved excitement. You felt that he and Tazio Nuvolari would have got along well.

Gilles and Didier Pironi lived in Monaco and commuted to Maranello for testing sessions. The sweeping stretch of highway from the French border at Ventimiglia to the Autostrada linking the Grand Prix Driverdom of Monaco with the Ferrari factory at Maranello has its place in racing folklore. That stretch of road illustrates a side of Grand Prix drivers that only they talk about. A side that probably only they believe. The pair often shared one of their twin GTB4 Ferraris and played a very special game to while away the trip. They played it on the stretch from Ventimiglia because of the challenge the road offered. The challenge was to see who could keep the Ferrari at peak revs in fifth gear for the longest time, a game guaranteed to eliminate boredom on the highway for all concerned. The passenger held the stopwatch and the driver kept the needle in the red. Passing those huge European trailer-trucks or any other traffic dawdling under 150 mph on either side was allowed in this ruleless, mindless game. The fact that the pair survived long enough to perish in official competition – Gilles in a Ferrari and Didier in a powerboat – becomes mildly surprising.

Harvey Postlethwaite was a designer with Ferrari when the drivers entertained themselves thus on the trip from Monaco. 'There were various roads from Monaco to Maranello but they all had to involve the Autostrada del Fiori [the Autostrada of Flowers]. It goes all along from Monte Carlo behind San Remo and the Italian Riviera resorts, all the way to Genoa. It's a fantastic road. Two lanes, three lanes, in and out of tunnels, round *mighty* corners. It must go for 200 kilometres and it's just flat strap all the way. Brilliant stuff. And they used to race down there.

'From Genoa you go over the mountains and that's autostrada that's *really* tight, then when you get off the mountains it's flat from Alessandria to the Autodromo at Maranello. They couldn't have driven the whole thing flat even though they might have said they did, but certainly they would have given it a good try. You could do the flat bits flat out . . . if you didn't end up in the back of a truck.'

Postlethwaite spent a lot of time away from the track with Villeneuve and he remembers his party trick after a meal at a restaurant in Modena or Maranello. Or anywhere that needed livening up. 'He would wind his Ferrari 308 on full lock, put his left foot flat on the clutch, his right foot flat on the throttle, tweak the key-start, wind the engine *straight* up to valve bounce, sideways off the clutch with his foot to start the wheels spinning, and because it's on full lock it goes round in a full circle on the front wheel axis with the rear tyres alight. He'd go twice round like that, roaring with laughter, catch it and zap straight out of the car park. *Huge* clouds of black smoke. Gilles eventually gave up driving any distance on the road and flew in his helicopter, but I wouldn't go up with him.'

The road was a medium Harvey could relate to, the sky was something else again.

Postlethwaite is excellent company at The Barley Mow now that he has returned as Director of Engineering at Tyrrell after a couple of separate stints at Ferrari. He came into Formula 1 with the Hesketh team and James Hunt, so he is a personality who has spanned the generation gap. I may be guilty of running with the hare and hunting with the hounds here. Harvey arrived in Formula 1 with Hesketh, the team for whom I had scant regard. Now I am letting him support my belief that the characters are lost from racing.

Eddie Irvine is a remnant from earlier days, but even the devil-may-care Irishman points out that if he plays around and enjoys himself, he is regarded as not showing sufficient respect for his profession – by people like me who bemoan the fact that there are no characters left in Formula 1. Harvey thinks that drivers in his early days had a totally cavalier attitude that most of them don't have now. He sees young Mika Salo in their team as a driver with spirit, but I wonder aloud whether that spirit wouldn't be dulled, brought into line, made to conform, if he won a Grand Prix.

I have a personal theory that any driver in Formula 1 is amusing and good company – until he becomes successful, until he starts winning. And by winning I mean on his way up, not lucking into a couple of wins when the front runners are out of the game. That's what Jenks calls 'finishing first, not winning'.

Postlethwaite agrees. 'It does change them. They come under pressure from sponsors, the media . . . And it's a shame . . . a pity.'

Inevitably Nigel Mansell looms into the conversation. 'He was a one-off. The fact that he came good when absolutely nobody said he would ever come good, left him with such a chip on his shoulder that he spent the rest of his professional life trying to get back at all the people who got at *him*. That was a shame because he didn't *need* to do that – what he did in a racing car spoke for itself. The impression you get, looking back, is that he was always trying to be somebody he wasn't, and if he could have been the guy he was when he started racing, he'd have been a much more sympathetic guy and I think everyone would have liked him more than the bitchy guy he became.'

Back to Irvine again and what he stands for in the squeaky-clean image-conscious world of Formula 1. 'Eddie really does seem not to give a shit and if he *really* doesn't give a shit then he might just survive at Maranello,' says Postlethwaite, who has been there. Twice. 'If he really doesn't go to bed at night and worry what the press are saying about him – and I think he probably doesn't – then he's probably going to be all right. He's got a cavalier approach and he's going to need it because we all know what it's going to be like there . . .

'The last two drivers who were really in that mould at Ferrari were Gilles and Jody, because since then every bloody one of them has been petrified. Scheckter probably didn't understand or read a word the Italian press were writing about anyway, and Gilles certainly couldn't. I mean, Jody couldn't read it in *English*, let alone Italian. And I don't think Gilles ever read a newspaper in his life!'

And as we are exploring the changed face of Formula 1 over lunch at The Barley Mow, I ask Postlethwaite how he regards the efforts of Hill and Schumacher to homogenise Formula 1. Hill had asked for definitive rules on what constituted an overtaking manoeuvre as though it was a board game, and Schumacher was talking to the press about crash bars between the wheels. Are they *really* trying to turn Formula 1 into a board game so that they can take all of the money but none of the risks, or is that being too simplistic, taking too much of a linen-helmet approach to motor racing in the '90s?

Postlethwaite bristles, rises to new heights in the conversation. 'It *is* Formula *1* we are talking about here, isn't it? You get *past* the f—ing bloke in front. Over him. Under him. Right of him. Left of him. Brake test him. Force him off. That's really what it's all about. And the driver, unless he's *really* stupid, won't carry out a manoeuvre that will take *both* of them off the road.'

Now we have reached a crossroads with the drivers wanting less aggression and the team owners baying for more.

Ayrton Senna never short-changed anyone at the aggression counter. Let Richard Williams have the last word on the way racing has changed, quoting again from his book *The Death of Ayrton*

Senna, where he talks of the various incidents when Prost and Mansell came off worst in on-track tangles with Senna.

'These were incidents through which the very nature of Grand Prix racing was changed utterly, and probably for good; and since Senna was not only their common denominator but also their catalyst, we can say that he was responsible for this great and disturbing change – by which a sport that had always depended on the inherent chivalry of its participants suddenly came to accommodate the possibility of the systematic application of controlled violence.'

CHAPTER FOURTEEN

Finale

LIFE IS VERY much what you make it. Perhaps I mirrored Denny Hulme in leaving home. It wasn't intentional. One of those things. Sandra and I had a great marriage for over 25 years, but we started to grow apart. It was my fault. Sandra was into horses and I wasn't. I was a pub person and Sandra wasn't.

Pubs are places of solace in most difficult situations, and The Barley Mow was my first refuge after I left home. John Woodiwiss offered me a room for as long as I wanted to stay, taking me in almost as a member of his family, and in my early 50s I was embarking on a new chapter in my life.

To a lot of regulars, running a pub of their own is a dream. It's a nightmare. I lived in 'The Barley' for a year, and the temptation of a permanent party downstairs every evening soon became wearing. How 'Woody' had coped for most of his life was beyond me. He and Val started at 6.30 am cleaning up from the night before and preparing for the day to come. It was an adventure at first, but I soon became aware of the sheer pressure of the life.

I bought a flat with huge rooms in an old rectory on the edge of the village. It is more like a hotel suite, and it suits me fine, a lock-it-and-leave-it apartment with a lot of style and easy walking distance to the shops, restaurants and railway station. The flat was a Barley Mow project. Val co-ordinated its redecoration from Construction Corner at the flagstone end of the bar. Roddy was in charge of painting and carpentry, Billy handled the electrical work, Steve sorted out the central heating installation and Mr Cuckow laid the carpets.

My friend Sue advised on how it should look, new bachelors being fairly hopeless at this side of it. She is part of my life, and she didn't want to be in this book. But she is. Sue comes to some of the races with me, rules my office with a rod of iron when I'm away, and insists that she won't walk through the door unless the place is tidy. Which means that I spend half the time between races making it untidy and the other half tidying it up. She has created a press-cutting service on race weekends, buying all the English newspapers, clipping the reports and faxing them to the Ford motorhome in the paddock of whichever track we are at in Europe, so that on Saturday and Sunday the Fleet Street scribes can see their work – or, more importantly, what the others have written – early each morning.

I was made an Associate Member of the British Racing Drivers' Club, the most prestigious club in international motor racing, and as near a knighthood as you can aspire to in the sport, especially as a journalist and not a racing driver. Nigel Roebuck and Alan Henry were made members a year later. Roebuck is a notorious non-joiner, saying that he would never want to be a member of any club you could *join*, and I wondered how he would take the BRDC honour. He was elated. Alan was ecstatic. I asked Roebuck what club regalia Alan was buying.

'Oh, nothing too ostentatious. Just two of everything . . .'

Someone famous was interviewed and asked which was his favourite restaurant.

'The one where they know me best,' he replied.

This is perhaps more important than it sounds. Restaurants are supposed to be comfortable places where you can relax over a good meal and enjoy the atmosphere. Tony Orlando, a dapper indefatigable Sicilian, owns the Meridiana Italian restaurant in East Horsley, a stone's throw from my flat. He built up a reputation with his La Baita restaurant in Bramley, a few villages away in Surrey, having bought the place from former racing driver Alan Brown, and served an enthusiastic Italian clientele from John Barnard's Ferrari design offices nearby. The Laughing Buddha is our local Chinese restaurant. They know me so well in there that I don't have to order. They recite each of my courses for me . . .

It was Denny Hulme who said earlier in this book 'You've got to be *happy*', and I had pointed out that his deciding to be happy didn't necessarily mean that everyone else was happy with the way that he had re-arranged his life. Now I know what he meant. In blunt terms it was a cop-out, but in reality it was starting out again.

Life in 1996 is like an adventure. In February I flew to New Zealand to visit daughter Selina, and Sandra was there too. We probably got on better than we had when we all lived under one roof. Selina has established herself in the international world of children's book illustration, and she lives with Tony Palmer in her own house in Lyttelton, a typically New Zealand Victorian hillside villa with panoramic sea views ideal for her work at home, a luxury I assume she inherited from me.

I stayed with Euan and Min Sarginson in Governors Bay at the far end of the Lyttelton inlet. Euan is a top photographer and Min is an estate agent. We have grown up together in one of those rolling relationships where we pick up effortlessly where we left off a year earlier. As though you'd just been away for the weekend. No forced politeness. This may be a New Zealand thing, but we seem to enjoy each other's company although we live a world apart.

On to Melbourne for the first world championship Grand Prix on the Albert Park track to see young Jacques Villeneuve come close to winning the race in his first drive with Williams. To Sydney then for Sir Jack Brabham's 70th birthday party, a black-tie bash on a boat cruising Sydney Harbour at night. Lots of names from the old days. Then a few days with dealer colleague Laurence and Gilly Edscer at the Boathouse Inn on the southern end of Phuket Island, a short flight from Bangkok. Bliss. The brochure said that the hotel had been designed for people who didn't like staying in hotels. It was fantastic. Temperatures in the 90s every day, but with no humidity. A curving mile of quiet beach. It was the sort of place where you pinched yourself each morning to make sure you weren't dreaming. Friendly people, good food, fine wines. Wonderful.

I missed the South American races, but snatched the chance to drive the F1 McLaren, the centre-seat road-going £540,000 supercar. David Clark, Sales Director at McLaren Cars, astounded me by letting me take the car away for an hour on my own.

'Drive it on roads you know,' he said. 'It'll be even more impressive then.'

It was quite the most amazing car I've ever driven, even though there is something almost obscene about driving a car that is *so* superior to anything else on the road. The ideal car for Mr Toad. Top speed was 231 mph from the 6.1-litre BMW V12 engine.

I will have been writing my weekly column in *Autocar* for 30 years come New Year 1997, and it continues to be fun to write. There are always more things to do. My 2.8-litre V6 Volkswagen Golf is quite the quickest car I have ever owned. It puts a smile on your face just driving to the office. I will drive a Bentley Turbo R to the British Grand Prix, a Porsche to the Goodwood Festival of Speed, and a BMW M3 to the French Grand Prix at Magny Cours. Mercedes had a car for me at Cologne Airport for the European Grand Prix at the Nurburgring, Chrysler had a car at San Francisco Airport for the Wine Country Classic races at Sears Point, Toyota provide cars in New Zealand, and I work with Ford, hosting a table at their hospitality motorhome at each of the Grands Prix in Europe. This summer I will have been to races in Australia, New Zealand, California, the Nurburgring, Silverstone, Imola, Monaco, Barcelona, France, Hockenheim, Hungary, Belgium and Portugal.

So life is good. I will be 57 when this book eventually reaches the shops, and I wake up wondering what each morning will bring. Because each one is different these days. A different country, a different car, perhaps a fax offering some exciting memorabilia in the office, or an eager subscriber from the other side of the world wanting to buy something exciting and expensive from my latest monthly catalogue. I sit in my kitchen having breakfast and watching the businessmen in their pinstripe suits with their umbrellas and briefcases hurrying to catch the train to Waterloo. It's therapeutic. I always imagine that they make more money than I do, but I'm having more fun. It definitely beats working . . .

Index